STUDENT MANUAL: THEORY AND PRACTICE OF GROUP COUNSELING

NINTH EDITION

STUDENT MANUAL: THEORY AND PRACTICE OF GROUP COUNSELING

Gerald Corey

California State University, Fullerton
Diplomate in Counseling Psychology,
American Board of Professional Psychology

CENGAGE
Learning

Australia · Brazil · Mexico · Singapore · United Kingdom · United States

For product information and technology assistance, contact us at **Cengage Learning Customer & Sales Support, 1-800-354-9706.**

For permission to use material from this text or product, submit all requests online at **www.cengage.com/permissions.** Further permissions questions can be emailed to **permissionrequest@cengage.com.**

ISBN: 978-1-305-40814-2

Cengage Learning
20 Channel Center Street
Boston, MA 02210
USA

Cengage Learning is a leading provider of customized learning solutions with office locations around the globe, including Singapore, the United Kingdom, Australia, Mexico, Brazil, and Japan. Locate your local office at **www.cengage.com/global**.

Cengage Learning products are represented in Canada by Nelson Education, Ltd.

To learn more about Cengage Learning Solutions, visit **www.cengage.com**.

Purchase any of our products at your local college store or at our preferred online store **www.cengagebrain.com**.

Printed in the United States of America
Print Number: 01   Print Year: 2014

Contents

PART 1

BASIC ELEMENTS OF GROUP PROCESS: AN OVERVIEW

CHAPTER ONE

Introduction to Group Work

Introduction to This Student Manual

This Student Manual is designed to accompany *Theory and Practice of Group Counseling* (ninth edition), by Gerald Corey (Cengage Learning, 2016). The manual is intended to help you gain practical experience in the various theoretical approaches to group work and to stimulate you to think about ethical and practical issues typically encountered by group leaders.

The design of the manual is based on the assumption that you will learn best by becoming actively involved in the learning process and by actually experiencing group concepts and techniques. Reading about them provides a foundation, but this knowledge remains abstract unless you can see how these theories are actually part of the group process.

Much of this material consists of things you can think about, experiment with, and do on your own. In addition, you can practice many exercises in small groups, both as a group facilitator and as a group member. You will be provided with opportunities to function in numerous role-playing situations. I encourage you to modify these exercises so that they will become personally meaningful. The material in the Exercises and Activities sections includes the following:

- Self-inventories to assess your attitudes about various theories
- Open-ended questions for you to explore
- Ideas and suggestions for role playing
- Techniques for group interaction
- Practical problems that occur in groups
- Group exercises for experiential practice
- Questions for reflection and discussion
- Ideas for writing in your journal
- Suggestions of how to apply what you are learning in the course to yourself as a person and as a group leader
- Each theory chapter features an expert in a particular theoretical model who offers his or her perspective on the approach by answering five questions.

Each chapter includes a comprehension check. When you take the quiz and score it, you will gain a sense of your mastery of the basic elements in the chapter. There is more material in this manual than a given course can cover thoroughly. However, my preference is to provide a wide variety of activities so that you can select the ones you find most meaningful. This Student Manual helps you focus on key concepts as you read, personalize the material, and apply it to the practice of group counseling.

A Word of Acknowledgment

I would like to extend my appreciation to Amelia Blevins, Associate Content Developer, for her participation in the process of the revision of the Student Manual, to Sean Cronin, Associate Content Developer, for coordinating the supplemental materials for the book and the accompanying manual, and to Michelle Muratori, Johns Hopkins University, for her review of the Student Manual and working on supplementary projects. Appreciation also goes to Kay Mikel, copy editor of this manual, who also edited the textbook.

About the Textbook

Theory and Practice of Group Counseling will introduce you to some basic issues of group leadership and group membership, and it will show you how groups function. Part One covers the basic elements of group process and practice that you will need to know regardless of the types of groups you may lead or the theoretical orientation you prefer. Chapter 2 deals with basic concerns of group leadership, such as the personal characteristics of effective leaders, the problems they face, the different styles of leadership, the range of specific skills required for effective leading, the attributes of an effective multicultural group counselor, and the need for practitioners to incorporate research in their group practice. Chapter 3 addresses important ethical issues that you will inevitably encounter as you lead groups. The emphasis is on the rights of group members and the responsibilities of group leaders. In Chapters 4 and 5 you are introduced to the major developmental tasks confronting a group as it goes through its various stages from formation to termination, including evaluation and follow-up. The central characteristics of the stages that make up the life history of a group are examined, with special attention paid to the major functions of the group leader at each stage. These chapters also focus on the functions of the members of a group and the possible problems that are associated with each stage in the group's evolution.

Part Two of the text is designed to provide you with a good overview of a variety of theoretical models underlying group counseling so that you can see the connection between theory and practice. Eleven models have been selected to present a balanced perspective. Each of these theoretical orientations has something worthwhile to offer you as a future group leader.

To provide a framework that will help you integrate the theoretical models, these eleven chapters follow a common outline. They present the key concepts of each theory and their implications for group practice, outline the role and functions of the group leader according to the particular theory, discuss how each theory is applied to group practice, and describe the major techniques employed under each theory. Illustrative examples make the use of these techniques more concrete. Each chapter contains my evaluation of the approach under discussion—an evaluation based on what I consider to be its major strengths and limitations—and a brief description of how the approach can be applied to group counseling in schools and with diverse client populations.

You will learn some essential aspects of the therapies explored, but this book is not designed to make you an expert in any one approach. My aim is to provide you with an understanding of some of the significant commonalities and differences among these theoretical models. My hope is that you will become sufficiently motivated to select some approaches and learn more about them by doing additional reading (there are suggestions after each chapter in Part Two) and by experiencing some of these group approaches as a participant. The ultimate goal is for you to develop your own personal style of group leadership and to begin thinking about how to translate theory into practice.

Part Three focuses on the practical application of the theories and principles covered in Parts One and Two, making these applications more vivid and concrete. Chapter 17 is designed to help you pull together the various methods and approaches, realizing commonalities and differences among them. I discuss the basic concepts and key techniques of various theories that can be used in many kinds of groups. Chapter 18 follows a group in action and presents Marianne Schneider Corey's and my version of an integrated model for group practice, drawing from various theoretical models as they apply to the different stages of a group that we facilitated together. You can see this group in action on the DVD program titled *Groups in Action: Evolution and Challenges*.

The DVD program *Groups in Action: Evolution and Challenges* is an integral supplement to this book. Part One (*Evolution of a Group*) depicts central features that illustrate the development of the group process and how coleaders facilitate a process as the group moves through the various stages: initial, transition, working, and ending. These samples of group work bring the theoretical perspectives to life, provide some flavor of the differences and similarities among the approaches, and show some ways of drawing on the diverse approaches in working with material that emerges from a group. Part Two (*Challenges Facing Group Leaders*) emphasizes the application of techniques for working with members who manifest problematic behaviors. Vignettes show the coleaders facilitating the group as members role-play difficult situations in the group.

Lectures by the Author of the Textbook

Theory and Practice of Group Counseling (ninth edition) comes with MindTap, an online learning solution created to harness the power of technology to drive student success. This cloud-based platform integrates a number of learning applications ("apps") into an easy-to-use and easy-to-access tool that supports a personalized learning experience. MindTap combines student learning tools—readings, multimedia, activities and assessments—into a singular Learning Path that guides you through your counseling course. This MindTap includes a series of audio lectures that I present for each chapter of *Theory and Practice of Group Counseling*, as well as an online video presentation of lectures that I give for each chapter, which are different from the audio lectures. These video lectures, titled *Gerald Corey's Perspectives on Theory and Practice of Group Counseling*, are available as an online program and also as a DVD. Visit the *Theory and Practice of Group Counseling* MindTap to watch Gerald Corey presenting lectures for each chapter of this book.

Be Active in Your Learning

I invite you to keep an open mind yet to read critically. By being an active learner and by raising questions, you will gain the necessary foundation for becoming an effective group leader. This *Student Manual for Theory and Practice of Group Counseling* has been designed as a supplement to the textbook. Your active involvement in the exercises and activities will give you real-time experience with the techniques you are studying.

Here are some suggestions for getting the maximum value from the textbook and the Student Manual. These suggestions are based on my experience in using the material in classes.

1. Look over the contents of the Student Manual to get an overview of the course and the reading program.

2. Before you read and study a chapter in the textbook, read any summary material in the corresponding chapter of the Student Manual, and then look over the questions and exercises, both in the manual and in the textbook. For the 11 chapters that deal with theories of group counseling (Part Two), complete the manual's corresponding Prechapter Self-Inventory, which is based on the key concepts discussed in the textbook. Completing these self-inventories will help you determine the degree to which you agree or disagree with the concepts of a given theory. Spending a few minutes reviewing these inventories will give you a clearer focus on the chapter you are reading in the textbook.

3. After reading and studying the text chapter, return to the Student Manual and do the following:

   a. If you have just finished a chapter on theory, review the Prechapter Self-Inventory to see if your views have changed.

   b. For the theoretical chapters, study the Summary chart that briefly describes the theory's view of the developmental stages of a group.

   c. Look over the basic assumptions of the theory and the summary of key concepts.

   d. Take and score the Comprehension Quiz for each chapter to check your level of mastery of a theory.

   e. Select some exercises to do on your own and some that you would be willing to do in your group or class.

   f. Choose some of the exercises and questions for reflection as catalysts for your journal writing.

4. The Student Manual is designed as a resource to help you eventually create your own theory and style of group leading. Toward this end, as you read and study the different theories, I recommend that you select specific aspects of each approach that appear to be suited to your personality. The Student Manual's main purpose is to make these theories come alive for you. To accomplish this aim, it is essential that you involve yourself actively by thinking critically, sharing your thoughts with others in class, and, if appropriate, investing yourself personally by bringing your own life experience into this course.

5. As you read and study, be alert for topics for class discussion and points that most interest you. Write down a few key questions and bring them to class. Look for concepts and techniques you can apply to the group you are leading or expect to be leading. As you work through the material, develop a capacity for critical evaluation by thinking about what you most like and least like about each of the theories. The Summary charts outlining the stages of development as applied to each theory are especially useful in this evaluation.

6. It is helpful to get some actual experience by working in small classroom groups with the concepts and techniques of the various counseling approaches. The more you are willing to become an active learner and a participant in your class or group, the more you will be able to see the possibilities for using these techniques as a group leader. I encourage you to use your ingenuity with the exercises presented here or others you create. Think of ways to apply the concepts and techniques to groups in various settings. As part of my course, students meet in small experiential groups (which are supervised) to practice being a group member and coleading a group. They work within the framework of the model they are studying in class, and in this way they get a better idea of how the various theoretical orientations are applied in practice.

7. The Exercises and Activities include a mixture of discussion questions and personal topics for self-exploration. Here are some cautions and recommendations about using these activities:

    a. The use of the exercises will depend largely on the format of your class. These exercises have been designed for use in a supervised group and for classes that include an experiential as well as a didactic component.

    b. Because many of the activities tap into personal material, you will need to decide what you are willing to disclose in your group. It is largely up to you. The purpose of the course is to learn about group process, not to experience group therapy. Yet it is possible to explore some of your personal concerns in a supervised group and at the same time learn how group process works by experiencing a group as a participant. Care should be taken, however, to avoid opening up deeply personal issues that cannot be adequately attended to in an academic course.

    c. It is essential that certain ground rules be established from the outset, especially rules about level of participation, "right to pass," and matters of confidentiality. The purpose and goals of your class need to be clearly defined and understood. Both your expectations and your instructor's expectations and requirements should be discussed early in the course.

    d. As you study the manual by yourself, you can benefit from reflecting on your personal concerns and by attempting to relate your life experiences to each of the therapies you study. These approaches will have more meaning for you if you apply them to understanding yourself. The manual can help you in this personal application and self-exploration even if you do not have opportunities to participate in a group.

    e. If you take the exercises seriously, your personal problems may come into focus for you. Although this process can lead to growth, it can also involve some anxiety. I hope you will consider becoming a member of a group (in addition to any group that might be a part of your course). Through such participation you can explore areas you want to change, and the experience can provide you with increased empathy for the members of the groups you will lead. Students often mention that their own experience as a client in counseling, especially group counseling, has been the most useful component in learning how to facilitate a group.

    f. I present a wide range of exercises that are based on particular therapeutic models. Let me emphasize that practitioners who adhere to a given approach may not use these exercises in the way I describe them. My aim is to help you find ways to use the concepts of each therapeutic model and to create exercises that you can practice, modify, and adapt to fit your situation. Use these exercises as a basis for creating approaches that will work for your groups.

8. Many students find it helpful to keep a journal as a part of their group course. This journal helps students keep track of their experiences as both members and facilitators of groups, and it motivates them to do writing on some of the exercises contained in the manual.

9. Look for opportunities to attend professional workshops and courses that deal not only with group work but also with specialized populations with whom you might work. Once you graduate you will need to attend professional workshops to continue to update your knowledge, refine your skills, and learn new therapeutic strategies.

Professional Organizations of Interest to Group Workers

As a student, consider joining the professional organization of your specialty field. There are many advantages in becoming involved in such organizations, including receiving journals and information about annual conferences and specialized workshops. I recommend that as a group worker you also join the **Association for Specialists in Group Work (ASGW),** a division of the American Counseling Association. As an ASGW student member, you qualify for a reduced fee and will receive the *Journal for Specialists in Group Work* four times a year.

Association for Specialists in Group Work
5999 Stevenson Avenue
Alexandria, VA 22304
Telephone: (800) 347-6647
Website: www. asgw.org

I also recommend joining the **American Group Psychotherapy Association (AGPA).** Membership includes a subscription to an excellent quarterly journal, the *International Journal of Group Psychotherapy*, which contains a variety of articles dealing with both the theory and practice of group therapy. Each year APGA offers a conference that features a variety of institutes, seminars, open sessions, and workshops. The AGPA has a student-member category.

American Group Psychotherapy Association, Inc.
25 East 21st Street, 6th Floor
New York, NY 10010
Telephone: (212) 477-2677 or Toll Free: (877) 668-2472
Fax: (212) 979-6627
E-mail: memberservices@agpa.org
Website: www.agpa.org

List of Professional Organizations

Contact the organization of your choice or visit the organization's website to find out what they can offer. Each of the following professional organizations has a code of ethics, which you may obtain by contacting the organization directly or by downloading the file from their website.

1. **American Counseling Association (ACA):** *Code of Ethics*, ©2014 Visit www.counseling. org/ for more information on this organization.
2. **National Board for Certified Counselors (NBCC):** *Code of Ethics*, ©2012 Visit www. nbcc.org/ for more information on this organization.
3. **Commission on Rehabilitation Counselor Certification (CRCC):** *Code of Professional Ethics for Rehabilitation Counselors*, ©2010 Visit www.crccertification.com/ for more information on this organization.
4. **Association for Addiction Professionals (NAADAC):** *Code of Ethics*, ©2011 Visit www. naadac.org/ for more information on this organization.
5. **Canadian Counselling and Psychotherapy Association (CCPA):** *Code of Ethics*, ©2007 Visit www.ccacc.ca/home.html for more information on this organization.
6. **American School Counselor Association (ASCA):** *Ethical Standards for School Counselors*, ©2010 Visit www.schoolcounselor.org/ for more information on this organization.

7. **American Psychological Association (APA):** *Ethical Principles of Psychologists and Code of Conduct,* ©2010 Visit www.apa.org/ for more information on this organization.

8. **American Psychiatric Association:** *The Principles of Medical Ethics With Annotations Especially Applicable to Psychiatry,* ©2013 Visit www.psych.org/ for more information on this organization.

9. **American Group Psychotherapy Association (AGPA):** *Ethical Guidelines for Group Therapists,* ©2002 Visit www.groupsinc.org/ for more information on this organization.

10. **American Mental Health Counselors Association (AMHCA):** *Code of Ethics,* ©2010 Visit www.amhca.org/ for more information on this organization.

11. **American Association for Marriage and Family Therapy (AAMFT):** *Code of Ethics,* ©2012 Visit www.aamft.org/ for more information on this organization.

12. **International Association of Marriage and Family Counselors (IAMFC):** *Ethical Code,* ©2011 Visit www.iamfc.com/ for more information on this organization.

13. **Association for Specialists in Group Work (ASGW):** *Best Practice Guidelines,* ©2008 Visit www.asgw.org/ for more information on this organization.

14. **National Association of Social Workers (NASW):** *Code of Ethics,* ©2008 Visit www.socialworkers.org/ for more information on this organization.

15. **National Organization for Human Services:** *Ethical Standards of Human Service Professionals,* ©2000 Visit www.nationalhumanservices.org/ for more information on this organization.

16. **American Music Therapy Association (AMTA):** *Code of Ethics,* ©2008 Visit www.musictherapy.org/ for more information on this organization.

Ways of Getting the Most From Your Group Experience

I hope your program will include some kind of therapeutic group experience, which is invaluable in the training of group counselors. Learning to be an effective group leader entails much more than simply taking a course and reading about group process. Your level of self-awareness and sensitivity to others are crucial factors in determining your effectiveness. If you are open to experiencing the group process and to committing yourself to becoming an active group participant, you can do a great deal to increase your chances of helping your clients see the value of a group experience.

How can you get the most from a group experience and maximize your learning? You can apply the recommendations below to both yourself as a member and to teaching others about groups. For a more detailed discussion of these points, I refer you to *Groups: Process and Practice* (M. S. Corey, G. Corey, & C. Corey, 2014), which is available from Cengage Learning.

1. Recognize that trust is not something that "just happens" in a group but that you have a role in creating it. If you are aware of anything getting in the way of a climate of safety, share your hesitations with the group.

2. Commit yourself to getting something from your group by focusing on your personal goals. Before each meeting, make the time to think about how you can get involved, what personal concerns you want to explore, and other ways to use the time in the group meaningfully.

3. Rather than waiting to be called on, bring yourself into the interactions at the beginning of each session by letting others know what you want from this particular meeting.

Although it is useful to have a tentative agenda of what you want to discuss, don't cling inflexibly to your agenda if other issues surface spontaneously within the group. Be open to pursuing alternative paths if you are affected by what others are exploring.

4. Realize that if the work other members are doing is affecting you, it is crucial that you let them know how you are reacting. If you are able to identify with the struggles or pains of others, it generally helps both you and them to share your feelings and thoughts.

5. Decide for yourself what, how much, and when you will disclose personal facets of yourself. Others will not have a basis for knowing you unless you tell them about yourself. If you have difficulty sharing yourself personally in your group, begin by letting others know what makes it hard for you to self-disclose.

6. Don't confuse self-disclosure with storytelling. Avoid getting lost and overwhelming others with mere information about you or your history. Instead, express what is on your mind and in your heart presently. Reveal the struggles that are significant to you at this time in your life, especially as they pertain to what others in the group are exploring.

7. Express persistent feelings that relate to what is emerging in the group in the here-and-now. If you are feeling intimidated by other people in the group, for example, announce that you feel that way. If you feel somewhat isolated, share this emotion. If you do not want to be a part of the group, it is essential that you talk about it. Be willing to assume responsibility for what you feel rather than blaming others.

8. Although silence may sometimes be golden, don't become a silent member. Realize that others will not know you if you do not let them know what issues are important to you, nor will they know that you identify with them or feel close to them unless you tell them.

9. Practice your attending and listening skills. If you can give others the gift of your presence and understanding, you are contributing a great deal to the group process.

10. Try to challenge yourself if you sense that you are taking too much group time for yourself. If you become overly concerned about measuring how much you are taking and receiving, you will inhibit the spontaneity that can make a group exciting and productive.

11. Use your group as a place to experiment with new behaviors. Allow yourself to try out different ways of being to determine how you may want to change. Discover how to extend new ways of thinking, feeling, and acting into your outside life. Between sessions, practice the skills you are learning in your group. Give yourself homework assignments, and let others in your group know how you are applying group learning to your behavior with family, friends, and associates.

12. Understand that making changes will not be instantaneous. You can also expect some setbacks. Keep track of any progress you are making, and remember to give yourself credit for your efforts and the subtle changes you are achieving.

13. Avoid giving others advice, giving intellectualized interpretations of their behavior, or using questioning as your main style of interacting. If you are inclined to ask a question, let others know why you are interested in hearing their answer. Or if you want to give advice, reveal to others what your investment is in giving this advice. Learn to speak *for* yourself and *about* yourself.

14. Concentrate on making personal and direct statements to others in your group. Direct communication with a member is more effective than talking about that person through the leader.

15. In giving feedback to others, avoid categorizing or labeling them. Instead of telling others who or what they are, tell them what you are observing, and let them know how they are affecting you. Rather than judging them as persons, focus on how you respond to some of their specific behaviors in the group.

16. Pay attention to any consistent feedback you might receive. If you hear that others perceive you as being somewhat judgmental and critical, don't be too quick to argue and convince others that you are open and accepting. Instead, take in what you are hearing, and consider their input to determine the degree to which what they are saying might apply to you.

17. Respect your defenses, and understand that they have served a purpose for you. When you become aware of feeling or acting defensively in your group, however, challenge your defenses by seeing what will happen if you strive to be less guarded. At least identify out loud that you are feeling defensive, and begin exploring what you might be resisting.

18. Provide support for others by expressing your care for them, but don't quickly intervene by trying to comfort others when they are experiencing feelings, such as expressing pain over an event. Realize that they need to experience, share, and work through certain feelings; they do not need reassurance that "all will turn out for the best." Let them know how their pain may be touching you, but don't attempt to "cure" them of their pain.

19. Take responsibility for what you are accomplishing in your group. Spend some time thinking about what is taking place in these meetings and evaluating the degree to which you are attaining your goals. If you are not satisfied with your group experience, look at what you can do to make the group a more meaningful experience.

20. Be aware of respecting and maintaining the confidentiality of what goes on inside your group. Even though you may not maliciously breach others' confidences, recognize how easy it might be to inappropriately talk to others who are not in the group about what members have revealed. How you handle confidentiality says a great deal about your professional character. If you have any concerns that what you are sharing is not staying within the group, be willing to bring this matter up in a session.

21. Be prepared if your friends and loved ones do not always understand or accept you, especially as you make changes. Some people may not support the new directions you choose to travel, and your changes may be threatening to them. It is a good idea to create a support system within your group. Ask selected members to help you remember the lessons you have learned in the group. Reporting to others in your group is an accountability procedure that will enable you to meet your personal goals.

22. Keep a personal journal in which you record impressions of your own explorations and learning in your group. The journal is a good place to enter your reactions to books you read for your personal development. A journal will be invaluable in keeping track of your progress and noting changes in your ways of thinking, feeling, and acting.

CHAPTER TWO

Group Leadership

Prechapter Self-Inventory for Group Leadership

Decide the degree to which you agree or disagree with these statements in this self-inventory. Respond to each statement, giving the initial response that most clearly identifies how you think or feel. I suggest that you go over your completed inventories and mark those items that you would like to discuss; then bring your inventories to class, and compare your positions with the views of others. Such comparisons can stimulate debate and help the class become involved in the topics to be discussed.

Using the following code, write next to each statement the number of the response that most closely reflects your viewpoint:

5 = I *strongly agree* with this statement.
4 = I *agree,* in most respects, with this statement.
3 = I am *undecided* in my opinion about this statement.
2 = I *disagree,* in most respects, with this statement.
1 = I *strongly disagree* with this statement.

_____ 1. The key to success as a group leader is a commitment to the never-ending journey toward becoming a more effective human being.

_____ 2. Group leaders promote a sense of empowerment by encouraging group members to become *client colleagues.*

_____ 3. Self-care is not a luxury but an ethical mandate, and group leaders need to commit to developing effective self-care strategies.

_____ 4. Beginning group leaders would do well to err on the side of caution rather than on the side of uninhibited and unexamined self-disclosure.

_____ 5. One way of interpreting is for leaders to share their hunches with members, asking them to reflect on how accurate these hunches are.

_____ 6. Confrontation has the potential of being detrimental both to the person being confronted and to the group process.

_____ 7. Feedback that is specific and descriptive rather than global and judgmental is the most helpful.

_____ 8. The leader's closing skills bring unity to the group experience and consolidate the learning that has occurred during a session.

_____ 9. Developing cultural competence enables practitioners to appreciate and manage diverse worldviews.

_____ 10. Part of your development as a group practitioner involves thinking of ways to make evaluation a basic part of your group practice.

Problems and Issues Facing Beginning Group Leaders

Group leaders (both those who are beginning and those who are experienced) typically face several common problems. Assume that you are now leading or coleading a group (even though you may not have done so), and give your reactions to each of the following situations. What do you imagine you'd think and feel in each of these cases? Think about your possible courses of action, and then discuss these situations in your class or group and exchange ideas. Many role-playing activities can be generated based on this material.

1. Imagine yourself getting ready to colead your first group. What emotions would you experience? What would be your main concerns before you actually began the first session? Assume you are meeting your coleader an hour before the group meets. What would you discuss? What would you do if you and your coleader had different ideas about how to open the first session?

2. Many beginning group leaders are afraid to make mistakes, and out of their fear they may be inactive and may not try interventions or follow their intuition. How does this description apply to you? Can you think of some ways to challenge yourself to be active as a leader? Are you willing to risk making mistakes? In small groups discuss how being afraid of making mistakes might get in your way of facilitating a group, and as well, how you can challenge your fears.

3. Again in small groups, discuss your thoughts on the topic of leader self-disclosure. How do you decide *what, when,* and *how* to disclose so self-disclosure facilitates rather than interferes with the group process? Tell others in your group what you are likely to disclose (or not disclose) in a group you are leading, and get their feedback. In your discussion groups, work toward developing a brief list of guidelines for appropriate leader disclosure that you can agree on.

4. It is extremely important for group counselors to be aware of the personal traits and characteristics needed to become effective leaders. Select some of the following questions to discuss in your class or small group, and use them as a basis for self-reflection on effective leadership:
   a. Why do you want to lead groups?
   b. What do you have to offer as a group counselor?
   c. What experiences have you had that you think will contribute to your success?
   d. What shortcomings do you have that may limit your effectiveness as a leader?
   e. Do you feel a sense of personal power in your own right, or do you depend on a role or position to give you power?
   f. In what ways do you appreciate, value, respect, accept, and like yourself?
   g. Do you see yourself as having courage? In what ways is courage important for a group leader?
   h. Do you have a sense of self-compassion? How might this be related to your ability to feel compassion for others?

5. How would you rate yourself on the following dimensions? For each dimension, circle the appropriate response. In a small group, discuss your ratings in terms of how they might affect your effectiveness as a group leader.

Need for control

1	2	3	4	5
Low				High

Tolerance for ambiguity

1	2	3	4	5
Low				High

Need for structure

1	2	3	4	5
Low				High

Ability to deal with conflict

1	2	3	4	5
Low				High

Inventiveness and creativity

1	2	3	4	5
Low				High

A sense of humor

1	2	3	4	5
Low				High

Authenticity and sincerity

1	2	3	4	5
Low				High

Stamina

1	2	3	4	5
Low				High

Commitment to self-care

1	2	3	4	5
Low				High

Ability to cope with anxiety

1	2	3	4	5
Low				High

6. Ideally, theory informs practice and is validated through research. Think about the ways research can inform your practice as a group counselor. In small groups, discuss the connections between research and clinical practice by considering some of these questions:

   a. Why might some group practitioners be reluctant to base their clinical practice on research outcome studies?

   b. What kind of research is most meaningful to you as a group practitioner?

   c. How can you learn about the potential applications of research to your practice as a group worker?

   d. How prepared are you to incorporate relevant research findings into your work as a group practitioner?

7. Obtain a research-based article about group work from a scholarly journal. Choose one that seems to have relevance to the type of groups you are interested in leading. With a small group of classmates, discuss the research and its implications for practice. What ideas presented in the article seem potentially useful to you as a practitioner? Specifically, how might these ideas inform your practice or deepen your understanding of group work? Also discuss the limitations of the research.

Checklist and Self-Evaluation of Group Leadership Skills

Table 2.1 in the textbook lists 22 specific group leadership skills. The following form will help you review these skills; it also provides a self-inventory of your strengths as a group leader and specific areas that need improvement. Read the brief description of each skill, and then rate yourself. Next, think about the questions listed under each skill; these will help you determine your level of skill development and examine your behavior as a leader. Ask yourself which skills you most need to develop or improve.

You can profit from this checklist by reviewing it before and after group sessions. If you are working with a coleader, it could be very useful to have him or her also rate you on each of these skills. These questions provide a systematic framework for exploring your level of skill development with fellow students and with your supervisor or instructor.

On these 22 skills, rate yourself on this 5-point scale:

5 = I do this most of the time with a very high degree of competence.

4 = I do this much of the time with a high degree of competence.

3 = I do this sometimes with an adequate degree of competence.

2 = I do this occasionally with a relatively low level of competence.

1 = I rarely demonstrate this or do it with an extremely low level of competence.

You are strongly encouraged to take this self-inventory at three points during the semester or quarter. The three blank spaces to the left of each number are for these ratings. I recommend that you cover your previous ratings with a piece of paper so that you are not influenced by them. It is ideal if you rate yourself (and have your coleader and supervisor rate you) about every 5 weeks. This will give you a regular pattern of your progress in developing group leadership skills. Above all, strive for the maximum degree of honesty with yourself as you complete this rating scale and as you reflect on the questions concerning each of these skills.

It is a good idea to circle the letter of the questions that are the most meaningful to you, as well as the questions that indicate a need for further skill development or special attention.

To what degree does the group leader demonstrate the following?

____ ____ ____ 1. *Active listening.* Hearing and understanding, and communicating that one is doing this.
   a. How well do you listen to members?
   b. How attentive are you to nonverbal language?
   c. Are you able to detect incongruity between members' words and their nonverbal cues?
   d. Are you able to hear both overt and subtle messages?
   e. Do you teach members how to listen and to respond?
   f. Do you focus on content to the extent that you miss how a message is delivered?

____ ____ ____ 2. *Restating.* Capturing the essence of what is said in different words with the effect of adding meaning or clarifying meaning.
   a. Can you repeat the essence of what others say without becoming mechanical?
   b. Do your restatements add meaning to what was said by a member?
   c. Do your restatements eliminate ambiguity and give sharper focus to what was said?
   d. Do you check with members to determine whether they think your restatement is accurate?

____ ____ ____ 3. *Clarifying.* Focusing on underlying issues and assisting others to get a clearer picture of what they are thinking or feeling.
   a. Do your clarifying remarks help members sort out conflicting feelings?
   b. Are you able to focus on underlying issues?
   c. Do members get a clearer focus on what they are thinking and feeling?
   d. Does your clarification lead to a deeper level of member self-exploration?

____ ____ ____ 4. *Summarizing.* Tying together loose ends, identifying common themes, and providing a picture of the directional trends of a group session.
   a. Do you use summarizing as a way to give more direction to a session?
   b. Do you tie together various themes in a group?
   c. Are you able to identify key elements of a session and present them as a summary of the proceedings at the end of a session?

____ ____ ____ 5. *Questioning.* Using questions to stimulate thought and action and avoiding a question/answer pattern of interaction between leader and member.
   a. Do you avoid overusing questioning as a leadership style?
   b. Do you use open-ended questions to encourage deeper exploration of issues?
   c. Do your questions lead clients in a definite direction? Do you have a hidden agenda? Do you have an expected answer?
   d. Do you avoid bombarding members with questions that set up a question/answer format?
   e. Do you ask "what" and "how" questions, or "why" questions?
   f. Do you keep yourself hidden as a counselor through questioning instead of making statements?

____ ____ ____ 6. *Interpreting.* Explaining the meaning of behavior patterns within the framework of a theoretical system.

    a. Can you present your interpretations in a tentative way, as a hunch or a hypothesis?

    b. Are your interpretations dogmatic and authoritarian? Do you have a need to convince members of what you see as "truth"?

    c. Do you have a tendency to rescue members from difficult feelings too quickly through the use of interpretations?

    d. Are you conscious of appropriateness and timing in making interpretations?

    e. Do you encourage members to provide their own meaning of their behavior?

    f. Do you invite other members to make interpretations?

____ ____ ____ 7. *Confronting.* Challenging members in a direct way on discrepancies and in such a manner that they will tend to react nondefensively.

    a. How do you confront members? What are the effects of your confrontations, generally?

    b. What kind of model do you provide for confronting others with care and respect?

    c. As a result of your confrontations, are members encouraged to look at discrepancies in a nondefensive manner?

    d. Do you confront people about their unused strengths?

    e. Are you sensitive to the timing and appropriateness of your confrontations?

    f. Are your confrontations related to specific behavior rather than being judgmental?

____ ____ ____ 8. *Reflecting feelings.* Mirroring what others appear to be feeling without being mechanical.

    a. Do you reflect feelings accurately?

    b. Do your reflections foster increased contact and involvement?

    c. Do your reflections help members clarify what they are feeling?

____ ____ ____ 9. *Supporting.* Offering some form of positive reinforcement at appropriate times in such a way that it has a facilitating effect.

    a. Do you recognize the progress that members make?

    b. Do you build on the strengths and gains made by members?

    c. Do you make use of positive reinforcement and encouragement?

    d. Does your support allow and encourage members to both express and explore their feelings? Or does your support tend to bolster members and aid them in avoiding intense feelings?

____ ____ ____ 10. *Empathizing.* Intuitively sensing the subjective world of others in a group, being able to adopt the frame of reference of others, and communicating this understanding to clients so that they feel understood.

    a. Are your life experiences diverse enough to provide a basis for understanding the subjective world of a range of clients?

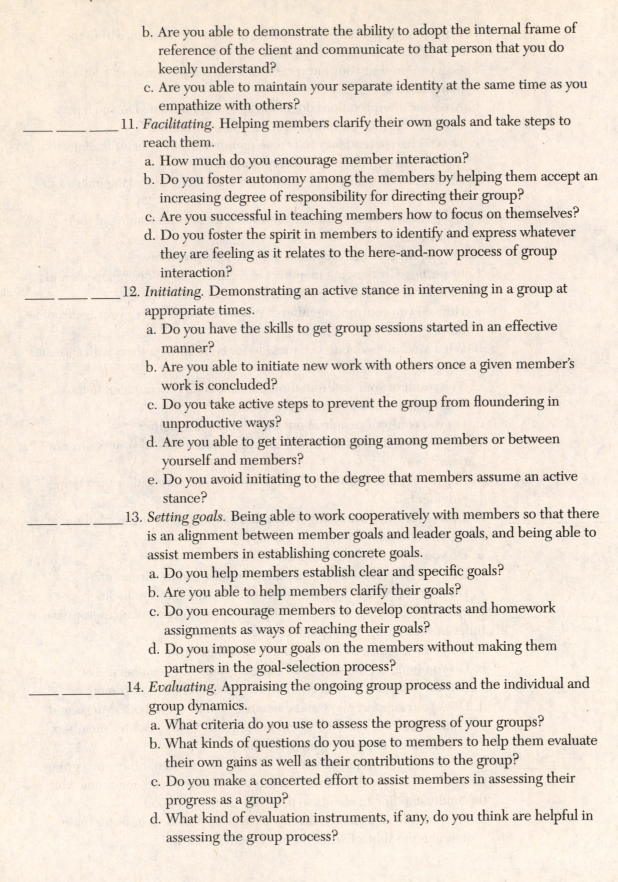

    b. Are you able to demonstrate the ability to adopt the internal frame of reference of the client and communicate to that person that you do keenly understand?

    c. Are you able to maintain your separate identity at the same time as you empathize with others?

_____ _____ _____ 11. *Facilitating.* Helping members clarify their own goals and take steps to reach them.

    a. How much do you encourage member interaction?

    b. Do you foster autonomy among the members by helping them accept an increasing degree of responsibility for directing their group?

    c. Are you successful in teaching members how to focus on themselves?

    d. Do you foster the spirit in members to identify and express whatever they are feeling as it relates to the here-and-now process of group interaction?

_____ _____ _____ 12. *Initiating.* Demonstrating an active stance in intervening in a group at appropriate times.

    a. Do you have the skills to get group sessions started in an effective manner?

    b. Are you able to initiate new work with others once a given member's work is concluded?

    c. Do you take active steps to prevent the group from floundering in unproductive ways?

    d. Are you able to get interaction going among members or between yourself and members?

    e. Do you avoid initiating to the degree that members assume an active stance?

_____ _____ _____ 13. *Setting goals.* Being able to work cooperatively with members so that there is an alignment between member goals and leader goals, and being able to assist members in establishing concrete goals.

    a. Do you help members establish clear and specific goals?

    b. Are you able to help members clarify their goals?

    c. Do you encourage members to develop contracts and homework assignments as ways of reaching their goals?

    d. Do you impose your goals on the members without making them partners in the goal-selection process?

_____ _____ _____ 14. *Evaluating.* Appraising the ongoing group process and the individual and group dynamics.

    a. What criteria do you use to assess the progress of your groups?

    b. What kinds of questions do you pose to members to help them evaluate their own gains as well as their contributions to the group?

    c. Do you make a concerted effort to assist members in assessing their progress as a group?

    d. What kind of evaluation instruments, if any, do you think are helpful in assessing the group process?

_____ _____ _____ 15. *Giving feedback.* Providing information to members in such a way that they can use it to make constructive behavior changes.

    a. Do you continually give concrete and useful feedback to members, and do you encourage members to do this for one another?

    b. Is your feedback both honest and personal?

    c. Do you teach members to sift through feedback and ultimately decide what they will do with this information?

    d. Do you offer feedback that relates to both the strengths and weaknesses of members?

    e. How do members typically react when you give them feedback?

_____ _____ _____ 16. *Suggesting.* Offering information or possibilities for action that can be used by members in making independent decisions.

    a. Can you differentiate between suggesting and prescribing?

    b. Do you give too many suggestions, and are they just ways of providing quick solutions for every problem a member presents?

    c. Do you rush in too quickly to give advice or information, or do you encourage group members to provide themselves with possible courses of action?

    d. Do you invite others in the group to offer suggestions for members to consider?

    e. Do your directions and suggestions actually restrict members from becoming autonomous?

_____ _____ _____ 17. *Protecting.* Actively intervening to ensure that members will be safeguarded from unnecessary psychological risks.

    a. Do you take measures to safeguard members from unnecessary risks?

    b. Do you show good judgment in risky situations?

    c. Do you intervene when members are being treated unfairly or are being pressured by others?

    d. Do you talk with members about the possible psychological risks involved in group participation?

_____ _____ _____ 18. *Disclosing oneself.* Willingly sharing with members any persistent personal reactions that relate to the here-and-now occurrences in the group.

    a. What is your style of self-disclosure? Are you aloof? Do you remain hidden behind a role? Do you model appropriate self-disclosure?

    b. What impact do your self-disclosures tend to have on the group?

    c. Are you willing to reveal your present feelings and thoughts to members when it is appropriate?

_____ _____ _____ 19. *Modeling.* Demonstrating to members desired behaviors that can be practiced both during and between group sessions.

    a. What kind of model are you for your clients?

    b. What specific behaviors and attitudes do you model?

    c. Are you doing in your own life what you ask the members in your group to do?

    d. What might the members of your group know about you by observing your actions in the group?

_____ _____ _____20. *Linking.* Promoting member-to-member interaction and facilitating exploration of common themes in a group.

    a. What interventions do you make that enhance interactions between members?

    b. In what ways do you attempt to foster a norm of member-to-member interactions rather than leader-to-member interactions?

    c. What are some specific instances when you would be most inclined to link the work of one member with that of other members?

_____ _____ _____21. *Blocking.* Being able to intervene effectively, without attacking anyone, when members engage in counterproductive behaviors.

    a. Do you take active steps to intervene when there are counterproductive forces within a group?

    b. Do you generally block the following behaviors when you are aware of them: scapegoating? group pressure? questioning? storytelling? gossiping?

    c. Do you block counterproductive behavior in a firm yet sensitive manner?

_____ _____ _____22. *Terminating.* Creating a climate that encourages members to continue working after sessions.

    a. Do you attempt to get members to transfer what they are learning in the group to their everyday lives?

    b. Do you assist members in reviewing and integrating their experiences?

    c. Do you create a climate in which members are encouraged to continue to think and act after sessions?

Suggestions for Using the Checklist

Obviously, all of the preceding 22 items are not merely skills to learn. Many of them represent attitudes related to your leadership effectiveness; some represent personal characteristics that many writers think are ideal qualities of group leaders. Again, you are encouraged to complete this self-evaluation three times during the course and to use it when you actually lead groups.

Finally, I recommend again that you look over the list and circle the numbers of those items that are most important to you. Then use the following guide to summarize your major strengths, the areas you most need to improve, and the areas that you would like to explore more fully in class. Also, it could be valuable to make comparisons of these ratings; for example, how does your self-rating compare with ratings by your supervisor, your coleader, and the members of your group?

1. Some areas where I feel particularly strong are: _____

_____

_____

_____

_____

2. Areas that need improvement most are: _____

_____

_____

_____

_____

3. Some specific steps I can take now to work toward improving these skills, attitudes, behaviors, and personal characteristics are: _____

_____

_____

_____

_____

Checklist for Becoming a Diversity-Competent Group Counselor

The Association for Specialists in Group Work (ASGW, 2008) document states that ethical practice requires leaders to be aware of the multicultural context in group work:

Group Workers practice with broad sensitivity to client differences including, but not limited to ethnic, gender, religious, sexual, psychological maturity, economic class, family history, physical characteristics or limitations, and geographic location. Group Workers continuously seek information regarding the cultural issues of the diverse population with whom they are working both by interaction with participants and from using outside resources. (Guideline B.8)

The cultural background of the members of your group affects the issues that they bring to a group and the ways in which they might be either ready or reluctant to explore these issues. As a group leader, you need to sensitize yourself to the clues members give indicating that they want to talk about some aspect of how their culture is affecting their participation in the group.

Although you will not have knowledge about every culture, it is important for you to have a basic knowledge of how culture affects group process. As a microcosm of society, groups provide a context for addressing issues of power, privilege, discrimination, social injustice, and oppression. As these themes emerge in a group, you have an opportunity to help members openly explore them.

Multicultural and social justice themes are intertwined in the practice of group work. In addition to becoming competent in working with diverse client populations, group leaders need to acquire social justice and advocacy competencies. The ASGW (2012) *Multicultural and Social Justice Competence Principles for Group Workers* specifically addresses the scope of competence in both multicultural and social justice areas. Examples of some of these competencies include the following:

- Group counselors discuss why social justice and advocacy issues are important in a group and how these issues influence the practice of group work.
- Group counselors address issues of status, privilege, and oppression that arise in group work facilitation.

- Group counselors are concerned with empowerment and build on the strengths of each group member and the resources of the group as a whole.
- Group counselors promote egalitarianism by educating group members about their rights and assisting them in assuming an active role in bringing about social change as well as individual change.
- Group counselors become familiar with ways that local, state, national, and international policies may influence their work with a diverse range of group members.
- Group counselors are prepared to intervene at an institutional level when working with culturally diverse groups.
- Group counselors expand the concept of being a client to include systems and communities when they are examining change.

Becoming a diversity-competent group counselor is basic to doing effective social justice–oriented group work. To deepen members' awareness of social justice as a basic value, you need to create a climate within your group that encourages open discussion of cultural diversity and social justice considerations, especially issues of power and privilege. As a group leader, your role is to bring certain cultural material to the surface so that misunderstandings or potential conflicts can be dealt with openly. If these themes are not addressed, it will be difficult for members to engage in productive work. Although members do share some universal human concerns, the members are also different from one another. A group is an ideal place for people to learn how to understand, appreciate, and respect cultural differences as they discover ways in which they all are bonded by common concerns.

The ASGW's (2012) *Multicultural and Social Justice Competence Principles for Group Workers* can help you gain a fuller appreciation of issues pertaining to cultural diversity and how diversity influences group process. I recommend that you download this document (go to www.asgw.org and follow the link under ASGW Standards and Practices) and carefully review it. The principles embodied in this document emphasize the acquisition of awareness, knowledge, and skills that will assist you, as a group leader, in working ethically and effectively with diversity issues in your groups.

After reading these standards and the sections in the textbook that deal with becoming a diversity-competent group counselor, reflect on the areas of competence you now possess as well as areas in which you need to acquire knowledge and skills. The following checklist can help you assess your current level of skill development in multicultural competencies. Strive to identify your strengths and limitations in working with groups from a multicultural perspective.

Beliefs and Attitudes of Diversity-Competent Group Leaders

Put a check mark in the box before each of the beliefs and attitudes you think you already hold or that represent an area of awareness you already possess.

With respect to beliefs and attitudes, diversity-competent group leaders . . .

❑ recognize and understand the stereotypes and preconceived notions they may hold toward other racial and ethnic minority groups.
❑ do not allow their personal biases, values, or problems to interfere with their ability to work with a diverse range of clients.

- ❑ believe cultural self-awareness and sensitivity to one's own cultural heritage are essential for any form of helping.
- ❑ are aware of their negative and positive emotional reactions toward other racial and ethnic groups that may prove detrimental to establishing collaborative helping relationships.
- ❑ are aware of how their own cultural background and experiences have influenced attitudes, values, and biases about what constitutes psychologically healthy individuals.
- ❑ have moved from being culturally unaware to knowing their cultural heritage.
- ❑ are able to recognize the limits of their competence with diverse client populations.
- ❑ seek to examine and understand the world from the vantage point of their clients.
- ❑ respect clients' religious and spiritual beliefs and values.
- ❑ recognize their sources of discomfort with differences that exist between themselves and others in terms of race, ethnicity, culture, age, gender, sexual orientation, and beliefs.
- ❑ welcome diverse value orientations and diverse assumptions about human behavior and, thus, have a basis for sharing the worldview of their clients as opposed to being culturally encapsulated.
- ❑ are able to accept and value cultural diversity rather than maintaining that their cultural heritage is superior.
- ❑ are able to identify and understand the central cultural constructs of their clients and avoid applying their own cultural constructs inappropriately to people with whom they work.
- ❑ respect indigenous helping practices and respect help-giving networks within the community.
- ❑ monitor their functioning through consultation, supervision, and further training or education.
- ❑ realize that traditional concepts and helping strategies may not be appropriate for all clients or for all problems.

Knowledge of Diversity-Competent Group Leaders

Put a check mark in the box before each of the areas of knowledge in this section that you think you already possess.

With respect to knowledge areas, diversity-competent group leaders . . .

- ❑ possess knowledge about their own racial and cultural heritage and how it affects them personally and in their work.
- ❑ possess knowledge and understanding about how oppression, racism, discrimination, and stereotyping affect them personally and professionally.
- ❑ acknowledge their own racist attitudes, beliefs, and feelings.
- ❑ do not impose their values and expectations on their clients from differing cultural backgrounds and avoid stereotyping clients.
- ❑ understand the worldview of their clients and learn about their clients' cultural backgrounds.
- ❑ understand the basic values underlying the helping process and attempt to learn about their clients' cultural values.
- ❑ are aware of the institutional barriers that prevent minorities from utilizing the mental health services available in their communities.
- ❑ have knowledge of the potential bias in assessment instruments and use procedures and interpret findings keeping in mind the cultural and linguistic characteristics of clients.

❑ possess specific knowledge and information about the particular individuals with whom they are working.

❑ are aware of the values, life experiences, cultural heritage, and historical background of their culturally diverse clients.

❑ possess knowledge about their social impact on others.

❑ are knowledgeable about communication style differences and how their style may clash with or foster the helping process with persons from different cultural groups.

❑ are knowledgeable about the community characteristics and the resources in the community as well as those in the family.

❑ have knowledge about sociopolitical influences that impinge on the life of ethnic and racial minorities, including immigration issues, poverty, racism, stereotyping, and powerlessness.

❑ view diversity in a positive light, which allows them to meet and resolve the challenges that arise in their work with a wide range of client populations.

❑ know how to help clients make use of indigenous support systems. In areas where they are lacking in knowledge, they seek resources to assist them.

Skills and Intervention Strategies of Diversity-Competent Group Leaders

Put a check mark in the box before each of the skill areas in this section that you think you already possess.

With respect to specific skills, diversity-competent group leaders . . .

❑ take responsibility for educating their clients about how the helping process works, including matters such as goals, expectations, legal rights, and the helper's orientation.

❑ familiarize themselves with relevant research and the latest findings regarding mental health and mental disorders that affect diverse client populations.

❑ are willing to seek out educational, consultative, and training experiences to enhance their ability to work with diverse client populations.

❑ are open to seeking consultation with traditional healers or religious and spiritual leaders to better serve diverse client groups, when appropriate.

❑ use methods and strategies and define goals consistent with the life experiences and cultural values of their clients and modify and adapt their interventions to accommodate cultural differences.

❑ are not limited to only one approach in helping but recognize that helping strategies may be culture bound.

❑ are able to send and receive both verbal and nonverbal messages accurately and appropriately.

❑ are able to exercise institutional intervention skills on behalf of their clients.

❑ become actively involved with minority individuals outside of the office (community events, celebrations, and neighborhood groups) to the extent possible.

❑ are committed to understanding themselves as racial and cultural beings and are actively seeking a nonracist identity.

❑ actively pursue and engage in professional and personal growth activities to address their limitations.

Once you've completed this checklist, take a few minutes to decide how you can develop or strengthen specific competencies that will enhance your ability to work more effectively with cultural diversity in your groups.

1. *Assessing Your Beliefs and Attitudes*

   a. What is your main strength in the area of beliefs and attitudes? _____

   _____

   _____

   _____

   _____

   b. What specific kind of belief or attitude would you most want to change? _____

   _____

   _____

   _____

   _____

   c. What steps can you take to bring about this change? _____

   _____

   _____

   _____

   _____

2. *Assessing Your Knowledge*

   a. What is your main strength in the area of knowledge? _____

   _____

   _____

   _____

   _____

   b. What specific kind of knowledge would you most want to acquire? _____

   _____

_____

_____

_____

c. What steps can you take to gain this knowledge? _____

_____

_____

_____

_____

3. *Assessing Your Skills*

a. What is your main strength in the area of skills? _____

_____

_____

_____

_____

b. What specific skill would you most want to acquire or refine? _____

_____

_____

_____

_____

c. What steps can you take to acquire or refine this skill? _____

_____

_____

_____

_____

Now that you have completed this checklist, you will have a good sense of your strengths and weaknesses in the area of multicultural counseling competencies. This assessment will be of major importance if it leads you to take action to enhance your awareness, knowledge, and skills.

Skills in Opening and Closing Group Sessions

Leaders in training are frequently ineffective in opening and closing group meetings. For example, I've often seen leaders quickly focus on one group member at the beginning of a session with no mention of the previous session. Members should at least be given a brief opportunity to share what they did in the way of practice outside of the group since the previous session. In addition, I find it useful to have each member briefly state what he or she wants from the upcoming session. Closing a group session should entail more than an abrupt announcement of the end of the meeting. It's more productive for the group leader to lead everyone in summarizing, integrating, and helping one another find ways of applying what they've learned to outside situations.

The phrases, statements, and questions in the next two sections will give you some concrete tools for opening and closing group sessions. Review these lists frequently, and experiment with parts of them at different times. Add your own opening and closing statements to help you get sessions moving well and to end each of your meetings most effectively. I hope you will not employ these phrases mechanically; rather, find ways to introduce them in a timely and appropriate fashion. Eventually, some of these catalytic statements may become a natural part of your own leadership style.

Guidelines for Opening Group Sessions

- What would you be willing to talk about in this session?
- Last week we left off with _____.
- Did anyone have any afterthoughts about our last meeting?
- I'd like to share some of my thoughts regarding our last session.
- My expectations and hopes for this session are _____.
- What did you do this week with what you learned in the last session?
- I'd like to go around the group and have each person complete this sentence: "Right now I'm feeling _____."
- How would each of you like to be different today from the way you were in the last session?
- If you don't participate in the group today, how will that be for you?
- How is each of you feeling about being here today?
- What are you willing to do to make this session productive?
- If you're not here by choice, are you still willing to keep yourself open to getting something from the session?
- Is there any unfinished business from the last session that anyone wants to pursue?
- I'd like to go around the group and have each person finish this sentence: "Today I could be actively involved in the group by _____."

Guidelines for Closing Group Sessions

- What, if anything, did you learn in today's session?
- What did you hear yourself or someone else say that seemed especially significant to you?
- If you were to summarize the key themes that we explored today, what would they be?
- Are there any issues anyone wants to work on at the next session?
- A homework assignment I'd like you to consider is _____.
- Are there any changes you'd like to make in the group?

- How would you evaluate your participation in this session?
- We had a very intense session today. Would you like to say how you're feeling or thinking now?
- Before we close, I'd like to share my own reactions to this session.
- I noticed that you were very quiet during the session. Are you willing to say how this meeting was for you?

Guidelines for Meeting With Your Coleader

In the textbook I make frequent reference to learning to work effectively with a coleader. If you are working with a coleader, I cannot overemphasize the value of making the time to meet regularly with this person both before and after group sessions. In addition to talking about the progress of members in the group and the progress of the group as a whole, you will find it helpful to talk about your relationship with your coleader. To provide you with a framework for assessing how well you and your coleader are functioning as a team, I've prepared the following questions. Look over this list in meetings with your coleader, and select those issues that pertain to your relationship at various times. You can identify the areas in which you see yourself functioning especially well and those areas that both of you need to work on improving.

1. Did you select your coleader, or were the two of you assigned to each other? To what degree is there a trusting relationship between you? Do you respect each other? Are your differences complementary, or do they present problems in your functioning as a therapeutic team?
2. Did the two of you make plans and preparations together as the group was being organized? Are both of you actively involved and interested in the group now?
3. Are you making the time to meet between group sessions on a regular basis? How productive are your meetings? To what degree do you focus on your group and the members?
4. Are your theoretical orientations compatible? How do your theoretical views affect the goals and procedures of your group?
5. Do you and your coleader agree on the division of responsibility between the leaders and the members? Are the two of you sharing leadership responsibility to the satisfaction of each of you?
6. Are the two of you together in your expectations for the group?
7. How are the members reacting to each of you as a leader? How are you and your coleader reacting to each member? Is either of you having particular difficulty with any member?
8. Do both of you feel free to initiate suggestions and techniques in the group? Is either of you "holding back" and hoping that the other will do most of the leading?
9. Are both of you paying attention to how you open the group sessions and how you bring each session to a close?
10. Does each of you think of ways to consistently evaluate the progress of individual members and the group as a whole? Do you have some systematic feedback from the members about how they respond to your leadership?
11. Are you in agreement with your coleader about self-disclosure? Do both of you reveal to the members your reactions to what is going on in the group? If you see things differently from your coleader, are you open about this in the group? How do you handle problems

between the two of you? Can you talk openly with the members about your relationship and the way you lead together?

12. What is the balance between challenge and support in your group? Does one of the team typically support the members and the other challenge them? Are both of you able to be appropriately supportive and challenging?

13. Are the two of you reviewing each session and paying attention to any changes in the direction of the group? Can you profit from any mistakes that you have made? What are you learning about yourself and about groups by coleading? Are you devoting some time to making plans for upcoming sessions? And are you able to abandon your plans if it is called for in a particular session?

At the conclusion of the group, it will be imperative for you and your coleader to process the experience and to examine how your coleading relationship influenced the group dynamics. In addition to discussing any unfinished business, you might share with each other how you initially viewed your relationship and how (or if) it evolved over time. If the group were to continue, you might consider how you would proceed as coleaders and identify personal goals and shared goals that you would strive to achieve.

CHAPTER THREE

Ethical and Professional Issues in Group Practice

Prechapter Self-Inventory for Ethical and Professional Issues

Decide the degree to which you agree or disagree with the statements in this self-inventory. Respond to each statement, giving the initial response that most clearly identifies how you think or feel. I suggest that you go over your completed inventories and mark those items that you would like to discuss; then bring your inventories to class and compare your positions with the views of others. Such comparisons can stimulate debate and help the class become involved in the topics to be discussed.

Using the following code, write next to each statement the number of the response that most closely reflects your viewpoint:

5 = I *strongly agree* with this statement.
4 = I *agree,* in most respects, with this statement.
3 = I am *undecided* in my opinion about this statement.
2 = I *disagree,* in most respects, with this statement.
1 = I *strongly disagree* with this statement.

_____ 1. A central ethical issue in group work pertains to the group leader's competence.

_____ 2. Informed consent is not a one-time event, and clients should be informed at the outset that informed consent is an ongoing process.

_____ 3. When groups are involuntary, every attempt should be made to enlist the cooperation of the members and encourage them to continue attending voluntarily.

_____ 4. Members have a right to know that absolute confidentiality in groups is difficult and at times even unrealistic.

_____ 5. Confidentiality and privacy issues take on special considerations when group members and their therapists communicate with each other online and when group members communicate with other members via the Internet.

_____ 6. It is critical that group counselors increase their awareness of how their personal reactions to members may inhibit the group process.

_____ 7. As a group counselor, it is critical that you are aware of and understand your own spiritual or religious attitudes, beliefs, values, and experiences if you hope to facilitate an exploration of these issues with members of your groups.

_____ 8. Ethical practice demands that group counselors possess the self-awareness, knowledge, and skills that are basic components of diversity-competent practitioners.

_____ 9. At their best, group techniques are invented in each unique client situation, and they are a collaborative effort between the leader and members.

_____10. In working with culturally diverse client populations, leaders may need to modify some of their interventions to suit the client's cultural and ethnic background.

A Self-Inventory of Your Views on Ethical Practice in Group Work

This inventory is designed to stimulate your thinking about what constitutes ethical practice when leading groups. There are also exercises and activities, consisting of case vignettes for you to evaluate, as well as a self-evaluation of your level of training. These activities provide material for reflection and lively discussion in class.

In taking this first self-inventory, decide for each item the degree to which you think the leader's behavior is proper or improper, using the following code:

1 = This behavior is *unethical*.
2 = This behavior is *somewhat unethical*.
3 = I am *uncertain* about this behavior.
4 = This behavior is *somewhat ethical*.
5 = This behavior is *ethical*.

You may have your own reaction to an item that is different from the five listed here. Bring any of your reactions to class to compare with others' ideas.

_____ 1. A leader has no formal training or courses in group work but maintains that the best way to learn how to conduct groups is to do them.

_____ 2. A leader does not screen prospective members, believing that members will screen themselves out of a group if they find it is not appropriate for them.

_____ 3. A leader does not screen prospective members primarily because her theory is based on the assumption that anyone applying for a group should be accepted.

_____ 4. A leader makes tapes of the group sessions without the knowledge and consent of the members, based on the rationale that telling them would inhibit their free participation.

_____ 5. A leader refuses to see members between sessions, even if they request such a private session, and instead asks them to bring up the issue at the next group meeting.

_____ 6. A leader makes it a practice to socialize with members of a psychoeducation group, maintaining that this practice does not inhibit his capacity to work effectively with members.

_____ 7. A group counselor says that she sees nothing wrong in dating a former group member.

_____ 8. A leader fails to intervene when several members focus on another member and pressure that person to make a life decision.

_____ 9. A leader does not modify her techniques, even though many of the culturally diverse members in her group seem to have difficulty with some of her interventions.

_____10. A leader does not discuss with members any personal risks associated with joining a group because he believes he should not instill fears in members that they might not already have.

_____11. A group counselor who works with ethnic groups different from her own obtains specialized knowledge to better work with them.

_____12. A group leader assumes that a given individual will be hesitant to share emotional material because of his cultural background and decides not to make interventions with this member that are likely to evoke emotions.

_____13. A group leader does not mention confidentiality at the beginning of a group, thinking that if this topic is important the members will eventually bring it up.

_____14. A leader consciously attempts to impose her values on group members, based on the assumption that people who attend a group need clear direction from her.

_____15. A group counselor is willing to engage in a bartering arrangement with certain group members who say they cannot afford to pay the regular fee.

_____16. A leader sees nothing wrong in influencing the group in a subtle manner to accept his values.

_____17. A leader conducts groups to get her personal needs met through this work.

_____18. A leader regularly uses the group as a place for working out her personal problems, stating that this is good modeling for the other members.

_____19. A group counselor asserts that it is acceptable for her to develop sexual relationships with former group members, so long as they wait at least one year after the termination of the group.

_____20. A leader allows one member to dominate the group and does not intervene when this member monopolizes the group's time.

_____21. A group counselor pressures a culturally different group member to "open up" and share details about her family, maintaining that her silence is causing others in the group to mistrust her.

_____22. Without getting her permission, a leader contacts the parents of an adolescent girl who has disclosed her conflict over whether to have an abortion or keep her child.

_____23. A group leader is conducting research that involves the group, but she does not disclose this fact to the members, thinking that this may inhibit their participation.

_____24. A leader is uncomfortable when members explore a conflict and steers them away from addressing it, claiming that avoidance of conflict creates greater harmony.

_____25. A group counselor excludes a gay man from his group, stating that he does not approve of homosexuality so it would be difficult for him to be objective or compassionate with the man's struggles.

_____26. A leader says to the members in her group that everyone shares the same struggles, regardless of his or her cultural background, and that everyone in the group therefore needs to be treated equally and in the same fashion.

_____27. A leader does not state the purpose or goals of the group at the initial session.

_____28. A leader allows the expression of pent-up rage in group sessions but does not take precautions to see that members are not physically injured in these exercises.

_____29. A leader coerces members to participate in nonverbal touching exercises, thinking that this type of pressure is needed if they are to challenge their inhibitions.

_____30. A leader presses members to experience intense emotions and pushes for a catharsis—even if they say they do not want to explore a struggle—out of the conviction that they need to experience their emotions to become free.

_____31. A leader encourages certain ethnic members to give up their collectivist values in favor of thinking more of their own individual welfare.

_____32. A leader does not explain the rationale for an exercise she will be using and does not give members a choice to participate or not in the exercise.

_____33. When confidentiality is broken in a group of high school students, the leader ignores the situation, assuming that to discuss the matter or to take action will make things worse.

_____34. A leader forms a group with elementary schoolchildren without getting parental permission.

_____35. A group leader discusses in some detail his involvement with drugs, thinking that this will promote openness and trust among a group of adolescents.

_____36. A group leader refuses to obtain additional diversity training because she believes she will learn everything she needs to know about diversity directly from her group members.

_____37. Since a group leader has not officially joined a professional organization, he does not feel obligated to follow risk-management practices, which clinicians use to protect themselves from malpractice suits.

_____38. As a way to instill hope, a leader promises members that they will feel better shortly.

_____39. A group leader needs one more group member to be given permission by her supervisor to hold a group, and she allows a person with severe psychological problems to join a group of high-functioning clients.

_____40. A group leader refrains from seeking supervision after a group member announces that she is unhappy with the group and is terminating prematurely because he does not want to give his supervisor the impression that he is incompetent in leading the group.

_____41. A group leader does not present information about the group at the first meeting based on her belief that members will raise their concerns once the group is in progress.

_____42. A group leader promises absolute confidentiality to the members of her group.

_____43. A group leader does not attend to the informed consent process because the participants are involuntary members.

_____44. When a member is considering leaving a group, this leader intervenes by asking other members to pressure her into remaining in the group.

_____45. The group leader makes a special point to introduce confidentiality and privacy considerations in the event that group members communicate with each other online.

_____46. A group counselor addresses the parameters of online behavior through informed consent and establishes ground rules regarding members' commitment to avoid posting pictures, comments, or any type of confidential information about other members online.

_____47. Some members of a group are socializing outside of the group and this is known to all in the group, but the leader does not address this because he believes they have the right to make that choice.

_____49. Based on her conviction that religion and spirituality are important aspects of the lives of many participants, the group leader introduces these topics into several sessions.

_____50. When a group member brings up a religious concern, the leader encourages this member to discuss the matter with a clergy person because addressing such topics in a group are controversial and sensitive matters.

Association for Specialists in Group Work: "Best Practice Guidelines" (2008)*

This section presents the Association for Specialists in Group Work (ASGW) "Best Practice Guidelines." These guidelines were initially prepared by Lynn Rapin and Linda Keel (the cochairs of the ASGW Ethics Committee at the time) and were approved by the Executive Board on March 29, 1998. Several years later, Valorie Thomas and Deborah A. Pender (the cochairs of the ASGW Ethics Committee) revised them, and they were approved by the Executive Board on March 23, 2007. The "Best Practice Guidelines" address group workers' responsibilities in planning, performing, and processing group work. These guidelines are placed early in this manual with the expectation that you will want to refer to them often during the course.

The Association for Specialists in Group Work is a division of the American Counseling Association (ACA), which means that members of ASGW are bound to practice within the framework of the *ACA Code of Ethics* (as revised in 2014). The ASGW "Best Practice Guidelines" are meant to clarify and supplement the *ACA Code of Ethics*, not to replace them. The "Best Practice Guidelines" define group workers' responsibilities and scope of practice consistent with current ethical and community standards.

* *Note:* The following ASGW guidelines fit well with the chapter on ethical issues in group work. I recommend carefully reading these guidelines and addressing the questions following the guidelines. You can also access the "Best Practice Guidelines" online: www.asgw.org. You will also find a wide range of information about ASGW at the main website.

ASGW Best Practice Guidelines
Association for Specialists in Group Work
Best Practice Guidelines

Approved by the ASGW Executive Board, March 29, 1998
Prepared by: Lynn Rapin and Linda Keel ASGW Ethics Committee Co-Chairs
Revised by: Valorie Thomas and Deborah A. Pender ASGW Ethics Committee Co-Chairs
Revisions Approved by the ASGW Executive Board, March 23, 2007

The Association for Specialists in Group Work (ASGW) is a division of the American Counseling Association whose members are interested in and specialize in group work. Group Workers are defined as mental health professionals who use a group modality as an intervention when working with diverse populations. We value the creation of community while recognizing diverse perspectives; service to our members, clients, and the profession; and value leadership as a process to facilitate the growth and development of individuals and groups within their social and cultural contexts.

Preamble

The Association for Specialists in Group Work recognizes the commitment of its members to the Code of Ethics (as revised in 2005) of its parent organization, the American Counseling Association, and nothing in this document shall be construed to supplant that code. These Best Practice Guidelines are intended to clarify the application of the ACA Code of Ethics to the field of group work by defining Group Workers' responsibility and scope of practice involving those activities, strategies and interventions that are consistent and current with effective and appropriate professional ethical and community standards. ASGW views ethical process as being integral to group work and views Group Workers as ethical agents. Group Workers, by their very nature in being responsible and responsive to their group members, necessarily embrace a certain potential for ethical vulnerability. It is incumbent upon Group Workers to give considerable attention to the intent and context of their actions because the attempts of Group Workers to influence human behavior through group work always have ethical implications. These Best Practice Guidelines address Group Workers' responsibilities in planning, performing and processing groups.

Section A: Best Practice in Planning

A.1. Professional Context and Regulatory Requirements

Group Workers actively know, understand and apply the ACA Code of Ethics (2005), the ASGW Professional Standards for the Training of Group Workers, these ASGW Best Practice Guidelines, the ASGW diversity competencies, and the AMCD Multicultural Counseling Competencies and Standards, relevant state laws, accreditation requirements, relevant National Board for Certified Counselors Codes and Standards, their organization's standards, and insurance requirements impacting the practice of group work.

A.2. Scope of Practice and Conceptual Framework

Group Workers define the scope of practice related to the core and specialization competencies defined in the ASGW Training Standards. Group Workers are aware of personal strengths and weaknesses in leading groups. Group Workers develop and are able to articulate a general conceptual framework to guide practice and a rationale for use of techniques that are to be used. Group Workers limit their practice to those areas for which they meet the training criteria established by the ASGW Training Standards.

A.3. Assessment

a. Assessment of self. Group Workers actively assess their knowledge and skills related to the specific group(s) offered. Group Workers assess their values, beliefs and theoretical orientation and how these impact upon the group, particularly when working with a diverse and multicultural population.

b. Ecological assessment. Group Workers assess community needs, agency or organization resources, sponsoring organization mission, staff competency, attitudes regarding group work, professional training levels of potential group leaders regarding group work; client attitudes regarding group work, and multicultural and diversity considerations. Group Workers use this information as the basis for making decisions related to their group practice, or to the implementation of groups for which they have supervisory, evaluation, or oversight responsibilities.

A.4. Program Development and Evaluation

a. Group Workers identify the type(s) of group(s) to be offered and how they relate to community needs.

b. Group Workers concisely state in writing the purpose and goals of the group. Group Workers also identify the role of the group members in influencing or determining the group goals.

c. Group Workers set fees consistent with the organization's fee schedule, taking into consideration the financial status and locality of prospective group members.

d. Group Workers choose techniques and a leadership style appropriate to the type(s) of group(s) being offered.

e. Group Workers have an evaluation plan consistent with regulatory, organization and insurance requirements, where appropriate.

f. Group Workers take into consideration current professional guidelines when using technology, including but not limited to Internet communication.

A.5. Resources

Group Workers coordinate resources related to the kind of group(s) and group activities to be provided, such as: adequate funding; the appropriateness and availability of a trained co-leader; space and privacy requirements for the type(s) of group(s) being offered; marketing and recruiting; and appropriate collaboration with other community agencies and organizations.

A.6. Professional Disclosure Statement

Group Workers maintain awareness and sensitivity regarding cultural meaning of confidentiality and privacy. Group Workers respect differing views towards disclosure of information. They have a professional disclosure statement which includes information on confidentiality and exceptions to confidentiality, theoretical orientation, information on the nature, purpose(s) and goals of the group, the group services that can be provided, the role and responsibility of group members and leaders, Group Workers qualifications to conduct the specific group(s), specific licenses, certifications and professional affiliations, and address of licensing/credentialing body.

A.7. Group and Member Preparation

a. Group Workers screen prospective group members if appropriate to the type of group being offered. When selection of group members is appropriate, Group Workers identify group members whose needs and goals are compatible with the goals of the group.

b. Group Workers facilitate informed consent. They communicate information in ways that are both developmentally and culturally appropriate. Group Workers provide in oral and written form to prospective members (when appropriate to group type): the professional disclosure statement; group purpose and goals; group participation expectations including voluntary and involuntary membership; role expectations of members and leader(s); policies related to entering and exiting the group; policies governing substance use; policies and procedures governing mandated groups (where relevant); documentation requirements; disclosure of information to others; implications of out-of-group contact or involvement among members; procedures for consultation between group leader(s) and group member(s); fees and time parameters; and potential impacts of group participation.

c. Group Workers obtain the appropriate consent/assent forms for work with minors and other dependent group members.

d. Group Workers define confidentiality and its limits (for example, legal and ethical exceptions and expectations; waivers implicit with treatment plans, documentation and insurance usage). Group Workers have the responsibility to inform all group participants of the need for confidentiality, potential consequences of breaching confidentiality and that legal privilege does not apply to group discussions (unless provided by state statute).

A.8. Professional Development

Group Workers recognize that professional growth is a continuous, ongoing, developmental process throughout their career.

a. Group Workers remain current and increase knowledge and skill competencies through activities such as continuing education, professional supervision, and participation in personal and professional development activities.

b. Group Workers seek consultation and/or supervision regarding ethical concerns that interfere with effective functioning as a group leader. Supervisors have the responsibility to keep abreast of consultation, group theory, process, and adhere to related ethical guidelines.

c. Group Workers seek appropriate professional assistance for their own personal problems or conflicts that are likely to impair their professional judgement or work performance.

d. Group Workers seek consultation and supervision to ensure appropriate practice whenever working with a group for which all knowledge and skill competencies have not been achieved.

e. Group Workers keep abreast of group research and development.

A.9. Trends and Technological Changes

Group Workers are aware of and responsive to technological changes as they affect society and the profession. These include but are not limited to changes in mental health delivery systems; legislative and insurance industry reforms; shifting population demographics and client needs; and technological advances in Internet and other communication devices and delivery systems. Group Workers adhere to ethical guidelines related to the use of developing technologies.

Section B: Best Practice in Performing

B.1. Self Knowledge

Group Workers are aware of and monitor their strengths and weaknesses and the effects these have on group members. They explore their own cultural identities and how these affect their values and beliefs about group work.

B.2. Group Competencies

Group Workers have a basic knowledge of groups and the principles of group dynamics, and are able to perform the core group competencies, as described in the ASGW Professional Standards for the Training of Group Workers. They gain knowledge, personal awareness, sensitivity, and skills pertinent to working with a diverse client population. Additionally, Group Workers have adequate understanding and skill in any group specialty area chosen for practice (psychotherapy, counseling, task, psychoeducation, as described in the ASGW Training Standards).

B.3. Group Plan Adaptation

a. Group Workers apply and modify knowledge, skills and techniques appropriate to group type and stage, and to the unique needs of various cultural and ethnic groups.

b. Group Workers monitor the group's progress toward the group goals and plan.

c. Group Workers clearly define and maintain ethical, professional, and social relationship boundaries with group members as appropriate to their role in the organization and the type of group being offered.

B.4. Therapeutic Conditions and Dynamics

Group Workers understand and are able to implement appropriate models of group development, process observation and therapeutic conditions.

Group Workers manage the flow of communication, addressing safely and pacing of disclosures as to protect group members from physical, emotional, or psychological trauma.

B.5. Meaning

Group Workers assist members in generating meaning from the group experience.

B.6. Collaboration

Group Workers assist members in developing individual goals and respect group members as co-equal partners in the group experience.

B.7. Evaluation

Group Workers include evaluation (both formal and informal) between sessions and at the conclusion of the group.

B.8. Diversity

Group Workers practice with broad sensitivity to client differences including but not limited to ethnic, gender, religious, sexual, psychological maturity, economic class, family history, physical characteristics or limitations, and geographic location. Group Workers continuously seek information regarding the cultural issues of the diverse population with whom they are working both by interaction with participants and from using outside resources.

B.9. Ethical Surveillance

Group Workers employ an appropriate ethical decision making model in responding to ethical challenges and issues and in determining courses of action and behavior for self and group members. In addition, Group Workers employ applicable standards as promulgated by ACA, ASGW, or other appropriate professional organizations.

Section C: Best Practice in Group Processing

C.1. Processing Schedule

Group Workers process the workings of the group with themselves, group members, supervisors or other colleagues, as appropriate. This may include assessing progress on group and member goals, leader behaviors and techniques, group dynamics and interventions; developing understanding and acceptance of meaning. Processing may occur both within sessions and before and after each session, at time of termination, and later follow-up, as appropriate.

C.2. Reflective Practice

Group Workers attend to opportunities to synthesize theory and practice and to incorporate learning outcomes into ongoing groups. Group Workers attend to session dynamics of members and their interactions and also attend to the relationship between session dynamics and leader values, cognition and affect.

C.3. Evaluation and Follow-Up

a. Group Workers evaluate process and outcomes. Results are used for ongoing program planning, improvement and revisions of current group and/or to contribute to professional research literature. Group Workers follow all applicable policies and standards in using group material for research and reports.

b. Group Workers conduct follow-up contact with group members, as appropriate, to assess outcomes or when requested by a group member(s).

C.4. Consultation and Training with Other Organizations

Group Workers provide consultation and training to organizations in and out of their setting, when appropriate. Group Workers seek out consultation as needed with competent professional persons knowledgeable about group work.

Questions to Consider in Examining the "Best Practice Guidelines"

As you work through these questions, pay particular attention to ways you might apply the "Best Practice Guidelines" to group practice. I hope these questions will raise further questions in your mind as you begin the process of developing your own ethical guidelines. Ask yourself what additional guidelines might be included, or consider guidelines you want to challenge. If you were a member of the ASGW Ethics Committee charged with the task of revising these guidelines, which ones would you most want to modify, and why? Do you think the guidelines are complete and comprehensive? Do you see any bias in these guidelines? Are there any specific areas that need to be addressed in more detail for group counselors? Take the time to thoroughly review each of these guidelines in a critical way, and discuss the issues raised by them in small groups in class.

1. Scope of Practice and Conceptual Framework
    a. To what extent are you committed to limiting your practice to those areas for which you have met the training criteria established by the ASGW Training Standards?
    b. How well are you able to articulate a general conceptual framework to guide your practice? Can you provide a rationale for the techniques you use?
2. Assessment
    a. To what degree are you able to assess your knowledge and skills against those required to effectively lead a specific group?
    b. How well are you able to assess your values, beliefs, and theoretical orientation? How do these factors influence your work with groups?
    c. To what extent are you aware of your own values, biases, assumptions, and beliefs that most apply to working with culturally different clients?
    d. How do you make decisions about which techniques and leadership styles are appropriate to the specific groups you offer?
    e. To what degree are you able to assess community needs?
    f. If you are working in an agency setting, how familiar are you with the organization's resources and mission, and with their attitudes about and commitment to group work? Can you comment on client attitudes regarding group work?
    g. How well are you equipped to deal with multicultural and diversity considerations? How are such considerations dealt with at the agency or organizational level (if applicable)?
3. Professional Disclosure Statement
    a. As a group worker, what kind of professional disclosure statement do you believe is appropriate and useful?
    b. What would you most want to include in this document?
4. Group and Member Preparation
    a. What kind of minimal information would you provide to a person wanting to join one of your groups?
    b. How do you think informed consent can best be accomplished in both voluntary and mandatory groups?
    c. What are some legal and ethical issues pertaining to informed consent?
    d. Is it unethical to fail to screen prospective group members?
    e. What are some alternatives when screening is not practical?
    f. How can screening and orientation be handled in mandatory groups?
    g. How would you explain what confidentiality is and its purpose to members of your groups?
    h. Under what circumstances are you ethically or legally required to breach confidentiality?
    i. How can confidentiality best be taught to group members and maintained?
    j. How would you explain to members of your groups that legal privilege does not apply to group work unless it is provided by state statute?
5. Professional Development
    a. What steps might you take to remain current and to increase your knowledge and skill competencies?
    b. As a group worker, when would you seek consultation or supervision?

c. If you were encountering difficulties leading a group, what steps might you take in getting supervision or consultation?

d. Can you think of any areas of unresolved personal problems that could impair your professional judgment or inhibit your effectiveness as a group leader?

e. If you became aware of countertransference issues or personal problems that affected your performance as a group worker, what would you do?

6. Group Plan Adaptation

a. At this point in time, how well would you be able to modify your knowledge, skills, and techniques to match the type of group you were leading and the group's stage of development?

b. What are some ways in which you can help members continually assess the degree to which they are meeting their own goals?

c. How would you monitor the group's progress toward the group goals and purpose of the group?

d. How would you establish appropriate boundaries with group members?

7. Therapeutic Conditions and Dynamics

a. How would you create a therapeutic environment that would protect group members from physical, emotional, and psychological trauma?

b. What are some of the main characteristics and conditions you would most want to see in your group?

8. Meaning

a. How could you assist group members in finding meaning through the group experience?

b. Do you have preconceived ideas about what needs to occur in a group so that the experience will be meaningful to members?

9. Collaboration

a. How comfortable are you with treating group members as collaborators or equal partners in the therapeutic journey?

b. What are some specific things you can say or do to let your members know that they are equal partners?

10. Diversity

a. As a group practitioner, what ethical issues might you expect to confront with respect to working with diverse client populations?

b. To what degree are you willing to seek information regarding the cultural issues of the diverse populations in your groups?

11. Processing and Reflective Practice

a. In what ways is it your ethical obligation as a group facilitator to be reflective and process the group's dynamics?

b. Would it be possible to overanalyze or excessively process the workings of a group? If so, how would you determine when that line is crossed?

12. Evaluation and Follow-Up

a. What are some ideas you have for evaluating the process and outcomes of your groups?

b. Is it unethical to fail to arrange for follow-up meetings?

c. What are some alternatives to follow-up meetings on either an individual or a group basis?

American Group Psychotherapy Association. Inc. (AGPA)
Ethical Guidelines for Group Therapists
(Revised, February, 2002)
Guidelines for Ethics
Introduction

The American Group Psychotherapy Association is a multi-disciplinary, membership organization dedicated to advancing knowledge, research, and training in group psychotherapy and other group interventions to benefit the client/patient population. The National Registry of Certified Group Psychotherapists advances group psychotherapy by certifying group psychotherapists according to nationally accepted criteria, and promotes these practitioners and principles to other mental health professionals, employers, insurers, educators, and clients for the purpose of maintaining the highest standards for group psychotherapy practice and quality care. Membership in AGPA and/or inclusion in the National Registry requires adherence to standards of ethical practice as outlined by state licensing boards and/or designated national professional organizations, whichever was applicable in establishing clinical credentials. Those who do not belong to a professional group having a published standard of ethics must follow the principles of ethics established by the American Psychological Association.

Ethical complaints about individuals who are members of AGPA and/or listed in the Registry should be directed to the state licensing board or, in the absence of a state license, to the designated primary professional organization of the individual. Should an ethical complaint be received regarding an individual who is a member of AGPA and/or listed in the Registry whose state does not have licensure and who does not belong to a primary professional organization, the complainant will be directed to the state or federal legal system to file his or her complaint.

In the event of the revocation, suspension or voluntary relinquishment of a clinical license to practice or membership/certification in the designated national professional organization, membership in AGPA and/or inclusion in the Registry will be revoked. In the event an individual referred to the governmental agencies or courts of law is found guilty, his or her AGPA membership and/or his or her inclusion in the Registry will be revoked. It is the responsibility of the individual to inform AGPA and/or the Registry of any revocation, suspension or voluntary relinquishment of licensure or membership/certification, whichever was used to verify clinical credentials for inclusion in the Registry.

Guidelines of Group Psychotherapy Practice

The following guidelines of group psychotherapy practice shall serve as models for group therapists' ethical behavior.

Responsibility to Patient/Client

1. The group psychotherapist provides services with respect for the dignity and uniqueness of each patient/client as well as the rights and autonomy of the individual patient/client.
   1.1 The group psychotherapist shall provide the potential group patient/client with information about the nature of group psychotherapy and apprise him or her of the risks, rights and obligations as a member of a therapy group.
   1.2 The group psychotherapist shall encourage the patient/client's participation in group psychotherapy only so long as it is appropriate to the patient/client's needs.
   1.3 The group psychotherapist shall not practice or condone any form of discrimination on the basis of race, color, sex, sexual orientation, age, religion, national origin or physical handicap, except that this guideline shall not prohibit group therapy practice with population specific or problem specific groups.
2. The group psychotherapist safeguards the patient/client's right to privacy by judiciously protecting information of a confidential nature.
   2.1 The group shall agree that the patient/client as well as the psychotherapist shall protect the identity of its members.
   2.2 The group therapist is knowledgeable about the limits of privileged communication as they apply to group therapy and informs group members of those limits.
   2.3 The group psychotherapist shall not use identifiable information about the group or its members for teaching purposes, publication or professional presentations unless permission has been obtained and all measures have been taken to preserve patient/client anonymity.

2.4 Except where required by law, the group psychotherapist shall share information about the group members with others only after obtaining appropriate patient/client consent. Specific permission must be requested to permit conferring with the referring therapist or with the individual therapist where the patient/client is in conjoint therapy.

2.5 When clinical examination suggests that a patient/client may be dangerous to himself/herself or others, it is the group psychotherapist's ethical and legal obligation to take appropriate steps in order to be responsible to society in general, as well as the patient/client.

3. The group psychotherapist acts to safeguard the patient/client and the public from the incompetent, unethical, illegal practice of any group psychotherapist.

3.1 The group psychotherapist must be aware of her/his own individual competencies, and when the needs of the patient/client are beyond the competencies of the psychotherapist, consultation must be sought from other qualified professionals or other appropriate sources.

3.2 The group psychotherapist shall not use her/his professional relationship to advance personal or business interests.

3.3 Sexual intimacy with patients/clients is unethical.

3.4 The group psychotherapist shall protect the patient/client and the public from misinformation and misrepresentation. She/he shall not use false or misleading advertising regarding her/his qualifications or skills as a group psychotherapist.

Professional Standards

The group psychotherapist shall maintain the integrity of the practice of group psychotherapy.

1. It is the personal responsibility of the group psychotherapist to maintain competence in the practice of group psychotherapy through formal educational activities and informal learning experiences.

2. The group psychotherapist has a responsibility to contribute to the ongoing development of the body of knowledge pertaining to group psychotherapy whether involved as an investigator, participant or user of research results.

3. The group psychotherapist shall accept the obligation to attempt to inform and alert other group psychotherapists who are violating ethical principles or to bring those violations to the attention of appropriate professional authorities.

Questions to Consider in Examining the AGPA "Ethical Guidelines for Group Therapists"

1. *Responsibility to Patient/Client*

   a. In what ways can you demonstrate to group members that you have respect for them and honor their uniqueness?

   b. If you have difficulty respecting the actions of certain individuals attending your group, what steps could you take to ensure that you provide effective services to them?

   c. How will you inform group members about the risks involved in group work? What will you say to them about the importance of maintaining confidentiality? Should these topics be raised only at the outset of the group, or should they be discussed throughout the group?

   d. What actions might you take if members make racist, homophobic, or sexist remarks in the group?

   e. Under what circumstances would you share information about group members with others? In such instances, how much information would be appropriate and ethical to divulge? With whom would you share this information?

   f. What type of dual or multiple relationships with group members should be avoided at all costs? Are there circumstances under which dual or multiple relationships would be appropriate or even beneficial to them?

2. *Professional Standards*
   a. How will you contribute to the ongoing development of the knowledge base pertaining to group psychotherapy?
   b. In what ways are you prepared to protect the reputation of the profession? If a colleague was behaving in an ethically inappropriate manner, how would you proceed?

Exercises and Activities

Case Vignettes: Practice With Ethical Decision Making

Directions: The following situations in groups are presented for your analysis and for class discussion. What do you see as the ethical issues in each situation? To what degree do you think the group leader in each situation acted in an ethical or an unethical manner? What do you think you would have done differently? How might the situation in each case be remedied? Do you have any thoughts about how an unethical practice might have been avoided?

The object of these exercises is to give you practice in ethical decision making and an opportunity to discuss ethical issues involved in the practice of group work. Read each of the case situations presented, and respond by placing the number in the blank that best represents your professional ethical opinion regarding the *group leader's behavior.* Use this code:

1 = unethical
2 = somewhat unethical
3 = uncertain
4 = somewhat ethical
5 = ethical

_____ 1. *Orientation and providing information.* The group leader assumes that the more information about group process she provides, the more the members will attempt to please her. She is opposed to giving prior information, either in writing or orally. If members flounder in defining goals, she believes this is part of the group process; therefore, she does not emphasize goal definition. She does not discuss the procedures she will use because she believes procedures are not possible without specified goals. Thus, procedures will be dictated by the eventual goals members define. This leader is convinced that informed consent is not really possible and thinks members should follow their own spontaneous paths rather than learning about group norms and other expected group behavior.

_____ 2. *Screening members.* This case involves a busy mental health clinic that is understaffed. Counselors are under some pressure to do group work as a way of dealing with more clients in a given time. A counselor decides to organize a group by putting a notice on the bulletin board in the clinic and by sending colleagues a memorandum asking for candidates. There are no provisions for individual screening of potential members, no written announcements informing members of the goals and purposes of the group, and no preparation for incoming members. No information is given to the members about the leader's background, possible techniques to be used, expectations, and so forth. No consideration is given to the leader's qualifications to work with special populations. The receptionist is asked to admit the first 12 people who come to sign up. The receptionist puts people into the group as they inquire, irrespective of the nature of their problems, and they are simply told to show up at the first meeting.

_____ 3. *Confidentiality.* A group leader discusses the legal aspects of confidentiality, the reasons for it, and the impact on the group when confidentiality is breached. He summarizes members' responsibility in keeping confidentiality by saying, "Anything that happens here, stays here." In discussing the importance of confidentiality in the group, he also points out how confidentiality can be violated in subtle ways and how confidences are often divulged without malice.

_____ 4. *Voluntary/involuntary participation.* A group leader agrees to accept court-ordered members into her group. In spite of her attempts to get these members involved, they consistently make it clear that they are there only as a condition of their probation and that they have no intention of getting personally involved. After the 10 required sessions, the group leader reports back to the probation officer that these individuals made satisfactory progress, mainly because they attended the sessions and she was convinced they must have learned something simply by listening to others even though they didn't share or participate.

_____ 5. *Leaving a group.* A leader says: "Because this is a voluntary group, your attendance cannot be required. If at any time you don't want to attend, use your judgment and stay away. If for any reason you find that this group is not meeting your needs, you're perfectly free to leave. We want you in this group only if you're choosing to be a member." Several members simply drop out of the group without telling the leader or the other members that this is their intention. The leader continues the group, making no references to the missing members.

_____ 6. *Coercion and pressure.* Joan is having difficulties with her husband, and she discusses her struggles with him in her group. Before she has had a chance to express the full range of her feelings and explore her own part in the conflict, many members intervene with advice, such as "Leave the guy," "You're better off without him," "Don't waste any more of your life—you deserve better," and "If someone did that to me, I sure wouldn't hang around." The leader intervenes and redirects the group discussion to Joan's feelings.

_____ 7. *Imposing leader values.* Imagine a group in which several value-laden issues, such as homosexuality, abortion, heavy drug use, and extramarital affairs, have come up for discussion. The leader, Catherine, has definite convictions on most of these issues, but she thinks that to express these values might have an undue influence on the group. Thus, each time she is asked directly about her position, Catherine turns it back on the members by saying: "It seems to be very important for you to know how I stand on this issue. Talk to me about this." She never does state her position on the issues.

_____ 8. *Equitable treatment.* This situation involves a leader who focuses his attention primarily on several younger women while ignoring most of the other members. He often cuts others short or seems rather impatient when they are working. Eventually, one of the male members confronts the leader on this issue; the leader asserts that the women are much more willing to work than the other members and continues with his selective style.

_____ 9. *Dual relationships.* Jack has been leading an ongoing group for several months. At times the members have parties, and they inform Jack that these gatherings have drawn them closer together than if they had restricted their time together to the group situation. They sense a gap with him, however, because they see him only in a professional role. They tell him that they miss him at these parties and that it would be good for him and for the group if he came to some of them. They clearly express their desire for more personal contact with him because they want to get to know him in a more informal situation. He decides to attend, hoping to increase the cohesion in the group.

_____10. *Use of techniques.* Steve, a relatively inexperienced group leader, attends a weekend workshop designed to liberate one's feelings through the use of techniques aimed at promoting catharsis. He is impressed with the power of this therapy and is eager to try out these techniques in the men's group he leads at a local prison. During one session, an inmate with a propensity for violence seems slightly agitated. Steve decides to use a technique to heighten or intensify his emotions and "let it all out." He hopes this will be a cathartic experience for the group member.

_____11. *Goal development.* Phil begins a group session with this statement: "I assume that you all want something from this group, so let's get down to business right away. Who wants to work?" Because of Phil's skills in working with members, there is rarely a dull session, and things seem to keep moving. He is active in using role-playing techniques, in suggesting homework assignments, in taking members on guided fantasies, and in providing structured exercises. He does not spend group time talking about the members' personal goals or how they might best accomplish what they came to the group to attain.

_____12. *Consultation.* Fran is conducting a short-term group in an elementary school aimed at helping children of divorce. At the beginning of the group, she lets the children know that for the most part, what they explore in the group will stay there. She becomes concerned about one of the children, Brad, thinking that he might be suicidal. She seeks consultation from the school psychologist and discusses her concerns about Brad with his teachers. She does not tell him that she is seeking outside consultation because she does not want to alarm him, nor does she want to convey the impression that she is sharing information from the group with other school personnel.

_____13. *Termination from the group.* Ken is just finishing a group that he has led weekly for a year. The group members express a unanimous desire to continue. They feel good about themselves and one another and are sad to leave these weekly sessions, which they believe have been very productive for them. They express anxiety about continuing to make it without group support and without Ken's direction. This is the final session, and now they ask him to keep the group going. He decides not to continue the group.

_____14. *Evaluation and follow-up.* Bart comes to the West Coast from the East Coast to offer an intensive personal growth workshop. During the workshop, many personal conflicts emerge and much emotion is expressed. There is no letup in the intensity because Bart assumes that the way to achieve breakthroughs is to "keep at it constantly" so that defenses are broken down. This leader believes people develop tough defenses and that the best way to crack them is through a sustained period of confrontations. No follow-up is planned, and Bart asserts, "Group members are responsible for themselves and will go only as far as they choose." The residential workshop ends and Bart leaves the state the next morning to conduct another group, providing no information on where the members can turn for further assistance.

_____15. *Referrals.* Paula is employed as a counselor at a community mental health agency where no groups are available. She believes in the value of group counseling after her clients have completed a number of individual sessions with her. In spite of her best efforts to begin a group at her agency, the director does not give her permission. Paula then suggests to some of her individual clients that she would be pleased to accept them into a group through her private practice. Because she knows they are financially strapped, she is willing to have them join her group at a reduced fee.

_____16. *Professional development.* Because of the demand, Rhonda agrees to organize and lead a group for battered women at the agency where she is employed. She is hesitant to lead the group because she did not have a course in group counseling in her graduate program, has not been in a group as a member, and has not had any supervision or training in group work. She finally agrees to set up the group because she thinks the techniques and skills she uses in individual counseling will easily transfer to a group situation. Because it is not realistic for her to obtain group training quickly, she convinces herself that the pressing demand for this group makes it acceptable for her to lead it.

_____17. *Countertransference.* Howard is a group psychotherapist in private practice. He recently got divorced and has bitter feelings toward his ex-wife. A new client, Diane, is the spitting image of his ex-wife and has joined one of Howard's groups to work through her past experiences as a victim of domestic violence. It has crossed Howard's mind to refer Diane to another therapist; however, he has decided to continue working with her. Faced with having to pay his ex-wife a great deal in alimony, he cannot afford to lose any income by referring clients.

_____18. *Coleader issues.* Lorenzo and George have been coleading a group for 2 months as part of an experiential group course. Although Lorenzo consistently makes himself available before and after the group to process each session, George does not. He claims to have other commitments; however, he has been caught lying on a couple of occasions. Consequently, Lorenzo no longer trusts George, yet he tries to "keep the peace" because he hates conflict. Lorenzo's unspoken resentment is beginning to become apparent to group members and has affected group cohesion. Despite being aware of this, Lorenzo has decided not to confront George, and instead just "get through the semester."

_____19. *An impaired colleague.* Hillary recently joined the staff of counselors at an alternative school serving high school students who have been engaging in delinquent behaviors. Toby, an older and more experienced counselor, runs a number of the groups there. Despite his popularity among the students, Hillary has observed that he seems burned out and disengaged. In fact, she suspects that he is drinking on the job. An outspoken young woman, Hillary decides to bypass confronting Toby directly and informs the principal.

_____20. *An online group.* Marisa is very adept at using technology and is also a skilled group leader. Thus, she has decided to combine her talents and start an online group for depressed teenagers. She is not overly concerned about privacy issues because she trusts that she will be able to develop a secure site. She likes the fact that her clients won't have to contend with transportation issues to get to therapy. They will be able to log on from their own computers at home. Some of Marisa's colleagues have been critical of this idea because they fear she won't be able to pick up on important cues over the Internet (such as body language or severity of depression). Marisa believes the potential advantages of facilitating an online group outweigh the potential risks.

Self-Evaluation of Your Level of Training as a Group Worker

Note: You can access the ASGW (2000) "Professional Standards for the Training of Group Workers" online: www.asgw.org. You will also find a wide range of information about ASGW at the main website.

The following activity allows you to assess your current level of knowledge and skills as a group counselor. It is based on "Professional Standards for the Training of Group Workers," which were expanded, revised, and adopted by the ASGW's Executive Board in 2000.* (Download this document by linking to the ASGW website.) These standards contain both knowledge competencies and skill competencies that the ASGW considers as core training in group work for all counselors. The ASGW also specifies 10 hours of observation of and participation in a group experience as the minimum level of supervised practice (with a recommended 20 hours of such experience). There should be a minimum of one course in basic group work that deals with knowledge and skills. In addition to the core group competencies, advanced competencies are specified for group work specialists in these four areas of group work: (1) task facilitation groups, (2) psychoeducation groups, (3) counseling groups, and (4) psychotherapy groups.

Directions: Rate yourself on the following competencies, using this scale:

5 = I am *especially strong* in this area.

4 = I am *very good to good* in this area.

3 = I am just *adequate* and could surely improve.

2 = I am *deficient* and need much improvement.

1 = I am *especially weak* in this competency.

Core Knowledge Competencies for Group Workers

To the following degree, I am able to:

_____ 1. state the four major group work specializations, the distinguishing characteristics of each, the commonalities shared by all, and the appropriate instances in which each is to be used.

_____ 2. identify the basic principles of group dynamics.

---

*The sections dealing with knowledge competencies and skill competencies are adapted by permission of the ASGW. The rating scale is an adaptation of the standards for the purposes of this manual.

Source "Association for Specialists in Group Work: Professional Standards for the Training of Group Workers," *Group Worker,* 28(3), Spring 2000, pp. 1–10. [Special insert]. Reprinted with permission of ASGW.

_____ 3. discuss the basic therapeutic ingredients of groups.

_____ 4. identify the personal characteristics of group workers that have an impact on members and know my personal strengths, weaknesses, biases, and values and their effect on others.

_____ 5. describe the specific ethical issues that are unique to group work.

_____ 6. discuss the body of research on group work and how it relates to my academic preparation.

_____ 7. define the process components involved in the typical stages of a group's development.

_____ 8. describe the major facilitative and debilitative roles that group members may play.

_____ 9. state the advantages and disadvantages of group work and the circumstances for which it is indicated or contraindicated.

_____ 10. identify therapeutic factors of group work.

_____ 11. identify principles and strategies for recruiting and screening prospective group members.

_____ 12. explain the importance of group and member evaluation.

_____ 13. deliver a clear, concise, and complete definition of group work.

_____ 14. explain and clarify the purpose of a particular form of group work.

Core Skill Competencies for Group Workers

To the following degree, I am able to:

_____ 1. encourage the participation of group members.

_____ 2. observe and identify group process events.

_____ 3. attend to and acknowledge group members' behavior.

_____ 4. clarify and summarize group members' statements.

_____ 5. open and close group sessions.

_____ 6. impart information in the group when necessary.

_____ 7. model effective group leader behavior.

_____ 8. engage in appropriate self-disclosure.

_____ 9. give and receive feedback in the group.

_____ 10. ask open-ended questions in the group.

_____ 11. empathize with group members.

_____ 12. confront group members' behavior.

_____ 13. help group members attribute meaning to their experience.

_____ 14. help group members integrate and apply their learning.

_____ 15. demonstrate the ASGW ethical and professional standards in group practice.

_____ 16. keep the group on course in accomplishing its goals.

Evaluating Group Leadership Competencies

_____ 1. Look over your knowledge and skill ratings to get a sense of your current level of proficiency. What do you think you can do to develop those areas that need strengthening? Form small groups in class to discuss your self-assessments. As a group, what ideas can you come up with to develop and maintain each of the knowledge and skill competencies?

_____ 2. Carefully look at the ASGW's recommendations for practice as a part of the core training in group work. What training experiences have you received to date? What supervised group experiences have you had? What experiences do you expect to have had by the time you complete your program?

_____ 3. Review the ethical issues involved in the training of group workers (described in Chapter 3 of the textbook). What ethical issues have the most relevance for your own training at this time? Three experiences as adjuncts to a training program for group workers are described: (1) participation in personal counseling, (2) participation in group counseling or a personal growth group, and (3) participation in a training and supervision group. What are your thoughts about the value of each of these aspects of training? How willing would you be to involve yourself through various means of self-exploration in becoming a group counselor? Again, form small groups in class and discuss the ethical issues each of you find most interesting regarding the training of group counselors.

_____ 4. In Chapter 2 of the Student Manual there is a checklist of 22 group leader skills. I suggest that you review and complete it several times during the course. These are concrete skills that are needed for effective group leadership. One way to improve your level of skill development is to periodically assess your areas of strength and specific areas needing improvement.

CHAPTER FOUR

Early Stages in the Development of a Group

Prechapter Self-Inventory for the Early Stages in the Development of a Group

Decide the degree to which you agree or disagree with the statements in this self-inventory. Respond to each statement, giving the initial response that most clearly identifies how you think or feel. I suggest that you go over your completed inventories and mark those items you would like to discuss; then bring your inventories to class, and compare your positions with the views of others. Such comparisons can stimulate debate and help the class become involved in the topics to be discussed.

Using the following code, write next to each statement the number of the response that most closely reflects your viewpoint:

5 = I *strongly agree* with this statement.
4 = I *agree,* in most respects, with this statement.
3 = I am *undecided* in my opinion about this statement.
2 = I *disagree,* in most respects, with this statement.
1 = I *strongly disagree* with this statement.

_____ 1. For a group to be successful, you need to devote considerable time to planning.

_____ 2. By learning about the problems and potential crises of each stage, you learn when and how to intervene.

_____ 3. Careful screening will lessen the psychological risks of inappropriate participation in a group.

_____ 4. As a group leader, you have a responsibility to determine whether a prospective member is suitable for a given group; this decision will protect both the prospective member and the group itself.

_____ 5. Screening, selecting, and orienting members to group procedures are especially critical in working with individuals from diverse cultural groups.

_____ 6. During the initial stage of a group, the members are tentative because they are discovering and testing limits and are wondering whether they will be accepted.

_____ 7. The leader's success in establishing a basic sense of trust and security depends in large part on how well he or she has prepared for the group.

_____ 8. The more unstructured the group, the greater the anxiety and ambiguity about how one is to behave in a group.

_____ 9. If a level of trust has been established during the initial stage, members are usually willing to express certain feelings, thoughts, and reactions that they may not have been willing to verbalize during earlier sessions.

_____10. Recognizing that conflict is often inevitable and that it can strengthen trust is likely to reduce the probability that members and the leader will try to dodge the conflicts that are a natural part of a group's development.

Suggestions for Writing a Proposal for a Group

A clear and convincing proposal is often essential for translating a good idea for a group into actual practice. If you are going to create a group under the auspices of your supervisors or an agency, you will probably have to explain your rationale and proposed methods, and you may be required to submit your ideas in written form. Writing out your proposal can help you conceptualize your goals, procedures, and strategies for evaluation. There are many different kinds of groups, so there is no standard form that you can follow in writing a proposal for a group. Tailor your proposal for your unique setting and population and provide a clear and comprehensive picture of what you intend to accomplish in your group.

To gain practice in developing, writing, and presenting a proposal, think of a group that you would eventually like to organize. Once you have decided on a particular type of group (for example, a group for parents who want to learn better child-rearing skills, a group for children in an elementary school, or a group for adolescents who are having problems in school), answer the following questions before drafting your proposal. These questions can assist you in the design and structure of your group. Later, spend some time in class discussing the various members' proposals and getting feedback from others on how to improve your proposal.

1. What type of group will you create? Will it be a counseling group? a therapy group? a psychoeducation group? a task group? Will it be long term or short term? Will it have a remedial (treatment) or a developmental (enhancement) focus?
2. Who is the group for? Is it for a particular population, such as children in an elementary school? for outpatients in a community mental health center? for substance abusers in a residential setting? for parents who are having major problems relating to their children? for couples who hope to learn better communication skills? for veterans returning from the Middle East?
3. What are your goals for this group; that is, what will members gain from participating in the group? What are the short-term goals? Are the goals and objectives specific? How will these goals be accomplished in a group setting? How will the long-range goals be evaluated during the course of the group and once it comes to an end?
4. In what ways would a group provide definite advantages over individual counseling?
5. What are your basic assumptions underlying this project? Do you have a clear and convincing rationale for your group?
6. Who will lead the group? What are the leader's qualifications? If you will be leading the group, will you be doing so alone, or will you be working with a coleader? What challenges might you face if you lead the group on your own? What would the challenges be in coleading a group?
7. How will you announce your group and recruit members for it? Where will you get members? What will you want to convey in any written announcements?
8. What kind of screening and selection procedures will be used? What is the rationale for using these particular procedures? Who will you include, and whom might you exclude?

9. How many members will be in the group? Where will the group meet? How often will it meet? How long will each meeting last? Will new people be allowed to join the group once it has started?

10. What structure will the group have? Will it be designed around special topics and issues? If so, what topics are likely to be the focus of the group?

11. How will members be prepared to derive the maximum benefit from the group? What ground rules will the group have?

12. Will you ask members to formulate contracts as a basis for structuring the sessions? What are some advantages and disadvantages of using contracts for your particular group?

13. How will you handle the fact that people will be taking some risks by participating in the group? What will you tell them about these risks, and what will you do to safeguard them from unnecessary risks? Will you take any special precautions with minors?

14. Will your group be voluntary or mandatory? If the members are required to attend, what measures are you taking to increase the chances of gaining their cooperation? How might you deal with the resistance of members who do not want to participate?

15. What ethical considerations need to be addressed? Does your proposal reflect an awareness of ethical practice? What ethical guidelines will you follow?

16. What legal considerations, if any, might be involved in setting up your group?

17. What risk-management procedures would you want to build into your group proposal?

18. What do you expect to be the characteristics of the various stages of the group? What do you see as your function at each of these stages? What expectations do you have for the members at each phase?

19. What techniques and procedures might you employ in the group? Will there be structured exercises? Will you emphasize role playing?

20. Will members be expected to practice new skills outside of the group sessions? What techniques might you use to get members to support one another in their efforts to change, both in the sessions and between meetings?

21. To what extent will you be available for individual consultation with group members? If the members are having difficulties resulting from the group, are you willing to meet with them privately, or do you expect them to bring up these problems in the group? When might you suggest a referral for a particular member?

22. What evaluation procedures are in your plan? Will you evaluate each session? If so, how? Once the group ends, what methods might you use to assess the overall effectiveness of the group?

23. What follow-up procedures might you use? Will you meet each member privately to discuss the degree to which he or she has met personal goals? Will you meet with the group as a whole one or more times for evaluation purposes?

24. How will you incorporate research findings into your practice as a group leader? What topics would be valuable to examine when you search the scholarly literature? How might your awareness of research enhance your skills and knowledge as a group leader?

25. To whom will you submit your proposal? What is the process for reviewing and approving proposals at your workplace? What steps can you take to increase the chances that your proposal will be accepted or approved? How will you proceed if you are asked to modify your proposal? What modifications would you be willing to make? Which parts of your proposal are nonnegotiable?

Exercises and Activities

Your knowledge of the stages in the development of a group can help you carry out the specific functions of a group leader at these various phases. You can provide needed structure, make appropriate interventions, and predict certain blocks to the group process.

Practicing Leadership Skills

These exercises and activities are designed to give you practice in your class or group in developing the leadership skills needed at each stage. As you read through these activities, select the ones that have the most meaning for you and bring them up in the class/group. You can use some of them on your own as a way of learning techniques for organizing groups, establishing and maintaining a working climate, terminating groups, and opening or closing group sessions.

1. *Interacting with prospective members.* Imagine talking to potential group members. Explain to them what your group is for and how you expect to lead it. Assume that these people have never been in a group before. What would you stress regarding the purposes and procedures of the group? How would you explain the informed consent process?

2. *Screening interview exercise.* Assume the role of a leader conducting a screening interview for members of a certain kind of group. Conduct a pregroup interview with a prospective member for about 10 minutes. Then the one who was interviewed can report on how he or she felt during the interview. What is your interviewing style like? What were some of your most effective questions or interventions? How could the interview have been improved? Next, interview another prospective member so you can gain from the feedback and try new ideas.

3. *Interviewing the leader.* Prospective members may want to talk with the leader before they commit themselves to a group. In this exercise the same format can be used as in Exercise 2, except group members (several people in class can volunteer for this role) ask questions of the group leader. This exercise can be done in dyads so that everyone has a chance to be both the member and the leader. Everyone can be invited to make observations and suggestions.

4. *Including versus excluding members.* Draw up a list of specific questions that you as a leader might ask at a screening interview. What would you look for? On what basis would you include or exclude members?

5. *Turning away individuals sensitively.* How would you turn away a person if you thought either that he or she was not appropriate for the group or that the group was not appropriate for him or her? You might set this up as a group/class exercise. How can you exclude a person from a group without conveying rejection? What might you do if the person feels rejected despite your best efforts to avoid conveying rejection?

6. *Working with involuntary members.* What screening methods, if any, can you apply to involuntary group members? Do you believe they can benefit from group participation? Why or why not? What would you do if the agency you worked for insisted that all clients attend the group, whether they wanted to or not? Assume that all the mental health workers there had to use group therapy as the primary treatment method.

7. *Open versus closed groups.* Discuss some problems you might encounter in an open group (one with changing membership) that you would not be so likely to face in a closed group. How do you expect to deal with the problems that arise in an open group?

8. *Private interviews*. What value, if any, do you see in arranging an initial private interview with each group member to explore matters such as goals, fears, expectations, questions, and concerns? How would you prepare members of your group?

9. *Initial stage of a group*. Try to recall what it was like for you when you first entered a counseling group or *any* group of strangers. Consider the possibility that your prospective group members feel the same way. Discuss with others in your class/group how you might be a more compassionate leader if you could keep these memories fresh.

10. *Trust building*. Think of the ways in which you would attempt to create trust within the group. What are some specific strategies you might use to foster the development of trust during the initial meetings? If you sensed that trust was not developing at a reasonable pace, how might you address that?

11. *Questioning your competence*. Assume that you are leading your first group and several members are questioning your level of expertise. How would you deal with this challenge?

12. *Identifying boundaries in the group leader role*. Imagine that group members are telling you they see you strictly as "the leader." They ask you to become more like them and to share more of yourself with them. How would you handle this situation? Explain to the group your understanding of the role of group leader.

13. *Patterns of resistance*. Examine your own patterns of resistance or reluctance as a group member. List some ways in which you have found yourself hesitant or cautious in this class/group. What has helped or hindered you in working through your own patterns of reluctance? Imagine that you are leading a group of people who have many of the same defenses, concerns, or reservations that you have. How would this be for you?

14. *Pressuring versus encouraging members*. If a member says she doesn't want to press onward with an issue on which she has been working, what courses of action would you be inclined to take? Do you see a difference between pressuring members to talk about a given issue and encouraging them to talk about possible fears that keep them from working on the issue?

15. *Handling difficult behaviors*. What can a leader do, in general, to effectively handle problematic behaviors that occur in a group? What are helpful leader behaviors in a group whose members exhibit problem behaviors? How might you address hidden agendas in the group?

16. *Avoiding labels*. Discuss the differences between reducing a person to a label (such as "the monopolist," "the help-rejecting complainer," "the bore," and so on) and describing a specific behavior (such as monopolizing or complaining). As a group leader, how can you encourage a member to recognize and deal with specific behaviors that are counterproductive to the progress of both the individual and the group?

17. *Working with defenses*. There is a danger in pushing people too soon to give up a defense. Ask yourself if you are able to handle the reaction of a person who relinquishes a defense. For example, if you encourage a member to feel his anger instead of intellectualizing it, could you handle the possible explosive expression of his anger should he experience it fully? How can you determine whether you are competent to deal with what lies behind a defense?

18. *Experiencing countertransference*. Your own objectivity can become distorted as a result of countertransference feelings that are aroused in you toward certain clients and that tend to be based on your unrecognized and unresolved personal issues. Put yourself into each of

the following eight common countertransference situations. How would you fit into each of these situations? What are you aware of in yourself that might prevent you from focusing on the needs and best interests of group members?

a. You have an inordinate need for reassurance and constant reinforcement; this includes the need to please all the members, to win their respect, to get them to approve of you, and to have them validate you as a "superb leader."

b. You see yourself in certain clients; you overidentify with some members to the extent that you take on their problems and seem to absorb their pain.

c. You develop sexual and romantic feelings toward certain members; you engage in seductive behavior and allow your sexual attraction to become a central focus in the group.

d. You give people advice in such a way that you tell others what to do based on your own needs and values.

e. You develop social relationships with some members outside of the group and find that you challenge them less during group sessions than you do other members.

f. You use power over members to prove your adequacy; you gain power through the use of certain highly directive techniques.

g. You attempt to persuade members to accept the values you hold; you are more interested in having members subscribe to your idea of the right way to live than in letting members decide on their own values.

h. You see clearly the faults of members and use what they do or don't do to justify poor results in a group; at the same time you are blind to your own shortcomings or your part in the group process.

19. *Demonstrating cultural sensitivity.* In working with diverse client or student populations, what steps will you take to ensure that your screening processes and interventions are culturally appropriate? What knowledge and skills do you need to acquire to practice in a multiculturally competent manner?

20. *Goal setting.* How might you assist group members in defining and clarifying their goals? Practice goal setting with your classmates or group members. How can you transform goals that are vague and general into ones that are specific and measurable? How might you help a member who has set unrealistic goals revise them so that they are achievable? What might you say to group members to make them more accountable for meeting their goals?

Helpful Intervention Phrases for the Initial Stage of a Group

A few well-chosen and well-timed words can give group members the guidance that will enable them to explore personal issues in a significant way. Following is a list of sentences and phrases leaders can use during the early stage of a group. These are not interventions meant to be memorized but ideas you can modify to fit your personal style as well as your specific group population. Although my coleaders and I use many of these interventions during the initial stage of a group, not all of them are used in a single group.

- Who in the group are you most aware of right now?
- How does it feel to be in the room right now?
- Are you here because you want to be?
- What do you most want to get from this group?
- What are you willing to do to get what you say you want?

- To what degree are you willing to try out new behaviors in this group?
- What are three things you want us to know about you?
- What expectations are you bringing with you to this group?
- If a friend of yours introduced you to this group, what might he or she say about you?
- I hope you challenge yourself early to get involved. The longer you wait, the more difficult it might become.
- What fears or doubts do you have about this group, if any?
- What do you fear most? What do you hope for most?
- Why would you want to change anything in your life now?
- What would you most like to say you have learned or decided to do when you leave the group?
- It is important that you express persistent thoughts and feelings.
- If you are in the group now because someone sent you here, how do you feel about that?

Helpful Intervention Phrases for the Transition Stage of a Group

The transition stage is an especially challenging time in a group's evolution. Defenses are typically high, and a leader's interventions need to be carefully made. The manner and tone in which you phrase your interventions affect a member's willingness to take risks and to respond to challenges. My coleaders and I find the following statements and questions to be generally facilitative:

- I notice that you have been hesitant to participate during many of these sessions. What has it been like for you to be here thus far?
- I am aware how quiet the group as a whole is. I wonder what is not being said in here that may be important to express.
- You say that you are unwilling to continue. What stops you?
- Who in this group were you thinking about last week, and what were you thinking?
- If you are experiencing difficulties in this group, would you be willing to talk about this?
- Imagine that this is the last chance you have to change your life.
- Rather than questioning people, would you say what is prompting you to ask your questions?
- Rather than telling others your solutions to problems, consider saying more about the problems you are struggling with.
- With whom do you have unfinished business?
- If this were the end of the group, would that be all right?
- How would it be for you if you continued the rest of your life the way you are now?
- What are you willing to do with the tension you feel?
- I am aware that several of you are hesitant to become involved. Do you have any reactions to my observation?
- Some of you say you are bored. What is not happening for you in here? What are you willing to do to change it?
- Take a moment to center yourself. If you had to pick just one problem right now, which one would you want to talk about?
- You are very willing to talk. I am concerned that I have not yet heard from several people, and I would like to check in with them.

- You say that you learn a great deal by observing others. What is it that you have been observing, and how have you been affected by this?
- I know this conflict is difficult and uncomfortable. We have a better chance to find clarity and understanding if we continue talking.

Groups in Action: Evolution and Challenges (DVD and Workbook)

Getting the Most From the DVD and Workbook Program

My colleague and I have developed a self-study student DVD and workbook combination titled *Groups in Action: Evolution and Challenges* that can be used as an integrated learning package with *Theory and Practice of Group Counseling. Groups in Action* consists of two separate programs. The first program, *Evolution of a Group* (2 hours) depicts central features that illustrate the development of the group process and how the coleaders facilitated that process as the group moved through the various stages: initial, transition, working, and ending. The second program, *Challenges for Group Leaders* (90 minutes) demonstrates ways to work therapeutically with a variety of difficult behaviors in groups and approaches to addressing diversity issues in group counseling. The DVD and workbook are sold as a package only, and the workbook, which utilizes an interactive format, requires that students become active learners as they study the group process in action. The *Groups in Action* program is published by Cengage Learning.

The aim of this interactive program is to raise questions and issues—and to help you understand the art of facilitating a group. The first DVD program (*Evolution of a Group*) shows significant incidents that emerged from the group process during a 3-day residential group therapy session. You will see how the coleaders (Marianne Schneider Corey and Jerry Corey) facilitated that process as the group moved through the four group stages: initial, transition, working, and ending.

Use the workbook that accompanies the DVD as your "interpreter" of the group process. The workbook provides a rationale for the interventions made, frequently discusses how an individual's work moved beyond what is shown in the video, and encourages you to interact with what you are observing. By completing the activities in the workbook, you will be actively experiencing how theory can be translated into practice.

Note: The page numbers shown in parentheses refer to pages in the textbook *Theory and Practice of Group Counseling* (9th ed.) where further information on these topics can be found.

Stage 1: Pregroup Issues—Formation of the Group (pages 70–78)

Before making the decision to be a part of this group, the potential group members met together with the coleaders to get acquainted with one another and to determine whether they wanted to participate in this type of special group experience. Of course, all the participants knew in advance that the purpose of this workshop was to produce an educational program.

During the formation of this group, we employed many of the procedures described in Chapter 4. For instance, we screened members, and we arranged for a pregroup meeting to prepare them for the group. We addressed topics such as confidentiality, dealing with genuine personal concerns, safeguards to protect members, and preparation for the actual weekend group that would be videotaped.

If you are using the DVD and workbook along with this text, you will see the detailed information that was provided when forming this special kind of group. Notice in the DVD how we asked members to begin by sharing any reactions they had about the pregroup meeting.

Stage 2: Initial Stage—Orientation and Exploration (pages 79–85)

1. *Characteristics of the initial stage.* Think about how the characteristics described in the text are evident in the initial stage of the group depicted in the DVD. For instance, in the DVD what are some expectations and concerns of the members? Did all the members feel a sense of inclusion in the group?

2. *Establishing trust.* Trust is the foundation of a group. As you view the DVD, answer these questions: What early concerns did the members voice? What were some of the fears of members? For this kind of group, how could the fact that it was being videotaped become a hidden agenda if the topic had not been thoroughly discussed from the outset? How did the coleaders steer the members of this group into a here-and-now focus from the beginning? What process was used to help the members get acquainted? How much trust seemed evident as you observed the initial session? What would it take for you to feel a sense of trust in a group? What did you learn about some ways to create trust in a group through viewing the early phase of the group?

3. *Role of the group leader.* What kind of roles did you see the coleaders assuming in the DVD group? What behaviors did the coleaders model? What did you notice about the way we worked together as coleaders? If you were leading this group, would you have a clear sense of what the members wanted to get from the group experience? What did you notice about the way the coleaders intervened to assist members in defining specific personal goals?

4. *Structuring and forming norms.* Structuring is an important process during the early stages of a group. What kind of structuring did you observe the coleaders providing? How might you provide a different kind of structuring? How did the coleaders deal with the issue of cultural diversity that emerged early in the life of the group? What specific norms are the coleaders attempting to shape early in the group?

Stage 3: Transition Stage—Dealing With Resistance (pages 85–93)

1. *Characteristics of the transition stage.* Before a group gets involved in doing a deeper level of work, it typically goes through a transition phase. As you view the DVD, what evidence do you see of the members dealing with anxiety, resistance, and conflict? What were some specific manifestations of resistance during the early stages? What characteristics unfold in this group during the transition stage? What lessons can you learn from this about dealing therapeutically with resistance?

2. *Anxiety among group members.* Some common anxieties typical during the transition stage include fears of rejection, of not being understood, of being judged harshly, or of losing control. What anxieties are voiced by members in this group? What did you learn about what is helpful in exploring these fears? What fears might you have if you were a member of this kind of group?

3. A member may say, "I'm being very careful in this group because I am afraid of being judged." As coleaders, we ask members to talk more about the fears or reservations they may be experiencing so we can intervene in a way that makes the room safer and provides a climate whereby members can talk about their hesitations. This comes about by exploring fears, not simply by being reassured. After viewing the DVD, what is the importance of carefully working with whatever members bring to a group regarding their fears and reservations? How is this transitional work essential if you hope to help a group move to a deeper level of interpersonal interaction? From reading this chapter and viewing the transition stage segment of the DVD, what are you learning about the leader's task during this crucial stage in a group?

4. *Conflict.* Although conflict often occurs during the transition stage, it can erupt during the initial group session. In the video group, conflict occurs during both the initial and the ending stages. What are the possible consequences of ignoring conflict or dealing with it ineffectively? Did you learn anything about how to deal with conflict from viewing the sessions, regardless of when it occurs?

5. *Resistance.* Resistance is a common phenomenon in groups that must be recognized and explored. You will notice that members in the DVD group are asked to share some of the ways they are likely to resist when they become anxious. What value do you see in asking members to identify and express what might get in their way of participating effectively in this group?

6. *Leader functions at early stages.* In viewing the DVD, did you notice the use of the go-around technique? What are some techniques you would want to use as a way to open a session in a group you are leading? From the DVD, what did you learn about leader functions in getting members to check in and state how they would like to use time for a session? What specific techniques for closing a session did you read about and also observe in this group?

CHAPTER FIVE

Later Stages in the Development of a Group

Prechapter Self-Inventory for the Later Stages in the Development of a Group

Decide the degree to which you agree or disagree with these statements in this self-inventory. Respond to each statement, giving the initial response that most clearly identifies how you think or feel. I suggest that you go over your completed inventories and mark those items that you would like to discuss; then bring your inventories to class, and compare your positions with the views of others. Such comparisons can stimulate debate and help the class become involved in the topics to be discussed.

Using the following code, write next to each statement the number of the response that most closely reflects your viewpoint:

5 = I *strongly agree* with this statement.

4 = I *agree,* in most respects, with this statement.

3 = I am *undecided* in my opinion about this statement.

2 = I *disagree,* in most respects, with this statement.

1 = I *strongly disagree* with this statement.

_____ 1. Groups do not have to experience conflict to become cohesive, but if conflict is present in the group and is smoothed over or somehow ignored, it can be expected to get in the way of building cohesion.

_____ 2. In a working group, the members are willing to work and practice outside the group to achieve behavioral changes.

_____ 3. Although clients' specific life circumstances may differ depending on their cultural background, groups allow a diverse range of people to discover what they have in common.

_____ 4. Experimentation with different modes of behavior is a significant aspect of the working stage, mainly because the group is now a safe place in which to try out novel behavior.

_____ 5. The expression of pent-up feelings can be therapeutic because it releases energy that has been tied up in withholding certain threatening feelings.

_____ 6. Groups offer members many opportunities to evaluate their thinking and to adopt constructive beliefs in place of self-limiting ones.

_____ 7. Self-disclosure is the principal vehicle of group interaction, and it is critical that group participants have a clear understanding of what self-disclosure is—and what it is not.

_____ 8. When confrontation takes place in the supportive environment of a group, it can be a true act of caring.

_____ 9. As a group leader, unless you recognize your own feelings about termination and are able to deal with them constructively, you are in no position to help members deal with their separation issues.

_____10. As a group leader, your central tasks in the final phase of a group's development are to provide a structure that enables participants to clarify the meaning of their experiences in the group and to assist members in generalizing their learning from the group to everyday situations.

Questions for Discussion

1. What characteristics distinguish a group in the working stage from a group in transition?
2. How is group cohesion a central variable at the working stage? What factors contribute to this cohesion? If a group you were leading seemed fragmented and lacked any sense of community, what might you say or do? Can you think of some reasons to explain the absence of cohesion?
3. Review the therapeutic factors of a group. What factors do you think are especially important?
4. Refer to the section of the textbook that deals with the characteristics of an effective working group. What factors do you think are most significant? Discuss your reasons.
5. How would you explain to a group member the nature and purpose of self-disclosure? What specific guidelines are useful in teaching participants the skills involved in appropriate self-disclosure?
6. What is the purpose of confrontation? What would you tell members about confronting (or challenging) in a constructive way?
7. How is feedback a key part of any group at all stages, but particularly during the working and ending stages? What would you most want to teach members about how to give and receive feedback?
8. How do the leader's and members' functions change when the group leaves the working stage and enters the ending stage?
9. How would you assist group members in consolidating their learning before the group ends?
10. What are the leader's responsibilities after a group ends?

Assessment Devices for Group Sessions

I present two forms here on which members can assess group sessions. Look over these evaluation forms as examples of assessment devices you might create for your own groups. As you consider the purpose of your groups, take what you consider to be the best elements of each of these forms and develop a form that will tap the information you are looking for. Complete the self-evaluation form now to help you answer the question, "What kind of group member am I?" The second form consists of 11 items that can be administered in a few minutes at the end of each group session. Tally the results, and if any problems are apparent, bring the matter up for discussion in your group. This form helps chart the results on a weekly basis so you can see trends in the groups you are leading.

Self-Assessment Scale: What Kind of Group Member Am I?

One of the best ways of preparing for effective group leadership is to first become an effective group member. This self-inventory is geared to help you determine your strengths and weaknesses as a group member. I hope you have already had some form of experience as a member of a group. If not, you can rate yourself on the inventory in terms of your behavior in the class you are in now.

After this inventory is completed, the class can break up into small groups; the groups can be composed of people who know one another best. Members of these groups should then assess the self-ratings and discuss how to become a better group member.

Rate yourself on a scale of 1 to 5, with 1 being "almost never true of me" and 5 being "almost always true of me" as a *group member*.

_____ 1. I am an active and contributing group member.

_____ 2. I am willing to raise personal concerns and explore them in the group.

_____ 3. I listen attentively to others, and I respond to them.

_____ 4. I confront others with care, yet I do so directly.

_____ 5. As a group participant, I not only give direct feedback to others but also am open to feedback from them.

_____ 6. I am willing to formulate specific goals and contracts.

_____ 7. I am willing to openly express my feelings about and reactions to what is occurring within the group.

_____ 8. I serve as a positive model to others in the group.

_____ 9. I am active in taking steps to create and maintain trust in the group.

_____ 10. I show that I am willing to put insights into action by practicing what I learn in the group in my life between sessions.

_____ 11. I prepare myself for the group by thinking about what I want from the sessions.

_____ 12. I am willing to get involved in role-playing activities.

_____ 13. I am able to provide support to others in the group at appropriate times.

Members' Weekly Evaluation of a Group

Directions: This evaluation exercise can be given to members at the end of each group session you may be leading to give you a quick index of the level of satisfaction of the members.

You can summarize the results and begin a session with the trends you are noticing from the evaluation sheets. Have the members circle the appropriate number for each item, using the following scale:

1 or 2 = very weak
3 or 4 = moderately weak
5 or 6 = adequate
7 or 8 = moderately strong
9 or 10 = very strong

1. What degree of preparation (reacting, thinking about the topic, reading, and writing) did you do for this week?

1 2   3 4   5 6   7 8   9 10

2. How would you rate your involvement in the group today?

    1   2   3 4   5   6   7   8   9   10

3. How would you rate the group's level of involvement?

    1   2   3 4   5   6   7   8   9   10

4. Rate yourself on the degree to which you saw yourself today as willing to take risks, to share with other members what you thought and felt, and to be an active participant.

    1   2   3 4   5   6   7   8   9   10

5. To what degree do you feel satisfied with your experience in the group?

    1   2   3 4   5   6   7   8   9   10

6. To what degree do you feel that the group dealt with issues in a personal and meaningful way (sharing feelings as opposed to intellectual discussion)?

    1   2   3 4   5   6   7   8   9   10

7. To what degree do you experience trust within the group?

    1   2   3 4   5   6   7   8   9   10

8. How would you rate the group leader's level of involvement and investment in today's session?

    1   2   3 4   5   6   7   8   9   10

9. Rate your leader on the dimensions of his or her ability today to create a good working climate as characterized by warmth, respect, support, empathy, and trust.

    1   2   3 4   5   6   7   8   9   10

Members can also evaluate the group by filling in these blanks:

10. A new behavior I tried was _____

    _____

    _____

    _____

    _____

11. What I would like to do differently at the next meeting is _____

    _____

    _____

_____

_____

_____

Exercises and Activities

The following exercises and activities can be incorporated into class discussions, used in a small group format, or used to guide your own self-reflection. Keeping a journal to write down your impressions and thoughts about these topics is strongly encouraged.

1. *Dealing with conflict.* Once conflict has been expressed and worked through and trust has been established, the group often becomes a cohesive unit. In a small group, discuss how conflict was dealt with in your family of origin and how that influences the way you deal with conflict today. How able are you to address conflict as a group leader? How will you react to members who are avoidant of conflict?

2. *Group cohesion.* Based on your observations and experiences, what conditions need to be present for a group to develop cohesion? How will you assess the level of cohesion in groups you lead or colead? What responsibility do you have as a leader to foster cohesion in the groups you facilitate? Share your responses in a small group.

3. *Encouraging hope.* Discuss the role hope plays in producing positive therapeutic outcomes. To what extent do you believe the therapeutic process can help your clients and group members work through their issues? When working with a group member who feels hopeless about his or her situation, how can you (as the leader) and other group members encourage hope?

4. *Creating the climate for emotional intimacy.* The group setting provides an ideal arena for members to discover their fears of getting close to others. Identify barriers that could potentially prevent emotional intimacy from developing in a group that you might lead. How would you address these barriers?

5. *Cognitive restructuring.* Groups offer members many opportunities to evaluate their thinking and to adopt constructive beliefs to replace self-limiting ones. Identify some of your own faulty beliefs or assumptions and encourage your classmates or group members to do the same. In a small group, discuss how these faulty or self-limiting beliefs are getting in your way, and identify ways you can actively challenge and replace these beliefs.

6. *Offering feedback.* The exchange of feedback among group members is widely considered to be a key element in promoting interpersonal learning and group development. As a role model, the leader must be adept at providing members with effective feedback. The text provides guidelines for offering feedback. Using these suggestions, practice giving feedback to your classmates. Create role-play scenarios in which you must offer group members difficult-to-hear feedback. As a leader, how would you present it? As the group member who is the recipient of feedback, how would it feel to be in that position? Experiment by playing the roles of both group leader and member. Be sure to process the experience afterward.

7. *Ending a group.* Leaders have the task of facilitating a discussion of the emotional aspects associated with termination. What emotions surface for you with regard to endings?

How can you help group members deal with their feelings about termination in a productive manner? What can you do to assist members in consolidating what they learned in a group experience as a group ends?

Helpful Intervention Phrases for the Working Stage of a Group

You might find the following sentences, questions, and phrases helpful once your group gets under way and people are working. Again, these are not to be used mechanically; rather, they can serve as constructive interventions if you use them in context, with a sense of timing. As you lead groups, think of the phrases that are useful to you. Here are some that my coleaders and I use:

- What would you like to do?
- Do any of you have any thoughts about our last session that you would like to share?
- What else needs to be said?
- How were you affected by _____?
- How does this issue relate to you? How are you affected by Sharon's work?
- I would like each person in the group to finish the sentence "_____."
- Could you say what you are experiencing right now?
- I like it when you _____.
- Right now I am aware of _____.
- Would you be willing to try this experiment to see how it works for you?
- Imagine that your mother were here now. What would you want to say to her?
- Instead of asking her questions, you could tell her what you are experiencing at this time.
- I notice that _____.
- You say that you are embarrassed by what you revealed. Look around the room and notice some of the people you are most aware of. What do you imagine they are thinking about you now?
- Would you consider _____.
- My hunch is _____.
- I notice tears in your eyes. What are you reacting to?
- You rehearse a lot before you speak. Could you rehearse out loud?
- You experienced a lot of emotions during this session. What did you learn about yourself?
- What decision did you make about yourself in that situation when you were a child?
- Become each part of your dream. Give each part a voice.
- Instead of talking about this situation, live it as though it were happening now.
- Instead of saying "I can't," say "I won't."
- What can you do between this session and the next to practice what you just learned?
- I think it is important that each of you ask if you are getting what you want from this group and whether there are any changes you would like to see.
- I would like to review our contracts to determine whether any of them need to be revised or updated.

Helpful Intervention Phrases for the Final Stage of a Group

During the consolidation stage of a group, it is important for members to think of ways to apply what they have learned in the group to everyday life, to take care of unfinished business, to express their feelings regarding separation, and to make sense of the total group experience.

My coleaders and I frequently use the following phrases and sentences during the ending stage of a group. As you review this list, think of additional statements and questions that would help members accomplish the tasks at this stage:

- What are some of the most important things you have learned about yourself in this group?
- Are there any things you want to say to anyone here?
- How do you feel about saying good-bye?
- What can you do to remember what you have learned in this group.
- How can you practice what you have learned here?
- With whom do you need to talk outside of the group? What is the essence of what you want them to hear?
- As a result of being in this group, what decisions have you made?
- If we were to meet a year from now as a group, what would you want to say that you had accomplished?
- If you had to say your message in one sentence, what would it be?
- How might you discount what you have learned in here?
- What steps will you take to translate your insight into actions?
- Can you identify at least one person in this group to contact if you discover that you are not putting your plans into action.
- Let's practice and role-play some of the situations each of you expects to encounter after you leave the group.
- To what degree did you attain your goals?
- What did it take and what steps did you go through to get what you wanted out of this group?
- If you could repeat this experience, what might you do differently?
- What kept you from becoming closer to others in this group?
- What did you learn about yourself in this group? What did you do to bring this learning about?
- What do you most want to take from this group and apply to your everyday life?
- Don't expect and insist that others in your life be different. If you are different with them, they are more likely to be different with you.
- When you talk with significant people in your life, remember that the focus needs to be on you.
- The trust and closeness you are experiencing in this group did not simply happen. Reflect on what each of you did to help create this.

Evolution of a Group: Getting the Most From the DVD Program

This is a continuation of the guide to using the first program in the DVD and workbook, *Evolution of a Group*, with this book. The specific topics covered in this section are in Chapter 5 of the textbook.

Note: The page numbers shown in parentheses refer to pages in the textbook *Theory and Practice of Group Counseling* (9th ed.) where further information on these topics can be found.

Stage 4: Working Stage—Cohesion and Productivity (pages 94–107)

1. *Characteristics of an effective working stage.* Identify the key characteristics of a group in a working stage. How do these characteristics apply to the group shown in the DVD? How does the group seem different at this stage from the earlier stages?

2. *Therapeutic factors of a group.* Therapeutic factors such as intimacy, hope, catharsis, cognitive restructuring, self-disclosure, acceptance, cohesion and universality, and feedback are discussed in the textbook. As you view the working stage of this group, look for specific illustrations of these therapeutic factors in the various members' work.

   Can you see how one member's disclosure and exploration of a personal issue can tap common issues in many other members (cohesion and universality)? As you view the working stage of this group, look for interventions used by the coleaders, such as dealing with relationships, talking to parents in symbolic ways, expressing pain that one has been carrying around for many years, and dealing with loss. What is the value of allowing members to express their feelings over painful issues?

   You will notice in this group that the coleaders attempt to link members by role playing. Instead of having members merely report events, the coleaders ask them to live out in a symbolic way painful events from their past. How does staying in the here-and-now enhance the depth of self-exploration? How does one member's work become a catalyst that brings others into the interactions? What are the values of linking members together with common themes and pursuing work with several members at the same time? How does role playing enhance the interactions within a group?

Stage 5: Final Stage—Consolidation and Termination (pages 107–112)

1. *Effective ways of terminating a group.* A number of tasks need to be accomplished during the final stage of a group. Many of these tasks are illustrated briefly in the group shown in the DVD. As you observe the program, ask yourself these questions: How are members in this particular group prepared for the termination of the group? How do the members conceptualize their learning? How does the group seem different at this stage from earlier phases of its development?

2. *Characteristics of the final stage.* What characteristics are common during the final stage of a group? What would you most want to teach members at this time in a group?

Stage 6: Postgroup Issues—Follow-Up and Evaluation (pages 112–114)

1. *Follow-up sessions.* If you were going to arrange a follow-up meeting with the members in the DVD group, what topics would you be most interested in exploring with them? How would you go about evaluating the results of this group experience on these members?

2. *Reviewing key points in the text and the video group.* After reading Chapters 4 and 5 in the textbook, assess what you have learned about how groups function most effectively.

   Review what you have learned from studying the DVD program (and participating in the workbook). After viewing the entire video, it is a good idea to study the video in segments, making full use of the workbook. Consider these questions as you consolidate your learning.

   - How was trust created and maintained in this group?
   - How did the coleader interventions during the initial and transition stages facilitate movement into a working stage?

- What risks did you observe members taking that resulted in deeper self-explorations? How did the self-disclosure of one member lead to disclosure by others in the group?
- How is working with reluctance of members a critical factor in preparing members to delve more deeply into personal issues?
- What did you learn about the importance of addressing conflict when it occurs in a group session?
- What specific therapeutic factors did you see operating during the working stage?
- What value did you see in role enactments and asking members to stay in the here-and-now? How did linking members promote personal exploration?
- What value do you see in encouraging members to express their feelings in a group setting? How did the emotional work of the members affect you?
- What did you learn about coleading a group as you studied this program? What did you learn about how groups either function or malfunction?
- What kind of personal work do you think you need to do as a group member to better enable you to meet the challenges of facilitating a group?
- What are the most significant turning points you observed in this group?

Comprehension Check: Quiz for Chapters 1–5*

_____ 1. The purpose of a course in group work is
   a. to offer students an experience in group therapy.
   b. to diagnose students' psychopathology.
   c. to help students understand group process.
   d. to train students to do group projects.

_____ 2. The author encourages group workers to
   a. join the Association for Specialists in Group Work (ASGW).
   b. join the American Group Psychotherapy Association (AGPA).
   c. attend professional workshops that deal with specialized populations with whom they might work.
   d. all of the above.

_____ 3. Which of the following suggestions does the author make about getting the most from a group experience?
   a. Recognize that trust is something that "just happens" in a group, so be patient and allow trust to naturally develop.
   b. Commit yourself to getting something from your group by focusing on your personal goals.
   c. Cling to your agenda even if other issues surface spontaneously within the group.
   d. Be willing and prepared to offer the group a great deal of background information when you self-disclose so that they will fully understand your stories.

---

*Note: Consult answer key in Appendix I for Chapters 1 to 5.

_____ 4. If a member is in touch with painful emotions during a group session, other group members

    a. should quickly intervene by trying to comfort him or her.

    b. should attempt to "cure" him or her of the pain.

    c. should realize that he or she needs to experience, share, and work through certain feelings.

    d. should reassure him or her that "all will turn out for the best."

_____ 5. Which of the following statements reflects realistic expectations with regard to participating in group work?

    a. Change is not instantaneous and setbacks can be anticipated.

    b. Moderate to dramatic changes usually are apparent shortly after joining a group.

    c. Personal growth will almost always be embraced by a group member's social network and family.

    d. Keeping a journal to track progress and note changes in thinking, feeling, and acting is necessary only for those practicing cognitive behavioral group therapy.

_____ 6. To promote growth in group members' lives, leaders need to

    a. live growth-oriented lives themselves.

    b. demonstrate that they have fully resolved their own issues.

    c. strive for perfection in their own lives in order to be excellent role models.

    d. have years of professional training and preferably a doctoral degree.

_____ 7. Having self-confidence and an awareness of one's influence on others is best described as

    a. arrogance.

    b. personal power.

    c. stamina.

    d. authenticity.

_____ 8. Highly effective therapists demonstrate which of the following abilities?

    a. An ability to deeply enter the world of another without losing a sense of self

    b. The ability to draw on their therapeutic power to help others while maintaining a sense of humility

    c. The ability to provide an emotionally safe environment for clients while challenging them

    d. All of the above

_____ 9. Some practical considerations that can limit practitioners' active participation in research include

    a. the constant pressure to meet clinical demands.

    b. a lack of time.

    c. a lack of financial remuneration for doing research.

    d. all of the above.

_____ 10. _____ find themselves slipping into distorted ways of thinking and engaging in negative thinking.

    a. Only beginning group leaders may

    b. Only deeply troubled group leaders

    c. Even the most effective group leaders may

    d. Qualified group leaders rarely, if ever,

_____11. Experiencing moderate anxiety as a beginning group leader
   a. is beneficial because it can lead to honest self-appraisal.
   b. is indicative that one does not have the temperament and personality for leading groups and therefore should find a different occupation.
   c. is a red flag that one may have an anxiety disorder.
   d. is predictive of failure according to recent group outcome studies.

_____12. It is _____ to disclose details of your past or of your personal life to make yourself known as a person or to empathize with the participants.
   a. unethical
   b. highly unprofessional
   c. not necessary
   d. recommended

_____13. By offering tentative hypotheses concerning certain patterns of behavior, the skill referred to as _____ helps group members see new perspectives and alternatives.
   a. active listening
   b. interpreting
   c. assuming
   d. restating

_____14. Feedback that is _____ is the most helpful.
   a. specific and descriptive
   b. global and judgmental
   c. general yet supportive
   d. presented cheerfully

_____15. Most students enrolled in master's programs
   a. receive ample training in research methods and feel adequately prepared to conduct clinical research.
   b. receive a moderate amount of exposure to research methods and feel adequately prepared to be consumers of clinical research.
   c. receive only basic research training and thus may not feel adequately prepared to understand the research literature, or to apply research findings to their clinical practice.
   d. receive no training in research methodology.

_____16. It is a good policy to provide a professional disclosure statement to group members that includes written information on a variety of topics pertaining to the nature of the group, including all of the following except
   a. therapists' qualifications.
   b. techniques often used in the group.
   c. the rights and obligations of group members.
   d. the benefits, but not risks, of participating in the group.

_____17. _____ is a process of presenting basic information about group treatment to potential group members to enable them to make better decisions about whether or not to enter and how to participate in a group.
   a. Informed consent
   b. Privileged communication
   c. A group lecture
   d. Mandatory consent

_____18. In the author's view, members
   a. do not have a responsibility to the leaders and other members to explain why they want to leave a group prematurely.
   b. have a responsibility to the leaders and other members to explain why they want to leave a group prematurely.
   c. are legally obligated to explain to the leaders and other members why they want to leave a group prematurely.
   d. have a responsibility to the leaders, but not to other members, to explain why they want to leave a group prematurely.

_____19. The _____ is not always recognized in a group setting, unless there is a statutory exception.
   a. ethical concept of confidentiality
   b. legal concept of confidentiality
   c. legal concept of privileged communication
   d. ethical concept of privileged communication

_____20. Expectations should initially be introduced and explained to potential group members during the
   a. screening and orientation session.
   b. initial stage of group development.
   c. transition stage of group development.
   d. working stage of group development.

_____21. As a group leader, you _____ in a group setting.
   a. cannot guarantee confidentiality
   b. must guarantee confidentiality
   c. can and should promise members a positive outcome
   d. can guarantee privileged communication

_____22. Which of the following describes a potential risk of participating in a group?
   a. Engaging in self-reflection
   b. Developing social interest
   c. Not being able to completely resolve personal problems
   d. Life changes that can potentially cause disruption

_____23. Leaders who develop sexual relationships with current group members are
   a. acting unethically.
   b. jeopardizing their licenses and their professional careers.
   c. degrading the profession at large.
   d. all of the above.

_____24. If _____ develop(s) among various _____ within the group, it is likely that the progress of the group will come to an abrupt halt.
   a. overt agendas; individuals
   b. hidden agendas; subgroups
   c. trust; subgroups
   d. conflict; individuals

_____25. Western psychological thought emphasizes which of the following?
   a. A collectivistic sense
   b. Indirectness of communication
   c. Dependence on one's family
   d. Self-sufficiency and a sense of autonomy

_____26. In working with people from culturally diverse backgrounds in a group, _____ issues often surface.
   a. legal
   b. confidentiality
   c. social justice
   d. privacy

_____27. _____ is a potential trap that all group counselors are vulnerable to falling into.
   a. Cultural encapsulation
   b. Multicultural awareness
   c. White privilege
   d. Universality

_____28. Group leaders can practice unprofessionally by
   a. using techniques with which they are unfamiliar.
   b. using techniques in a mechanical way.
   c. using techniques to enhance their power.
   d. all of the above.

_____29. Techniques have a better chance of being used appropriately when
   a. the group leader is a licensed psychologist rather than a licensed social worker or counselor.
   b. they are highly emotive and are aimed at promoting catharsis.
   c. there is a rationale underlying their use.
   d. all of the above.

_____30. Professional competence is
   a. arrived at once and for all when one becomes licensed.
   b. an ongoing developmental process that spans the duration of one's career.
   c. achieved upon receiving one's graduate degree.
   d. largely achieved through extensive reading.

_____31. Which stage of group development is characterized by dealing with conflict, defensiveness, and resistance?
   a. Formation stage
   b. Orientation or initial stage
   c. Transition stage
   d. Working stage

_____32. Planning a group should begin with drafting a written proposal containing all of the following elements except
   a. the basic purposes of the group.
   b. the population to be served.
   c. a clear rationale for the group.
   d. an analysis of outcomes.

_____33. If screening members is not realistic for any number of reasons,
   a. the initial group meeting can be used as an information and screening session.
   b. the leader should abandon the idea of establishing the group.
   c. this step in the process can be skipped.
   d. screening can be incorporated into all stages of the group.

_____34. Which of the individuals below would be a strong candidate for a heterogeneous, outpatient, intensive-therapy group?
   a. A brain-damaged person
   b. A paranoid client
   c. A client with a sociopathic personality
   d. None of the above

_____35. The leader's theoretical orientation, the type of group, and the membership population are some factors that determine
   a. the amount and type of structuring employed.
   b. whether he or she should bother to prepare and submit a proposal for the group.
   c. whether confidentiality should be considered a priority.
   d. whether members are allowed to leave the group prematurely.

_____36. Although many variables are related to creating norms and trust during the early phase of development, _____ is one of the most important.
   a. gender balance among group members
   b. the optimum balance between too much and too little leader direction
   c. the leader's theoretical orientation
   d. the leader's ability to adopt a neutral stance

_____37. Which of the following statements is true with regard to conflict in groups?
   a. Conflict can be dealt with constructively even if members have not recognized its existence.
   b. Conflict can and should be avoided in groups because it destroys trust.
   c. Too often both the members and the leader want to bypass conflict out of the mistaken assumption that it is something to be feared and avoided at all costs.
   d. Ignoring conflicts and negative reactions is advisable in certain types of groups.

_____38. Intermember conflict is often the result of
   a. transference.
   b. countertransference.
   c. psychopathology.
   d. the aggressive impulses of dominant group members.

_____39. Confronting the leader is often a participant's first significant step toward
   a. victory.
   b. self-direction.
   c. being asked to leave the group.
   d. a violent outburst.

_____40. _____ must be recognized as a protective force that reduces members' anxiety.
   a. Resistance
   b. Countertransference
   c. Hallucinations
   d. Catharsis

_____41. In actual practice there is _____. This is especially true of movement from the transition stage to the working stage.
   a. considerable overlapping of stages
   b. occasional overlapping of stages
   c. very little overlapping of stages
   d. no overlapping of stages

_____42. A higher degree of cohesion, a clearer notion of what members want from their group, and a more intensive level of interaction among the members are characteristic of the _____ stage.
   a. formation
   b. orientation
   c. transition
   d. working

_____43. _____ involves a sense of belonging, inclusion, solidarity, and an attractiveness of a group for its members.
   a. Group think
   b. Group chemistry
   c. Group cohesion
   d. Social interest

_____44. A working group can be identified by which of the following features?
   a. Here-and-now focus
   b. Willingness to work and practice inside, but not outside, the group to achieve behavioral change
   c. A sense of commitment to the group by the vocal members and passive participation by the more reserved members
   d. Anxiety about self-disclosure

_____45. Which of the following is considered a therapeutic factor that operates in groups?
   a. Subgrouping
   b. Development of transference toward the leader
   c. Reliance on ego defense mechanisms
   d. Acceptance of self and others

_____46. After catharsis, _____ is often necessary to help members make new decisions based on what they experienced emotionally.
   a. critical incident stress debriefing
   b. cognitive work
   c. a break
   d. empty chair work

_____47. _____ is an invitation to examine discrepancies between what one says and what one does, to become aware of unused potential, and to carry insights into action.
   a. Therapeutic coercion
   b. Constructive confrontation
   c. Tough love
   d. A therapeutic directive

_____48. Which of these suggestions should not be used when offering other group members constructive feedback?
   a. Difficult-to-hear feedback should be timed well and given in a nonjudgmental way.
   b. Before offering another member feedback, explore your fears about giving and receiving feedback.
   c. Offer corrective comments before giving positive feedback.
   d. Concise feedback given in a clear and straightforward manner is more helpful than qualified statements and interpretive or mixed feedback.

_____49. Which of the following are essential tasks to address during the termination phase of group therapy?
   a. Review and reinforce changes made by each of the members of the group.
   b. Assist members in reexamining their relationship with the group leader and other group members.
   c. Help participants to face future challenges with the tools they acquired in the group.
   d. All of the above.

_____50. During the final phase of a group, which characteristic tends not to be evident?
   a. There may be some sadness and anxiety over the reality of separation.
   b. Members may express their hopes and concerns for one another.
   c. There is a low level of trust in the group.
   d. Members are deciding what courses of action they are likely to take.

PART 2

THEORETICAL APPROACHES TO GROUP COUNSELING

CHAPTER SIX

The Psychoanalytic Approach to Groups

Prechapter Self-Inventories: General Directions

The purpose of the self-inventories is to identify and clarify your attitudes and beliefs about the different theoretical approaches to group therapy. Each of the statements on these inventories is *true* from the perspective of the particular theory in question. You decide the degree to which you agree or disagree with these statements. Complete each self-inventory before you read the corresponding textbook chapter. Respond to each statement, giving the initial response that most clearly identifies how you think or feel. Then, after reading the chapter, look over your responses to see whether you want to modify them in any way. These self-inventories will help you express your views and will prepare you to actively read and think about the ideas you encounter in each of the chapters on theory.

I suggest that you go over your completed inventories and mark those items that you would like to discuss; then bring your inventories to class, and compare your positions with the views of others. Such comparisons can stimulate debate and help the class become involved in the topics to be discussed.

Using the following code, write next to each statement the number of the response that most closely reflects your viewpoint:

5 = I *strongly agree* with this statement.
4 = I *agree,* in most respects, with this statement.
3 = I am *undecided* in my opinion about this statement.
2 = I *disagree,* in most respects, with this statement.
1 = I *strongly disagree* with this statement.

Prechapter Self-Inventory for the Psychoanalytic Approach

_____ 1. Self-disclosure and transparency have become more acceptable to contemporary psychodynamic group practitioners.

_____ 2. In group work it is particularly important to focus on experiences from the first 6 years of life because the roots of present conflicts usually lie there.

_____ 3. Group work encourages participants to relive significant relationships, and the group ideally functions as a symbolic family so that members can work through these early relationships.

_____ 4. Insight, understanding, and working through repressed material should be given a primary focus in psychoanalytic group therapy.

_____ 5. Well-timed and accurate interpretations help group members integrate new information that can lead to new insights.

_____ 6. Transference should be encouraged in a group because it is through this process that members come to an understanding of unresolved conflicts from past relationships that are affecting their current relationships.

_____ 7. Brief dynamic therapy tends to emphasize a client's strengths and resources in dealing with real-life issues rather than focusing on an exploration of early childhood experiences.

_____ 8. Brief psychodynamic therapy is an opportunity to begin a process of change that will continue long after therapy is terminated.

_____ 9. Group leaders need to be continuously aware of ways in which their own feelings (countertransference) can affect the group.

_____10. The group serves as a mirror for members to see themselves as they are and to get a perspective on how they cope with anxiety in situations outside of the group.

Summary of Basic Assumptions and Key Concepts of the Psychoanalytic Approach to Groups

1. Psychoanalytic therapists pay particular attention to the unconscious and to early childhood as crucial determinants of personality and behavior. Normal personality development is based on a successful resolution of conflicts at various stages of psychosexual development.

2. Psychoanalytic group work focuses on the influence of the past as a determinant of current personality functioning. Experiences during the first 6 years of life are seen as the roots of one's conflicts in the present. Traditional analytic group work focuses on the historical basis of current behavior for the purpose of resolving its persistence in the present.

3. The group provides a context for the re-creation of the original family so that members can work through their unresolved problems. The reactions of members to one another and to the leader are assumed to reveal symbolic clues to the dynamics of their relationships with significant figures from their family of origin. The present reactions of members are traced back and analyzed in terms of past influences.

4. The group context provides opportunities to observe defensive behaviors that were used in childhood. Through feedback, individuals can gain awareness of their defensive styles of interaction, and with this awareness they can eventually choose constructive forms of dealing with anxiety.

5. More traditional analytically oriented group practitioners tend to remain relatively anonymous and encourage group members to project onto them feelings that they have had toward the significant people in their lives. However, modern analytically oriented practitioners are leaving behind the "detached-observer" model of classical analysis in favor of a more intersubjective style, called relational analysis, which puts more emphasis on therapist self-disclosure, responsiveness, reciprocity, and mutuality.

6. Both transference and countertransference are central aspects in the relationship. The focus is on resistances that occur in the therapeutic process, on interpretation of these resistances, and on working through transference feelings. Through this process, group members explore the parallels between their past and present experience and gain new understanding that can be the basis for personality change.

7. Some of the unique advantages of analytic group therapy are as follows: members reexperience relationships that are similar to their own early family relationships; there are opportunities for multiple transferences; members can gain insight into their defenses and resistances more dramatically than they can in individual therapy; and dependency on the authority of the therapist is lessened because members get feedback from other members.

8. A basic tenet of psychodynamic group therapy is the notion that group members, through their interactions within the group, re-create their social situation so that the group becomes a microcosm of their everyday lives.

9. Brief psychodynamic therapy uses key psychoanalytic and psychodynamic concepts such as the enduring impact of psychosexual, psychosocial, and object relational stages of development; the existence of unconscious processes; the reenactment of the client's past emotional issues in relationship with the therapist; the therapeutic alliance; and repetitive behavior.

10. Group therapists can assist members in identifying and dealing with the influence of environmental situations on their personality development. The goals of brief psychodynamic therapy can provide a new understanding for current problems. With this briefer form of psychoanalytically oriented therapy, group members can relinquish old patterns and establish new patterns in their present behavior.

11. There likely will be continuing pressure to provide group treatment as effectively and inexpensively as possible. For time-limited psychodynamic groups, members must formulate clear and precise treatment goals that are directly related to the organizing group theme. In these groups, the leader assumes a more active role than would be typical in a long-term psychodynamic group. Here-and-now behaviors and interactions are given more attention in time-limited groups.

Glossary of Key Terms for Psychoanalytic Theory

- **Anal stage** The second stage of psychosexual development, when pleasure is derived from retaining and expelling feces.
- **Anxiety** A feeling of impending doom that results from repressed feelings, memories, desires, and experiences emerging to the surface of awareness.
- **Attachment** Emotional bonding with another who is perceived as a source of security.
- **Attachment theory** Developed by Bowlby, this theory emphasizes the importance of attachment, separation, and loss in human development.
- **Borderline personality disorder** A pattern characterized by instability, irritability, self-destructive acts, impulsivity, and extreme mood shifts. Such people lack a sense of their own identity and do not have a deep understanding of others.
- **Brief psychodynamic therapy (BPT**) Applies the principles of psychoanalytic theory and therapy to treating selective disorders within a preestablished time limit of generally 10 to 25 sessions.
- **Countertransference** The therapist's unconscious emotional responses to a client, resulting in a distorted perception of the client's behavior; unresolved conflicts of the therapist that are projected onto the client.
- **Denial** An effort to suppress unpleasant reality and cope with anxiety by "closing our eyes" to the existence of anxiety-producing reality.
- **Dialectical behavior therapy (DBT)** A blend of cognitive behavioral and psychoanalytic techniques that generally involves a minimum of one year of treatment.

STAGES OF DEVELOPMENT OF THE PSYCHOANALYTIC GROUP*

Dimension	Initial Stage	Working Stage	Final Stage
Key developmental tasks and goals	Key task is uncovering and exploring unconscious material. Focus is on historical causes of present behavior. Unconscious processes are made conscious by promoting freedom to express any thought or feeling. Focus is on re-creating, analyzing, discussing, and interpreting past experiences and on working through defenses and resistances. Here-and-now experience connects with past experience.	The group resembles the original family, allowing members to relive their childhood and get to the roots of their conflicts. Key tasks include recalling early childhood experiences and reworking past traumas. The basic work entails recognizing and working through resistances and transferences. Multiple transferences occur in the group; members become aware of past relationships that are brought into the present situation in the group.	Key task is the development of insight into causes of problems. Analysis and interpretation of transference continues. Focus is on the conscious personal action that members can take and on social integration. Main goals are for members to analyze and resolve their own transferences toward other members and the group leader and to work through the repetition of behavior from early years. Personal autonomy is the goal of the final stage of group.
Role and tasks of group leader	Leader offers support and creates an accepting and nonstructured climate. Leader's tasks include setting limits, interpreting, and getting a sense of the members' character structures and patterns of defense.	Leader makes timely interpretations that lead to insight; helps members deal with anxiety constructively; is aware of counter-transference; and helps members deal effectively with resistances and transferences in the group.	Leader relinquishes much of the leadership functions to allow the members a greater degree of independence; guides the members to fuller awareness and social integration.
Role of group members	Members build rapport by reporting dreams and fantasies. They are expected to free-associate with one another's dreams. They are expected to work through resistances that prevent unconscious material from becoming conscious. Members encourage one another to examine their projections. Through mutual sharing and exploration, members gradually give up some defenses. Members need to identify ways in which they experience resistance in a group and they need to challenge themselves.	Members produce material in a free-floating manner; they ventilate and express feelings over past traumas. Emphasis is on working through transferences with leader and members. Members function as adjunct therapists by saying whatever comes to their mind; they may suggest interpretations for others. From observing the work of others in a group, the members learn that it is acceptable to have and express intense feelings that they may have kept out of awareness.	Unfinished business and transferences are worked through, and the focus is on self-interpretation and reality testing. Members become able to spot their own transference figures and relationships; they also contribute to the interpretation of the transference of others. Members gain increased awareness of how they dealt with competition as children and how their earlier experiences now affect their present relationships with others.

Techniques	Individual sessions are used to create readiness for a group. "Go-around" technique is used as a free-association device, where members respond spontaneously to one another. Initial resistance anxieties and expectations are identified.	Main techniques include free association, interpretation, analysis of resistance and transference, interpretation and analysis of dreams, and use of pregroup and postgroup sessions. Emphasis is given to the quality of the relationships between leaders and members.	Attempts are made to help members integrate what they've learned in the group, and they apply new learning to daily life. Members review insights gained. Members focus on putting a new perspective on their problems and past experiences.
Questions to consider	At the first group meeting, how can anxieties pertaining to joining the group best be dealt with? What are some ways to use here-and-now material in the group to understand a member's past? How can one's past provide a framework for understanding current behavior? What are some ways to encourage members to give unrehearsed reactions to one another? What are some values of simply reporting and sharing dreams in a group? How can free association be promoted by the go-around technique? Are members looking to the leader for direction and cues? How can a trusting environment best be created? What are ways that members can be both supported and challenged?	How are members relating to others in the group in ways that are similar to relations in their original family? How can the group be formed so that it can best work with the recalling of early childhood experiences? What are some advantages and disadvantages of the leader encouraging transference? How can this transference toward the leader be worked with therapeutically? As a leader, how can you utilize the projections of group members? What techniques can you develop to work with projections? What are some ways to make interpretations of individuals in a group without promoting their dependency on you? How can your interpretations stimulate their searching? How can you deliver interpretations in a tentative and respectful manner?	During the final stage, how can members be encouraged to take action based on their insight? What are some ways of helping members understand and resolve their transferences to the leader and others in the group? What are some ways of letting go of the leadership of the group so that the members are encouraged to become increasingly independent? What are some signs that a member is ready to terminate a group? How can the group be structured to promote a degree of independence in the members? What are some dangers of continuing the group for an indefinite period of time? What are the values of long-term group therapy? How can termination best take place in an analytic group?

*The transition stage has been omitted from these charts because there are no clear demarcations between the initial and working stages. The intent of this table is to give you an idea of the early, middle, and ending stages of a group.

Reactions: Summarize your reactions to the psychoanalytic perspective of group developmental stages. What do you like *most? least?* What aspects of this approach would you incorporate in your style of leadership?

- **Displacement** An ego-defense mechanism that entails redirection of some emotion from a real source to a substitute person or object.
- **Dream analysis** Viewed as "the royal road to the unconscious" by psychoanalysts, dreams express unconscious needs, conflicts, wishes, fears, and repressed experiences. Dream analysis enables members to deal in a concrete way with feelings and motivations that they otherwise would not face.
- **Ego** Part of the personality that performs various organizing functions, including keeping in contact with reality. The ego should not be equated with consciousness.
- **Ego-defense mechanism** A device protecting the ego from threatening thoughts and feelings.
- **Ego psychology** The psychological approach of Erik Erikson, emphasizing the development of the ego or self at various stages of life.
- **Electra complex** Unconscious sexual desire of the daughter for her father, along with feelings of hostility toward her mother.
- **Fixation** The condition of being arrested, or "stuck," at one level of psychosexual development.
- **Free association** A basic technique for uncovering repressed or unconscious material by communicating whatever comes to mind, with as little censoring as possible.
- **Genital stage** The final stage of psychosexual development. It begins at the time of puberty and lasts until senility sets in, at which time the individual tends to regress to earlier stages.
- **Identity crisis** A development challenge, occurring during adolescence, whereby the person seeks to establish a stable view of self and to define a place in life.
- **Insight** A cognitive and emotional awareness of the connection of past experiences to present problems.
- **Interpretation** A technique used to explore the meanings of free association, dreams, resistances, and transference feelings. Well-timed and accurate interpretations help clients integrate new data that can lead to new insights.
- **Latency stage** A period of psychosexual development, following the phallic stage, that is relatively calm before the storm of adolescence.
- **Latent content** The disguised, unconscious motives that represent the hidden meaning of the dream.
- **Manifest content** The dream as it appears to the dreamer; the conscious content of the dream.
- **Multiple transferences** A process whereby members develop intense feelings for certain others in a group; an individual may "see" in others some significant figure such as a parent, life-partner, ex-lover, or boss.
- **Narcissistic personality disorder** A pervasive pattern of grandiosity, hypersensitivity to the evaluations of others, and lack of empathy.
- **Object relations theory** A contemporary trend in psychoanalytic thinking, focusing on predictable developmental sequences in which early experiences of self shift in relation to an expanding awareness of others. It holds that individuals go through phases of autism, normal symbiosis, and separation and individuation, culminating in a state of integration.
- **Oedipus complex** Unconscious sexual desire of the son for his mother, along with feelings of hostility and fear toward his father.

- **Oral stage** The initial phase of psychosexual development, during which the mouth is the primary source of gratification; a time when the infant is learning to trust or mistrust the world.
- **Phallic stage** The third phase of psychosexual development, during which the child gains maximum gratification through direct experience with the genitals.
- **Projection** An ego-defense mechanism that involves attributing our own unacceptable thoughts, feelings, behaviors, and motives to others.
- **Psychoanalytic group** Group that promotes healing through reenacting the family of origin in a symbolic way so that the historical past of each group member is repeated in the group's presence. This approach enables members to work through their unresolved problems in the group.
- **Psychodynamics** The interplay of opposing forces and intrapsychic conflicts, providing a basic understanding of human motivation.
- **Psychosexual stages** The Freudian chronological phases of development, beginning in infancy. Each is characterized by a primary way of gaining sensual and sexual pleasure.
- **Psychosocial stages** Erikson's turning points, from infancy through old age. Each presents psychological and social tasks that must be mastered if maturation is to proceed in a healthy fashion.
- **Psychosocial theory** Erikson's theory that stresses the integration of the biological, psychological, and social aspects of development.
- **Rationalization** An ego-defense mechanism whereby we try to justify our behavior by imputing logical and admirable motives to it.
- **Reaction formation** A defense against a threatening impulse, involving the expression of the opposite impulse.
- **Regression** An ego-defense mechanism whereby an individual reverts to a less mature form of behavior as a way of coping with extreme stress.
- **Relational analysis** A contemporary form of psychoanalytic therapy that places emphasis on both the client's and the therapist's reactions and experiences within the therapeutic relationship. Transference is regarded as an interactive process between therapist and client.
- **Repression** An ego-defense mechanism whereby threatening or painful thoughts and desires are excluded from awareness.
- **Resistance** Reluctance to bring into conscious awareness threatening unconscious material that has been repressed or denied; anything that prevents members from dealing with unconscious material.
- **Therapeutic alliance** A working relationship in which the therapist communicates commitment, caring, interest, respect, and human concern for the group member.
- **Therapeutic regression** A process that involves reexperiencing primitive patterns associated with earlier developmental stages and is a necessary element of the analytic group process.
- **Transference** The client's unconscious shifting to the therapist of feelings, attitudes, and fantasies that stem from reactions to significant individuals from the past. Transference reflects the patterning of old experiences and earlier acquired distortions as they emerge in present relationships.
- **Unconscious** The thoughts, feelings, impulses, motivations, and events that are kept out of awareness of the conscious ego as a protection against anxiety.

- **Working through** Repeating interpretations and overcoming resistance of group members to resolve dysfunctional patterns that originated in childhood and enable members to make choices based on new insights.

Exercises and Activities for the Psychoanalytic Approach

Rationale

For the exercises in this section I've selected several group techniques based on psychoanalytic concepts and procedures and modified them considerably in the hope that you will be able to apply some of them in your group work. The following exercises are geared to stimulate your thinking on issues such as the value of *working with the past,* being open to what you can learn from the *unconscious,* experimenting with techniques like *free association,* understanding *dream work,* and increasing your appreciation of the importance of central concepts such as *resistance, transference,* and *countertransference.* Regardless of their theoretical orientation, group practitioners can benefit from understanding these concepts. As you work through these exercises in your class or group, remain open to how you can incorporate some of these psychodynamic concepts into your style of leading groups.

Some of these exercises can tap emotional material; therefore, it is best to restrict them to a supervised group situation. Some of these exercises may not be appropriate for the format and purpose of your class.

Exercises

1. *Working with your past.* The analytic approach is based on the assumption that past experiences play a vital role in shaping one's current personality. The following short exercises and questions are designed to assist you in remembering and exploring in your group selected dimensions of your past.

   a. Recall and reconstruct some childhood experiences. Examining pictures of yourself as a child, interviewing people who knew you well, looking over diaries, and so on can be useful means of stimulating recall. Share in your group what you consider to be some significant influences from your past. How have these factors contributed to the person you are now?

   b. Write an outline (such as you might find in the table of contents) of a book that you could write about your life. Pay attention mainly to chapter headings. Examples might include: "The child who was never allowed to be a child"; "A time of confusion"; "My most joyous memories"; "Dreams I had as a child"; "The things I wanted to be as a child." You could also write the preface to this book about your life and include an acknowledgment section. Who are the people you'd most want to acknowledge as having a significant impact on your life? In what ways have they made a difference?

   c. In the outline for the book on your life, include a chapter in which you rewrite your past the way you would have wanted it to be. Share your ideas for this chapter with your group.

   d. Make a list of your current struggles, and see if you can trace the origins of these conflicts to childhood events.

2. *Free association.* A key method of unlocking the unconscious is free association; the therapist asks clients to clear their mind of day-to-day thoughts and simply report in a spontaneous way whatever comes to mind. There are several ways to use free association in a group:

   a. Members can be encouraged to say whatever comes to them. Participants often censor their contributions; they rehearse what they will say for fear that "it won't come out right." Some members agonize over what to bring up in a group and exactly how to present a personal issue.

   It might also be a productive exercise in your group to make up incomplete sentences, finish them, and then find ways to free-associate with what seems to be significant material. For example, you might work with sentences such as these:

   When I'm in this group, I feel _____.
   One way I attempt to avoid things in this group is by _____.
   One fear I have in this group is _____.

3. *Dream work.* Report the key elements of one of your dreams to your group. You might try the following suggestions as a way of learning something about yourself through your dreams.

   a. Select any part of your dream and free-associate with that part. Say as many words as fast as you can without censoring them. After you've done this, see what your free-association work tells you.

   b. Give an initial interpretation of your dream. What themes or patterns do you see?

   c. Next, ask group members to give their reactions to your dream. What do they think your dream might reveal about you?

   d. You might want to begin keeping a dream journal. Write down your dreams. Record what you remember. Then look at the patterns of your dreams and interpret their meaning.

4. *Resistance.* Brainstorm all the possible ways in which you might resist in a group. What resistances have you experienced to simply getting into a group? List some avoidance patterns that you have seen in yourself in a group. How can you help group members recognize and work through resistances that could prevent them from effectively working in a group? What are some ways that resistance can be addressed therapeutically? What purposes do these member resistances serve?

5. *Transference.* To get some idea of this process, try some of these exercises in your group:

   a. Think of the people in your group. Does anyone remind you of a significant person in your life? Discuss the similarities.

   b. You can explore possible transferences that occur outside of the group. Have you ever experienced strong, immediate, and even irrational reactions to a person you hardly knew? Discuss what you can learn about unfinished business from your past by focusing on such occurrences.

   c. Be aware of transference onto the leader as an authority figure. Discuss the ways in which you might work with this therapeutically. How might such transferences either facilitate understanding or block growth?

6. *Countertransference.* Ideas for exploration in a group:

   a. What kind of client do you think you'd have the most difficulty working with in a group? Why? How do you imagine you'd handle a client who had very strong negative feelings toward you, especially if you felt that these feelings were inappropriate and a function of transference?

b. Select a client who you think is a difficult group member and who you anticipate will cause you problems. Take on the identity of this client. Others in the group can function as members, and one person can be the group leader and attempt to work with you. After you've had a chance to take on the role of this "problem member" for a while, explore what this experience was like for you. How did the other members respond to you? How did the group leader respond to you?

c. Identify a possible form of countertransference of yours that could interfere with your effectiveness in leading groups. For example, you may have an extreme need to be appreciated, which could determine your leadership style. Discuss this personality characteristic with your group. Although it may be unrealistic to expect a solution, you can talk about steps you could take to work on this problem.

7. *Being a group member.* What do you imagine it would be like for you to be a member of an ongoing analytic group? What issues do you think you'd want to pursue in such a group? What kind of member do you think you'd be?

8. *Role of group leader.* Review the section in the textbook on the role of the analytic group leader. What would it be like for you to work within the framework of this model? Would there be any differences in your ability to function within a psychodynamic model between brief therapy and long-term therapy? Could you function within this model if it were your primary orientation? Why or why not?

9. *Personal critique.* Devote some time to a personal evaluation of the strengths and weaknesses of the analytic approach to group therapy. What specific techniques do you think are valuable? Why? What concepts could you draw on from this model in your work with groups, regardless of your orientation? What are the major contributions of the analytic model? What are the major limitations? Does brief dynamic therapy address the limitations of the model? With what kind of population do you think this model would be most appropriate? least appropriate?

Reminder: If you've not yet read the last two chapters in the textbook (Chapters 17 and 18), I suggest that you do so at this point. The comparison of theories and the case of a group in action will help you get an overall picture of how these theories are related. As you read and study the theory chapters, the last two chapters will give you an increased appreciation of how diverse theories can be applied to the different stages of a group's development.

Questions for Reflection and Discussion

1. To what extent are psychoanalytic groups appropriate for all sociocultural and socioeconomic groups? For what populations do you think they are best suited? In what cases do you think they are not suitable?

2. Compare and contrast psychoanalysis in groups with one-to-one therapy. What are some advantages of group treatment over individual therapy? What are some limitations and disadvantages?

3. In general, psychoanalytic groups focus on the intrapsychic dynamics of the individual and emphasize relating everything that occurs in the group to historical determinants. What do you think of this focus on individual dynamics? What are some advantages and disadvantages of such a focus?

4. The psychoanalytic group in some ways replicates the original family of the members. Emphasis is put on recognizing and exploring multiple transferences in a group as a way of dealing with early familial issues. What are the possibilities of such a focus? To what degree do you think doing this can be an emotionally corrective experience?

5. Review the psychosexual and psychosocial stages of human development, which consist of an integration of Freud's and Erikson's ideas. How do these stages apply to you? Were there any critical turning points in your life that had an impact on who you are today? What applications of this developmental framework are useful for group counseling?

6. What concepts and techniques from the psychoanalytic approach would you be most interested in incorporating in your style of group leadership?

7. To what degree do you think psychodynamically, even though you might not use psychoanalytic techniques in a group?

8. From an analytic perspective, therapists are not totally free of countertransference reactions. What kind of members do you think you'd have the greatest difficulty in understanding and working with therapeutically? How do you see your reactions to certain types of members as related to your own unresolved personal issues?

9. The more traditional psychoanalytic group therapists maintain a stance characterized by objectivity, warm detachment, and relative anonymity. More contemporary psychoanalytic group therapists (relational or interpersonal therapists) have a style that involves psychological presence, self-disclosure, mutuality, and reciprocity. What advantages do you see with each style? Which style do you prefer and why?

10. Brief psychodynamic groups represent a modification of traditional psychoanalytic groups. What are some of the key elements of the time-limited approaches to group therapy that you particularly value?

11. Brief therapy provides an opportunity to begin a process of change that will continue long after therapy is terminated. What are some ways you can think of to encourage members to continue the work they began in a group once they terminate treatment?

12. What psychoanalytic ideas can you apply to better understand yourself?

An Expert's Perspective on Psychoanalytic Groups: by William Blau

WILLIAM BLAU, PhD, is a licensed psychologist in private practice and teaches as an adjunct instructor at Copper Mountain College in Joshua Tree, California. Although his theoretical orientation is psychoanalytic, he often uses techniques from other approaches.

1. What attracted you to this particular theoretical orientation? How does this theory fit for the person you are?

My study of psychology has always been a search for an understanding of mind and human experience. Throughout my training, I found psychoanalytic thought to be the theoretical model that most effectively combined exploration of the complex terrain of intrapersonal dynamics with systematic observation of interpersonal behavior. As a therapist I am privileged when I am deemed trustworthy enough to participate in a client's attempts to understand his or her inner world and, perhaps, to play a role in alleviating suffering and turmoil. I find efforts to "predict and control" behavior without understanding and empathy to be empty at best. Hence, I strongly endorse the nonjudgmental stance that is at the heart of the psychoanalytic therapeutic frame.

2. What Key Concepts (1 to 3) of this theory are most applicable to the practice of group counseling?

Recapitulation of the family group: Even if the group leader focuses on the here-and-now group process in conducting groups, it can be valuable, conceptually, to recognize that group members will engage in behavior that reflects prior experience in their family of origin.

Transference and countertransference: The multiple transferences in group counseling provide opportunities for understanding and insight. The group leader also experiences countertransference feelings that are both multiple and complex. For example, if I experience a strong liking for one group member, and another member is hostile to that person, my countertransference with the first person may affect my feelings for the hostile group member. Such interaction effects complicate the self-monitoring of countertransference that is an essential facet of effective group work.

Stages of development: Psychoanalytic stages of development have parallels with the stages of group development and are also relevant to understanding the developmental issues of individual group members. I find Erikson's identification of specific crises and tasks associated with each stage, from infancy to old age, to be of particular value in group work.

3. What Techniques (1 to 3) from this theory have the most practical value for group work practitioners?

The therapeutic frame: The leader establishes the group as a "safe place" in which to explore feelings, thoughts, impulses, and memories that are problematic or disturbing. The nonjudgmental stance of the leader helps establish a group environment that allows members to express material that might be dangerous in the outside world. Details of the frame may vary, depending on factors that include the composition of the group and the setting in which the group takes place, but all members should fully understand the frame, including any limitations on confidentiality. Confidentiality is always limited in a group, compared to individual treatment, because the leader cannot force all members to follow the agreed upon rules.

Listening to the unconscious: This is an application of psychoanalytic free association to group counseling. Once the therapeutic frame has been established, the leader stops talking and just listens. This technique typically elicits some anxiety as group members struggle to initiate the group process on their own. The "leaderless" period is often highly productive and reveals a great deal about the dynamics that will emerge throughout the life of the group. As a psychoanalytically oriented leader, I use this period to listen for clues about each member's unconscious, just as I would listen to an individual client who was free associating. I do not rigidly maintain the silence, and I do increasingly engage actively in the group process as it develops. Nevertheless, whenever I feel stuck as to what to say, my default is to "shut up and listen" until I feel I have a contribution that is coherent with the dynamics present in the group. This technique is not useful in all groups, and clients whose emotional stability is fragile or who are not committed to doing group work may require more structure. Nevertheless, I have found that a willingness to "shut up and listen" is very useful in my own work, and student group leaders who feel pressured to "do something" in the group have effectively used it as well.

Interpretation: Skillful interpretations can elicit insight and are important elements of a psychoanalytically oriented group. Each interpretation I make is only a hunch for the client to consider. Interpretations should start near the surface of the unconscious, acknowledging material that is barely conscious or almost conscious, and gradually address deeper content, as accepted by the individual client. My guiding principle is to focus on the effect of the interpretation on the client and avoid attachment to the "correctness" of any interpretive hypothesis. Interpretations by other group members are useful and often powerful; nevertheless, it is important to gauge not only the interpretation's impact on the client whose behavior is being interpreted, but also the intention of the interpreting member. Interpretations in group counseling are more likely to refer to here-and-now behavior than to incidents in the client's past.

4. **How does this theory have particular relevance for addressing diversity and social justice issues in group work?**
Psychoanalytic theory has played a part in cross-cultural studies since Freud's early work on psychoanalytic anthropology. Psychoanalytic theorists and researchers have consistently demonstrated the deleterious effects of discrimination, providing strong support for opposing racism and supporting social justice. The nonjudgmental stance of the psychoanalytic therapeutic frame provides a basis for treatment that naturally allows for diversity and celebrates freedom from the "tyranny of the shoulds" imposed by rigid cultural taboos internalized by the super-ego.

Ego-defense mechanisms, particularly projection, displacement, denial, and reaction formation, provide an understanding of the mechanisms underlying intolerance and prejudice. Following psychoanalytic theory, I treat pathological defense mechanisms as I would any symptom of posttraumatic stress disorder. Therefore, I see group counseling as a vehicle for mild exposure therapy for whatever prejudices are activated in the group. To whatever degree clients defend their egos with racist, sexist, classist, homophobic, or other prejudices, these clients may experience healing through having an experience in which one or more members of the feared group are part of the recapitulated family group. As in any desensitization exposure treatment, exposure must be gradual and gentle; repetition of a traumatic experience may cause harm if the client's ego does not "know" it to be harmless. The group leader must actively control the group to minimize this risk; the nonjudgmental stance of the therapist applies to feelings, not to behavior that could entrench the prejudices or cause harm to any member.

Psychoanalytically oriented group treatment has an advantage over long-term individual treatment in treating low-income clients who lack the time, money, or inclination to spend months or years in treatment.

5. Raise a question from this theoretical framework that you consider especially important for group work practice.

Psychoanalytic therapists see conscious problems as manifestations of unconscious dynamics involving primitive urges, catastrophic fears, and intense inner conflicts. In group counseling, any or all members of the group may attack and batter a client's defenses and potentially provoke an eruption of unconscious material that may threaten the client's mental stability. How can the group leader or leaders minimize this risk?

The leader can actively support the bullied member's most healthy defenses. The attack may, then, turn against the leader, but that's OK—taking such abuse is part of the leader's role. Psychoanalytic interpretations help "make the unconscious conscious," but bullying is typically an expression of the transference of the aggressor(s). In contrast to doing "attack therapy," as has been used in some addiction recovery programs, I encourage psychoanalytic group leaders to offer interpretations as hypotheses and to begin with material that is close to the member's awareness.

Your Thoughts on Dr. Blau's Psychoanalytic Perspective on Group Therapy

1. What value do you see in the concept of the recapitulation of the family group in groups you may be leading?
2. What aspects of Dr. Blau's perspective did you find most interesting and why?
3. What do you understand by the "therapeutic frame," and what importance do you place on this for the practice of group therapy?
4. What role do you believe that interpretation plays in effective group therapy?

Quiz on Psychoanalytic Approach to Groups: A Comprehension Check   Score ____%

Note: Refer to Appendix I for the scoring key for these quizzes. Count 5 points for each error, and subtract the total from 100 to get your percentage score. I recommend that you review these comprehension checks when preparing for tests in your class. I also suggest that you bring to class questions that you would like clarified. If you get a wrong answer that you believe is right, bring it up for discussion.

True/false items: Decide if the following statements are "more true" or "more false" as they apply to the psychoanalytic approach to groups.

T   F   1. Most interpretations in a psychoanalytic group are made by the individual client and other members; the group therapist infrequently makes interpretations.

T   F   2. In an analytic group, dealing with transference and resistance constitutes the bulk of the work.

T   F   3. Countertransference refers to the irrational feelings that the members project onto the group therapist.

T   F   4. Insight is not deemed to be either useful or necessary in the psychoanalytic group.

T   F   5. In analytic group work, resistance is viewed as the result of ineptness and lack of therapeutic skill on the part of the leader.

T   F   6. Attachment theory, which can be considered an offspring of object relations theory, is a part of the newer relational models within the psychodynamic approach.

T   F   7. Ego integrity involves feeling optimistic about what one is planning to do with one's life.

T   F   8. Therapists from the dominant culture may ignore the cultural, ethnic, and racial aspects of transference and countertransference.

T   F   9. An interpretation is simply a hypothesis; no matter how elegantly conceived, it is still subject to confirmation or refutation.

T   F   10. The contemporary theoretical trends in psychoanalytic thinking center on predictable developmental sequences in which the early experiences of the self shift in relation to an expanding awareness of others.

Note: Another suggestion for feedback and for review is to retake the prechapter self-inventory. All 10 of the items are true statements as applied to the particular therapy, so thinking about them is a good way to review.

Multiple-choice items: Select the *one best answer* among the alternatives given. Consider each question within the framework of psychoanalytic theory and practice.

_____11. Resistance in the psychoanalytic approach is viewed
   a. as an unconscious dynamic.
   b. as a conscious refusal of a member to explore a threatening topic.
   c. as a result of lack of skill on the leader's part.
   d. as a sign that the group is a failure.
   e. generally as a way to avoid intimacy.

_____12. The primary goal of analytic group work is to work toward
   a. adequate social adjustment.
   b. uncovering early experiences.
   c. helping members develop social interest.
   d. formulating a concrete plan for changing specific behaviors.
   e. teaching members problem-solving strategies.

_____13. In a group setting, free association could be used for
   a. uncovering repressed material.
   b. helping members develop more spontaneity.
   c. working on dreams.
   d. promoting meaningful interactions within the group.
   e. all of the above.

_____14. Psychoanalytic dream work consists of
   a. asking the member to act out all parts of the dream.
   b. having the member analyze and interpret his or her own dream.
   c. interpreting the latent meaning of the dream.
   d. the leader avoiding suggesting any meanings the dream might have.
   e. looking for universal and spiritual symbols in the dream.

_____15. The advantage of using groups with the psychoanalytic approach is that
   a. members can benefit from one another's work.
   b. multiple transferences can be formed.
   c. members can learn to identify their own transferences.
   d. the group can become the family of yesterday.
   e. all of the above.

_____16. Modern analytic practitioners are leaving behind the "detached-observer" model of classical analysis for

   a. a more intersubjective style.

   b. a form of relational analysis.

   c. both (a) and (b).

   d. a short-term therapy based on empirical findings.

   e. a model based on friendship.

_____17. Relational analysis, in contrast to classical analysis, puts more emphasis on

   a. therapist self-disclosure.

   b. responsiveness.

   c. reciprocity.

   d. mutuality.

   e. all of the above.

_____18. Brief psychodynamic therapy (BPT) generally has a time limit of

   a. 10 to 25 sessions.

   b. 1 to 6 sessions.

   c. never more than 6 sessions.

   d. 52 sessions.

_____19. Brief psychodynamic therapy (BPT) is

   a. mainly designed for borderline personality disorders.

   b. suitable for all clients regardless of diagnosis.

   c. appropriate for a variety of clients' needs.

   d. primarily aimed at working with narcissistic personality disorders.

_____20. Brief psychodynamic therapy (BPT) calls upon the therapist to

   a. assume a nondirective and even passive role.

   b. assume an active role in quickly formulating a therapeutic focus that goes beyond the surface of presenting problems.

   c. deal exclusively with a single presenting problem.

   d. avoid treating any underlying issue.

CHAPTER SEVEN

Adlerian Group Counseling

Prechapter Self-Inventory for the Adlerian Approach

Directions: Refer to page 77 for general directions. Indicate your position on these statements using the following code:

5 = I *strongly agree* with this statement.
4 = I *agree*, in most respects, with this statement.
3 = I am *undecided* in my opinion about this statement.
2 = I *disagree*, in most respects, with this statement.
1 = I *strongly disagree* with this statement.

_____ 1. People are best understood by looking at their movement toward goals and at where they are going rather than at where they have been.

_____ 2. Group counseling is especially appropriate as an intervention because people are strongly motivated by social connectedness and because they cannot be fully understood apart from their social context.

_____ 3. Although people are influenced by their early childhood experiences, they are not passively shaped and determined by these experiences.

_____ 4. A useful focus in group counseling is the interpersonal and social nature of a member's problems.

_____ 5. The Adlerian approach is basically a growth model; our destiny is never fixed as we are always in the process of becoming.

_____ 6. Recalling one's earliest memories is a useful group technique.

_____ 7. Although insight into our problems can be useful, it is essential that this awareness leads to constructive movement toward desired goals.

_____ 8. Each person develops a unique lifestyle that can be examined in group sessions.

_____ 9. The group leader's goals and the members' goals need to be aligned for effective work to occur.

_____10. An analysis of each member's family constellation is highly useful to successful group work.

Summary of Basic Assumptions and Key Concepts of the Adlerian Approach to Groups

1. The underlying assumptions of the Adlerian approach are as follows: humans are primarily social beings, motivated by social forces and influenced largely by social interactions;

conscious, not unconscious, processes account for much of behavior; people are creative, active, self-determined, autonomous beings, not the victims of fate; people are significantly influenced by their perceptions and interpretations of past events; as people gain awareness of the continuity of their lives, they are able to modify their faulty assumptions.

2. All people have basic feelings of inferiority that motivate them to strive for superiority, success, mastery, power, and perfection or completion. Their lifestyles comprise unique behaviors and habits that they develop in striving for power, meaning, and personal goals. Lifestyle is influenced first by the family constellation and family atmosphere, especially by relationships among siblings. This lifestyle, which is formed early in life to compensate for perceived feelings of inferiority, also influences a person's view of the world.

3. Group participants learn about social problems and their solutions firsthand, and they give support to others and get help from others. Members come to see that many of their problems are interpersonal in nature, that their behavior has social meaning, and that their goals can best be understood in the framework of social purposes. One of the major goals of a group is to increase members' social interest and community feeling.

4. Adlerians relate the past to the present only to indicate the continuity in a maladaptive style of living, not to show a causal connection between the past and the present. In contrast to the psychoanalytic emphasis on the past, Adlerians are more interested in the future. The three aspects of time are dynamically interrelated. Adlerians look for continuity or a pattern in a client's life, but the emphasis is always on the goal-directed nature of behavior. The individual's movement through life is unified and directed by the person's self-selected life goal.

5. Everything we do is related to our fictional life goal. Adlerians refer to the life goal as fictional finalism, or the imagined central goal that gives direction to behavior and unity to the personality. It is an image of what people would be like if they were perfectly secure. Adlerian group counselors work with both the patterns for living and the logic supporting them as a way to facilitate a more socially useful life goal.

6. The goals of Adlerian group counseling correspond to the four phases of group work, which include establishing and maintaining the proper therapeutic relationship, exploring the dynamics operating in the individual, communicating to the individual an understanding of self, and seeing new alternatives and making new choices.

7. The group setting provides a context for people to experience social interest; they come to care for the group as a community, as well as for individual members in the group. Group members are given opportunities to offer feedback and to support others, which is an example of social interest in action.

8. Group counseling is not simply a matter of an expert group leader making prescriptions for change. It is a collaborative effort in which members and the leader work toward mutually accepted goals. Change is aimed at both the cognitive and behavioral levels. Adlerians are mainly concerned with challenging clients' mistaken notions and faulty assumptions.

9. Adlerian group therapy has a psychoeducational focus and a present and future orientation, not a past orientation. Adlerian group leaders recognize that many of the changes in the members take place between group sessions, and leaders create a structure that will help members stay focused on specific personal goals. Adlerians recognize that focus, combined with time limits and encouragement, helps members gain hope that change is possible.

10. Adlerian group therapy lends itself to a time-limited approach. The core characteristics associated with brief group therapy include quickly establishing a strong therapeutic alliance; a clear problem focus and goal alignment; rapid assessment; emphasis on active and directive therapeutic interventions; a focus on strengths and abilities of clients; an optimistic view of change; a focus on both the present and the future; and an emphasis on tailoring treatment to the unique needs of clients in the most time-efficient manner possible.

11. Adlerian group counselors make use of several assessment techniques. Assessments of the members' family constellation, relationship difficulties, early recollections, dreams, and art work provide clues to life goals and lifestyle. The leader's task is to integrate and summarize themes from the lifestyle investigation and to interpret how mistaken notions are influencing group members. Adlerian group leaders tend to encourage members to become actively involved with other people and to develop a new lifestyle through these relationships.

12. The Adlerian approach offers a range of cognitive and action-oriented techniques to help people explore their concerns in a cultural context. Adlerian practitioners are flexible in adapting their interventions to each client's unique life situation, which makes this approach suitable for working with a wide range of client problems.

13. Adlerian group leaders promote an egalitarian, person-to-person relationship. Group leaders serve as models for the members, who often learn more from what leaders *do* in the group than from what they *say*.

14. Interpretation is a technique that facilitates the process of gaining insight into one's style of life. Interpretations are never forced on the client; they are presented tentatively in the form of hypotheses. Interpretations offered in this collaborative manner as hunches about possible meanings leave group members free to consider what they hear without feeling that they must accept the interpretation of the group leader.

15. Leaders challenge members to have faith and hope, to develop the courage to face life actively, and to choose the kind of life they want. Group members are invited to live as if they were the way they want to be. Encouragement is used throughout all phases of the group to assist members in creating new patterns of behavior and developing strengths, assets, resources, and abilities.

Glossary of Key Terms for Adlerian Therapy

- **Acting as if** A technique in which group members are encouraged to reflect on how they would be different if they were the person they desired to be.
- **Basic mistakes** Faulty, self-defeating perceptions, attitudes, and beliefs that may have been appropriate at one time but are appropriate no longer. These myths are influential in the development of personality. Examples include overgeneralizations, misperceptions of life and its demands, denying one's worth, an exaggerated need for security, and impossible goals.
- **Catching oneself** Helping clients identify signals associated with their problematic behavior or emotions so that clients can then make decisions that stop their symptoms from taking over.
- **Community feeling** An individual's awareness of being part of the human community and the individual's attitudes in dealing with the social world; a sense of striving for a better future for humanity.

- **Early recollections** Specific, detailed childhood memories that can be thought of as capsule summaries of one's present philosophy of life.
- **Emotional intelligence** A concept related to social interest that includes the ability to control impulses, empathize with others, form responsible interpersonal relationships, and develop intimate relationships.
- **Encouragement** The process of increasing members' courage to face life tasks; used throughout therapy as a way to counter discouragement and to help people set realistic goals; implies faith in people as they are and focuses on assets and strengths to build self-esteem.
- **Family atmosphere** The climate of relationships among family members.
- **Family constellation** The social and psychological structure of the family system; includes parental relationships, birth order, the individual's perception of self, sibling characteristics, and ratings.
- **Fictional finalism** An imagined central goal that gives direction to behavior and unity to the personality; an image of what people would be like if they were perfect, perfectly secure, or complete.
- **Holism** Characterizes the whole, indivisible person; all parts work together in harmony in movement toward goals. People are integrated beings who proceed with others through life; a reaction against separating personality into parts and a focus on the unity of personality.
- **Individual Psychology** Adler's term for his approach, reflecting his belief in the uniqueness and unity of the individual.
- **Inferiority feelings** The ever-present determining force in behavior; the source of human striving. Humans attempt to compensate for both imagined and real inferiorities, which helps them overcome handicaps.
- **Insight** Understanding that can be translated into constructive action.
- **Interpretation** The process by which individuals are helped to gain insight into their lifestyle.
- **Lifestyle** The individual's basic orientation to life and the themes that characterize the person's existence; a blueprint for living that each individual develops based on a subjective view of self and the world. The convictions individuals develop during the first 6 years of life to help them organize, understand, predict, and control their life experiences.
- **Life tasks** Adler's notion that all humans must face and solve certain problems universal in human life, including the tasks of friendship (community), work (making a contribution), and intimacy (love and marriage).
- **Mistaken goals** Related to patterns of misbehavior such as attention getting, power struggle, revenge, and inadequacy or withdrawal.
- **Phenomenology** The belief that humans actively and creatively interpret their life experiences in a personal and unique way; a focus on the subjective fashion in which people perceive their world.
- **Priorities** Characteristics that involve a dominant behavior pattern with supporting convictions that an individual uses to cope; examples include significance, control, comfort, and pleasing.
- **Private logic** Basic convictions and assumptions of the individual that underlie the lifestyle pattern and explain how behaviors fit together to provide consistency.

- **Reorientation** The phase of the counseling process wherein members are helped to redirect their mistaken goals and basic mistakes.
- **Social interest** The sense of connectedness with others and the desire to contribute usefully to society by dealing with the tasks of work, friendship, and intimacy—a sense of identification and empathy with others, a feeling of belonging, a striving for a better future for humanity.
- **Socioteleological approach** Belief that people are primarily motivated by social forces and are striving to achieve certain goals.
- **Striving for superiority** A strong inclination toward becoming competent, toward mastering the environment, and toward self-improvement; this striving for perfection or completion is a movement toward enhancement of self and is known as the "growth force."
- **Style of life** An individual's way of thinking, feeling, and acting. A conceptual framework by which the world is perceived and by which people are able to cope with life tasks; the person's personality.
- **Teleology** The study of goals and the goal-directedness of human behavior. Humans live by goals and purposes: they are moved by anticipation of the future; they create meaning.

Exercises and Activities for the Adlerian Group

Rationale

Many of the Adlerian concepts relevant for group practice involve issues such as the influence of one's family on one's current personality, reviewing one's past to determine its present impact, striving for goals that define a unique lifestyle, and identifying ways of developing social interest and community feeling. The basic concepts of the Adlerian approach will assume a more concrete meaning for you if you personalize them. It is up to you to decide how personal you want to be in sharing aspects of your life with others in your class or group. Remember that you can be personal without sharing your deepest and most private experiences. The following exercises and questions give you opportunities to experience some of the themes stressed in Adlerian groups.

Lifestyle Assessment

Adlerians often begin a group with a structured interview to obtain information about the members' family constellation, early recollections, life goals, and childhood experiences. If you have a basic grasp of the concepts of Adlerian psychology, you can develop your own inventory for getting some of this information. Although there are set formats for the lifestyle questionnaire, the purpose of this exercise is to provide you with the experience of gathering data about yourself that you could use if you were a member of a group. By practicing on yourself I hope you will gain some ideas for what to look for in interviews with members of the groups you will lead. Assume that you are interested in joining an Adlerian group *as a member,* and answer these questions as directly, simply, and honestly as you can.

1. What would you tell others about who you are? What are three adjectives that describe you?
2. How well are you dealing with current life tasks? In addressing this question, examine these areas of your life: leisure, friendship, being part of a family, relationships with others, meaning in life, being a parent, adjustment to work, finding hobbies, your feelings about self, the spiritual dimension of your life, and any other areas important to you.

STAGES OF DEVELOPMENT OF THE ADLERIAN GROUP

Dimension	Initial Stage	Working Stage	Final Stage
Key developmental tasks and goals	Central developmental tasks are establishing empathy and creating acceptance, setting goals and making commitments, understanding one's current lifestyle, and exploring one's premises and assumptions. The psychological investigation that occurs in the group involves exploration of the family atmosphere and subjective interpretation of childhood events.	Members are helped to understand their beliefs, feelings, motives, and goals; they develop insight into their mistaken goals and self-defeating behaviors; they work through interpersonal conflicts; and they explore the beliefs behind their feelings. A goal is to create meaning and significance in life. Through group interaction, one's basic values and lifestyle become evident.	This is a time when members explore multiple alternatives to problems and make a commitment to change. They translate insights into action and make new decisions. A goal is to facilitate members' awareness of their mistaken notions through observation of fellow group members and reality testing. A main goal is to promote social interest of members.
Role and tasks of group leader	Main goal of the group leader is to establish a collaborative relationship and to decide with clients on the goals of the group. Leader's tasks include providing encouragement, offering support and tentative hypotheses of behavior, and helping members assess and clarify their problems. Role of leader is to observe social context of behavior in group and to model attentive listening, caring, sincerity, and confrontation. Leader helps members recognize and use their strengths.	Functions of leader include interpreting early recollections around family patterns, helping members identify basic mistakes, helping members become aware of their own unique lifestyles, challenging them to deal with life tasks, and helping them summarize and integrate what they've learned so they can make new plans. Leader assumes that members can best be understood by looking at their strivings and goals and helping them create new and more functional beliefs.	The focus is on reeducation at this time. Leader helps members challenge attitudes and encourages them to take risks and experiment with new behavior by translating their new ideas into actual behavior outside the group. Leader's tasks include helping members recognize their mistaken beliefs and become aware of their own self-defeating beliefs and behaviors. Leader offers encouragement as members put their insights into action. Leader assists in fostering social interest.
Role of group members	Members state their goals and may establish contracts. They are expected to be active in the group and begin to assume responsibility for the ways in which they want to change. Members begin to work on trust issues, which are important in the encouragement process and in developing good morale within the group. Because of the way the group is structured, members meet their needs for belonging.	Members become increasingly aware of their lifestyle. They analyze the impact of the family constellation; they also begin to recognize that they are responsible for their own behavior. Members support and challenge others so that they can explore their basic inferiority feelings. Participants learn to believe in themselves by taking action to change their lives. They explore their mistaken attitudes and faulty motivations.	Members are expected to establish realistic goals. They see new options and more functional alternatives. They learn problem-solving and decision-making skills. This is a time of reorientation. Members encourage one another to redirect their goals along realistic lines. Members help one another in considering alternatives and in making new choices. Members are encouraged to act as *if* they were the person they want to be.

Techniques	Basic listening skills are crucial at this time. Analysis and assessment of one's lifestyle and how it affects current functioning are conducted. Other techniques include questioning, reflection, and clarification.	Some of the techniques used at this stage are confrontation, interpretation, modeling, paraphrasing, encouragement, "catching oneself" in old patterns, acting "as if," and teaching. Leader can adapt a variety of techniques to help members work.	Basic procedures at the final stage consist of encouraging members to act and change. Contracts are reestablished and role-playing techniques are used to help members reorient their goals. There is a continuation of the encouragement process.
Questions to consider	How can you as a leader establish a collaborative relationship with the members? Adlerians are concerned with the ways in which people strive for significance. How can the group itself be used to help members understand how they find meaning and how they meet the challenge of life? How well are the members dealing with current life tasks? Why are the members seeking this group now? In obtaining the lifestyle assessment of members, how would you address: • Parental influence? • Family information? • Memories of each sibling? • Role in the family? • Earliest recollections? • Critical turning points in life? • Basic mistakes?	What are the values of focusing on members' beliefs and motives with the intention of helping them develop insight into their mistaken goals? How can early recollections and family patterns be interpreted in light of the members' current behavior in the group situation? Leaders might think of this question in helping members become aware of their lifestyle: Under what circumstances does the person acquire a particular lifestyle, and how is it being maintained currently? What are some techniques for helping members catch themselves in old patterns and begin to behave in new and more effective ways? How can the cultural context best be taken into consideration so that techniques can be applied in flexible ways?	How can members be challenged to make a commitment to change? How can insights be translated into action? What are some of the ways members can apply problem-solving and decision-making skills acquired in the group to actual behavior in or outside of the group? To what degree are the members behaving as active and autonomous beings as opposed to acting as victims of fate? To what extent have the members become actively involved with other people and developed a new lifestyle through relationships? Can members summarize changes in attitudes, beliefs, goals, and behaviors? Are members feeling encouraged to take risks by acting on these changes?

Reactions: Summarize your reactions to the Adlerian perspective on group developmental stages. What do you like *most? least?* What aspects of this approach would you incorporate in your style of group leadership?

3. How have your parents influenced your life? Answer these questions for each parent:
   a. Describe the parent. What kind of person is he or she? What three adjectives describe this person?
   b. What ambitions did the parent have for you?
   c. What relationship did this parent have with each child in the family?
   d. What were your main feelings toward the parent when you were growing up? What are your feelings toward him or her now?
   e. In what ways are you similar to and different from the parent?
   f. How would you describe the relationship your parents have with each other?

4. What other family information do you recall? What aspects of your family life are relevant to the person you are now?

5. Describe your brothers and sisters (from the oldest to the youngest). What do you remember about each sibling? How would you compare yourself with each sibling? Who is most like you, and in what respect? Who is most different from you, and in what way? How would you describe your position in the family? What expectations did you have for each sibling? What were their expectations for you?

6. What are your earliest recollections? What specific incidents stand out for you? Do you recall how you felt in selected situations? Can you recall any reactions that you had in these situations?

7. What do you recall about your growth and development? In addressing this question, think about specific areas such as physical development, major changes in childhood and adolescence, social development, sexual development, spiritual development, childhood fears, ambitions and goals, special talents, assets, liabilities, school experiences, and work experiences.

8. Can you identify any basic mistakes (self-defeating perceptions) that you acquired in childhood or adolescence? Some examples include the following:
   a. Faulty generalizations, such as "Nobody really cares about me" and "I am always singled out as the one nobody likes."
   b. Denial of your value as a person, such as "I am basically unlovable" and "I will never accomplish what I want to in life."
   c. Misperceptions of reality, such as "Because people expect so much of me, I'll never measure up, and I'll always be frustrated."
   d. Write a brief summary of the key characteristics of your family constellation and your early recollections. From what you know of yourself, what might you select to explore in a group?
   e. What do you see as your major assets? What about your liabilities? What would you most want to change in your past if you could relive your childhood?

Personal Exploration and Suggested Activities

1. Adlerians use a technique known as *"the question."* It consists of asking a client "How would you be different if _____?" The end of the sentence refers to being free of a problem or a symptom. If you were troubled with migraine headaches, for example, you would be asked how you'd be different if you no longer had them. Apply this question to a specific problem you have. Explore how your life might be different without

this problem. How do you think your problem may be useful to you? Are you "rewarded" for some of your symptoms?

2. What are some of your *earliest memories*? Are they mainly joyful or painful? Consider sharing one specific early memory in your group or class and talking about the significance it has for you. What value do you see in the Adlerian technique of having clients recall their earliest memories? Can you think of ways to use this technique in groups you may lead?

3. Adlerians stress *birth order and the family constellation*. Share with others in your class or group what it was like to be the firstborn child, the last-born child, the middle child, or the only child. What does your group think are the advantages and disadvantages of each of these positions?

4. According to Adler, each of us has a *unique lifestyle,* or personality, that starts to develop in early childhood to compensate for and overcome some perceived inferiority. How does this notion apply to you? In what ways might you feel inferior? Could you interpret what you do as your way to strive for mastery and significance and to overcome basic inferiority? In describing your lifestyle, consider these questions: What makes you unique? How do you strive for power? When do you feel the most powerful? What goals do you most strive for? What do you most often tell others about yourself on a first meeting? How do you typically present yourself?

5. Adlerian therapists often ask group members to live *as if* they were the person they wanted to be. For example, you may want to be far more creative than you are now. Assume that you are more creative, and then describe yourself to your group. Think of other ways to present yourself as if you were the person who you would ideally like to be. What stops you from being this kind of person? What can you do to begin moving in this direction? What ways can you think of to use this "as if" technique in a group? What value do you see in applying the "as if" technique to yourself?

6. Adlerians center on "basic mistakes," or faulty assumptions, that people make about themselves. These mistaken ideas lead to self-defeating behavior. For example, you may believe that to feel successful you must be perfect. Because you'll never feel perfect, you will constantly put yourself under needless stress and experience little joy in your accomplishments. Select one faulty assumption you have made about yourself or the world. In your group discuss how this mistake affects you. If you were to change this assumption, how might your life be different? Can you identify any ways in which your basic mistakes affect the kind of group leader you are?

7. Adlerians stress self-determination by maintaining that we are not the victims of fate; rather, we are creative, active, choice-making beings whose every action has purpose and meaning. How does this notion fit you as you look at the patterns in your life?

8. In Adlerian groups the members are best understood by looking at where they are going. Teleology, or striving for goals, is a key Adlerian concept. Apply this idea to yourself and talk about what direction you are striving toward. How do you see your goals as influencing what you are doing now? How do you think your past has influenced your future goals? In what ways can you apply this purposive, goal-oriented approach in your work with groups?

9. What ideas from the Adlerian approach can you apply to better understanding yourself?

10. Adlerians emphasize developing *social interest,* which includes satisfying a need for social connectedness. What are some of the most important relationships in your life that meet your need for this sense of belongingness? Apply the concept of social interest to yourself

by considering the five life tasks that Adlerians contend we must face and resolve: How do you relate to others (friendships)? At work, what contributions do you make, and what meaning do you derive? What sense of belonging and acceptance do you experience with members of your family and those you love? How well do you get along with yourself? How satisfying is the spiritual dimension of your life (including your values and your relationship to the universe or cosmos)?

11. Adlerians place a great emphasis on family processes, especially the family atmosphere and the family constellation. Consider describing what it was like for you to grow up in your family. How would you characterize your relationship with each of your siblings? Focus on what you learned about yourself and others through these early family experiences. How do these experiences affect the kind of helper you are or the kind of group leader you are?

12. Our *private logic* is composed of core beliefs that we develop in early childhood. These beliefs provide the lens through which we view the world, and they may or may not be appropriate later in life. How has your behavior been shaped by beliefs that you developed in childhood? Which of these core beliefs are no longer serving you well? What might you do to challenge these beliefs?

Questions for Discussion and Reflection

1. What are your thoughts about Adler's idea that inferiority can be the basis for success? What are some possibilities of introducing the concept of inferiority and striving for superiority in group work with children or with adolescents? What therapeutic value might there be in encouraging young people to share ways they experience inferiority?

2. Adler talks about the family constellation and birth order as important factors that influence one's personality. What implications do these concepts have for group counseling? How can a group replicate a family? To what extent would you explore family constellation issues in the groups you lead? With what kind of age population or client population might you not be inclined to explore family constellation matters?

3. Social interest is a key Adlerian concept. How can a group increase social interest, and how is the group an appropriate form of intervention in light of Adlerian principles? In what ways can you think of addressing the implications of social interest if you were leading a group with school-age students?

4. How might you work with the concept of style of life in a group setting? In what ways could you get information about the development of a member's style of life by observing this person's interactions in the group?

5. Adlerians do not tend to conduct pregroup screening interviews. What are your thoughts about this? What do you think about screening potential members for a group? What advantages might you see in screening members for your groups? Are there any disadvantages?

6. Adlerians see group counseling as a form of teaching and learning, and because of this they make use of advice and information. What possible advantages and disadvantages do you see in this focus? How would this educational focus fit if you were leading a group with school-age children?

7. A group leader's interpretations are often linked to specific group behavior that is happening in a session. Members themselves can be invited to make their own interpretations.

What are your thoughts about the way in which Adlerian group counselors offer an inter-pretation in a collaborative way for members to consider?

8. For what kind of clients do you think Adlerian groups would be best suited? Do you think they would be appropriate for all populations? Explain. What are the implications for work-ing with multicultural populations?

9. Community embodies feeling connected to all of humanity—past, present, and future—and being involved in making the world a better place. How can you be an advocate for the community you serve in your role as a group worker? What can you do to empower group members to become actively involved in their communities?

10. A person's private logic may be influenced by the culture in which he or she is raised. How can group leaders work with members' private logic in a way that is culturally sensitive?

11. What is your evaluation of Adler's view that we can be understood only by looking at our goals and our future strivings? How might you integrate this idea in actual practice in a group? With what client populations would you particularly focus on goals and future strivings?

An Expert's Perspective on Adlerian Group Counseling: by James Robert Bitter

JAMES ROBERT BITTER, EdD, is a Professor of Counseling in the Department of Human Development and Learning at East Tennessee State University

1. What attracted you to this particular theoretical orientation? How does this theory fit with the person you are?

What attracted me to Adlerian theory were the notions of community feeling and social interest. I was disappointed that religion could not provide for me a way to live a useful and productive life. I sought a lot of answers from psychology, which also left gaping holes in my human process until I read Adler. Adler provided me with the perfect blends of freedom and responsibility, of concern for others as well as self, for developing empathy but also providing guidance, of rational thinking, and a full experiencing of life. Adler was neither the complete mirror required for person-centered therapy nor the overbearing directiveness of rational emotive behavior therapy. It blended both with compassion and understanding.

2. What Key Concepts (1 to 3) of this theory are most applicable to the practice of group counseling?

Social embeddedness: We do not live alone. We live within and because of families, friends, and associates. In turn, these people are influenced by ethnicity, culture, gen-der, and a host of other aspects (including religion) that frame the context within which we live. The very notion of individual therapy is at odds with this group experience we call life. An individual focus is also at odds with the democracy we seek to employ as a means for governing our collective politics. If we are to enhance democracy and support contextualized change, then group counseling is so much more important than individual therapy.

Community feeling and its action line "social interest": Adler used the term *gemein-schaftsgefuehl,* or community feeling, to emphasize the importance of our connectedness to others. A community feeling is larger than merely being part of a community or working for social justice, although these can certainly reflect the feeling that Adler described. To have a community feeling is to feel connected to the whole of humankind, to all people who have come before us and who will come after us, to both genders, all cultures, to the spirituality of human life, and to nature. Social interest is the enacting of community feeling in daily life. It is the opposite of being self-absorbed or selfish, or self-elevating. Community feeling and social interest are at the center of psychological well-being. It is literally caring more about the well-being of others than we do about ourselves. And it is in this context that the great paradox of mental health exists. We are well as individuals by engaging in a life that makes a contribution to others.

Lifestyle and lifestyle assessment: Adler focused not on a personality we were or had, but rather on how we choose to move through life. This movement, this style of living, is created by each of us, and it becomes who we are. We are both the painter and the painting in our own lives. This style of moving through life is unified and made whole when we choose a goal of completion or wholeness or perfection that orients and guides our movement through life; that is, we understand the movement by understanding the goal it intends, the purpose it serves, the endpoint we seek. No form of therapy more clearly reveals this movement than asking people to work within the therapeutic structure of group process.

3. **What Techniques (1 to 3) from this theory have the most practical value for group work practitioners?**

Establishing group agreements: Some approaches to group process advocate pre-screening and the establishment of group rules. Typically, Adlerians do not believe in prescreening because it seems to us that it is designed more to protect the therapist or counselor than it is to help the group. Indeed, most prescreening eliminates the people who could use the group experience the most—the lost, the disenfranchised, and the socially withdrawn. In an Adlerian group, ground rules are replaced with agreements. These agreements are what we need to effectively participate in the group. If we all participate in generating them, then we are all responsible for maintaining and reassessing them too, and it is more likely that the agreements will have real meaning in the group process.

Family constellation and life task assessment: We do not merely live life; we live the story of our lives. That story is constantly unfolding. And even though we cannot tell where the story will end or how we will get there, we can rely on an understanding of where we have been and the meaning we've created to provide a foundation for the next part of the story. We all started in the care of other people. For most of us that was in the family with a parent or parents, sometimes with grandparents and siblings and aunts and uncles and cousins and friends, the concrete aspects of our social embeddedness. In addition, Adler noted that we all must answer the fundamental questions of our existence: Who am I and what am I worth? We do this by addressing three necessary and unavoidable tasks in life, the task of friendship (the social task); the task of occupation (work); and the task of intimacy (love and sometimes marriage). These tasks emerge out of evolutionary imperatives, and they are all addressed in Adlerian groups.

Early recollections: If family constellation and life tasks provide a beginning or foundation for our life story, early memories or early recollections tell us what it all means. Adler noted that we might have thousands of experiences before the age of 9, but we often have difficulty remembering more than 3 to 12 of them. Early memories are one-time events that the person can visualize: "One time, something happened. . . ." What is remembered is not as important as why we choose to remember it. These memories tell us something about how we see ourselves, others, life, and the world in this journey we are taking through what time we have on earth. These memories often include the ethical convictions that guide our lives. To understand an individual's early memories within a group is to understand everything that the person brings and contributes to the group process.

4. How does this theory have particular relevance for addressing diversity and social justice issues in group work?

Because social embeddedness is considered central to an understanding of the person, an appreciation of diversity is also required. Here, we are not just talking about diversity of culture, race, gender, sexual orientation, abledness, class, and socioeconomic status. We are also talking about a diversity of perspectives and experiences even within these larger classifications. Focusing on the uniqueness of individuals requires that we understand the uniqueness of their upbringing, their growth and development, their perspectives, and their convictions. These, in turn, become the basis for helping others develop empathy, to walk in the shoes of another, to understand people as different from self, and how others contribute to the wholeness of humanity.

Similarly, community feeling and social interest call upon us to address issues related to what Adler and Dreikurs called *social equality*, and this is the foundation for social justice. No one functions well in a position of subservience or inferiority, and even dominance and privilege have their drawbacks. Because we are all connected, we all have an obligation to care for each other, and also to develop empathy for each other. To paraphrase Abraham Lincoln, "We know that marginalization is bad simply because none of us would want to be marginalized."

5. Raise a question from this theoretical framework that you consider especially important for group work practice.

What do each of us bring to the group process that might enliven the lived experiences of others? This is a highly pragmatic question at the heart of the requirements for social interest. I never know the answer to this until we meet as a group and the process evolves.

Another prominent Adlerian, Dr. Jon Carlson, Distinguished Professor in the Division of Psychology and Counseling at Governors State University, also provided his thoughts on why he became an Adlerian and what he values from the Adlerian approach.

"I was originally trained as a behaviorist and was not particularly interested in the Adlerian approach. I took classes at the Chicago Adlerian school because they were the only group that was offering training on the practice of psychotherapy. Everyone else was interested in theory and research. I remember taking the classes and translating the Adlerian concepts into behavioral terms (for example, encouragement is positive reinforcement; logical consequences are punishment). Later, as I matured as a person and therapist, I became so taken by the relational nature of Adler's work and the emphasis on others, especially social interest because it fits so closely with what I believe a therapist's personal life needs to be like. Some of the aspects of this theory that have most applicability to group counseling are the importance of relationships and the social focus of the theory; the positive psychology emphasis through ideas such as encouragement; the idea that we are all trying to belong in the social world; mentally healthy people get along with the important people in their life; and the concept of social interest and caring for others."

Your Thoughts on Dr. Bitter's Adlerian Perspective

1. What value do you see in establishing group agreements in a collaborative way as opposed to leaders issuing ground rules that members are expected to follow?
2. What do you think of the idea of not screening members for a group that you might be leading?
3. To what degree do you agree with the notion that community feeling and social interest are at the center of being a healthy person? How can a counseling group be built on the principle of social interest?

Quiz on Adlerian Theory: A Comprehension Check   Score ____%

Note: Please refer to Appendix I for the scoring key. Count 5 points for each error, and subtract the total from 100 to get your percentage score.

True/false items: Decide if the following statements are "more true" or "more false" as they apply to the Adlerian approach to groups.

T F 1. According to Adler, feelings of inferiority are the wellspring of creativity.
T F 2. In the Adlerian group, interpretation is done in relation to the lifestyle.
T F 3. Insight and interpretation are basic aspects of Adlerian group counseling.
T F 4. In the Adlerian group, little attention is paid to one's past experiences.
T F 5. Encouragement is one of the most distinctive procedures used in Adlerian group work.
T F 6. Phenomenology implies an objective approach to therapy.
T F 7. The Adlerian group leader functions in a very nondirective manner.
T F 8. Another label for Adlerian psychology is ego psychology.
T F 9. Adler asserts that the earliest impressions lay the foundation for one's lifestyle.
T F 10. Adlerians contend that people remember only those past events that are consistent with their current view of themselves.

Multiple-choice items: Select the *one best answer* among the alternatives given. Consider each question within the framework of Adlerian therapy.

_____11. Which of the following did Adler *not* stress?
   a. the unity of personality
   b. a focus on reliving early childhood experiences
   c. the direction in which people are headed
   d. a unique style of life that is an expression of life goals
   e. feelings of inferiority

_____12. The phenomenological orientation pays attention to the
   a. events that occur at various stages of life.
   b. manner in which biological and environmental forces limit us.
   c. manner in which people interact with one another.
   d. internal dynamics that drive a person.
   e. way in which individuals perceive their world.

_____13. The concept of fictional finalism refers to
   a. an imagined central goal that guides a person's behavior.
   b. the hopeless stance that leads to personal defeat.
   c. the manner in which people express their need to belong.
   d. the process of assessing one's style of life.
   e. the interpretation that individuals give to life events.

_____14. _____, derived from the German word *Gemeinschaftsgefühl*, is a fundamental tenet of Adler's theory.
   a. Socialism
   b. Social interest
   c. Self-absorption
   d. Self-interest
   e. The subconscious

_____15. During the _____ phase, members are encouraged to take action based on what they have learned from their group participation.
   a. establishing and maintaining the relationship
   b. assessment and analysis
   c. insight
   d. reorientation
   e. encouragement

_____16. Who developed Adlerian group methods?
   a. Viktor Frankl and Rollo May
   b. Rudolf Dreikurs and Manford Sonstegard
   c. Abraham Maslow and Carl Rogers
   d. J. L. Moreno and Fritz Perls
   e. Alexander Wolf and Alexander Lowen

_____17. Adler stressed
   a. the value of transference for group therapy.
   b. the importance of the group leader being a "blank screen."
   c. mother–child bonding as a foundation for later interpersonal relationships.
   d. the purposeful nature of behavior.
   e. the power of the group leader.

_____18. Which of the following is *not* a key concept of the Adlerian approach?

a. holism

b. creativity and choice

c. psychic determinism

d. teleology

e. social interest

_____19. Which concept helps us explain how all human behavior fits together so that there is some consistency to actions?

a. holism

b. fictional finalism

c. ego integrity

d. lifestyle

e. social interest

_____20. Goal alignment refers to the state whereby

a. all the members develop common goals.

b. both the leader's and the members' goals are the same.

c. members are willing to carry out new behavior beyond the group session.

d. members accept the goals of society by adjusting to the dominant norms.

e. members are willing to abide by the group leader's rules governing the group.

CHAPTER EIGHT

Psychodrama in Groups

Prechapter Self-Inventory for Psychodrama

Directions: Refer to page 77 for general directions. Indicate your position on these statements using the following code:

5 = I *strongly agree* with this statement.
4 = I *agree,* in most respects, with this statement.
3 = I am *undecided* in my opinion about this statement.
2 = I *disagree,* in most respects, with this statement.
1 = I *strongly disagree* with this statement.

_____ 1. There can be therapeutic value in releasing pent-up feelings, even if this process does not lead to changing external situations.

_____ 2. A theme in psychodrama is: "Don't tell me *about* it, show us as if it's happening now."

_____ 3. A basic tenet of psychodrama is that reliving and reexperiencing a scene from the past gives participants both the opportunity to examine how that event affected them at the time it occurred and a chance to deal differently with the event now.

_____ 4. Group members can learn a great deal about themselves by observing and experiencing the psychodramas of other members.

_____ 5. It is important to "warm up" a group before moving into action.

_____ 6. Playing both one's own role and the role of a significant other person can increase awareness of oneself.

_____ 7. After intensive group work it is very important for members to share their feelings, thoughts, and reactions and discuss how they perceive the work.

_____ 8. A group leader's task is both to encourage catharsis and to help members understand emotional experiences.

_____ 9. Group members (protagonists) should always have the right to choose what conflict or problem situation they will portray, and it is their right to decide how far they will explore a situation in the group context.

_____ 10. Unless a group is cohesive, it is unlikely that members will risk role-playing of important life problems.

Summary of Basic Assumptions and Key Concepts of Psychodrama

1. Psychodrama frees people from old feelings so that they can develop new ways of responding to problems. Some basic elements of psychodrama include spontaneity, creativity,

fantasy, improvisation, and role playing. Psychodrama is a blend of philosophy, theory, and techniques that weaves together imagination, intuition, and physical action to explore a wide range of psychological problems.

2. The underlying philosophy of psychodrama is consistent with many of the premises of existential therapy, person-centered therapy, and Gestalt therapy, all of which emphasize understanding and respecting the group member's experience and the importance of the therapeutic relationship as a healing factor. Although group counselors who employ psychodramatic methods assume an active and directive role in facilitating a group, these methods are most effective when the leader maintains the person-centered spirit.

3. Psychodrama offers a dynamic approach to life's problems and provides members with alternative ways of coping with their concerns. In psychodrama, group members can demonstrate a variety of ways of responding to situations and thus provide them with new and different perspectives.

4. Psychodrama is an integrative approach that provides a context for applying its methods in a variety of therapeutic group settings.

5. Psychodrama emphasizes enacting or reenacting events (anticipated or past) as though they were occurring in the present. It places importance on the past, present, *and* future; the past can come to life when it is brought into the here-and-now, as can the future. Members are encouraged to speak in the present tense and to use action words.

6. Feelings are released through verbally and physically dramatizing emotion-laden situations. Catharsis is generally a natural part of the psychodramatic process, but it is not in itself a goal. Simply rediscovering buried emotions will not bring about healing; these feelings must be worked with for integration to occur. After a catharsis, members often gain a new perspective on an old problem and begin to think and feel differently about a situation.

7. Through recapitulating and reworking a situation from their life, psychodrama participants can gain insights into an event and learn new ways of coping with interpersonal problems.

8. Insight is the cognitive shift that connects awareness of various emotional experiences with some meaningful narrative or some growing understanding. Insight adds a degree of understanding to the catharsis.

9. The psychodramatic group offers an opportunity to find out how others feel and what the results of certain behaviors might be. The group is like a laboratory that offers a relatively safe setting for *reality testing,* or trying out behaviors that may not generally be socially acceptable in real-life situations.

10. The psychodrama director's tasks include being a producer, catalyst/facilitator, and observer/analyzer. The director organizes the psychodrama, plays a key role in warming up the group, and pays careful attention to what emerges in the drama. The director assists the protagonist in developing a scene or series of scenes and facilitates the free expression of feelings.

11. A basic assumption underlying psychodrama is that members of the group can benefit vicariously by identifying with a protagonist. Many people can become involved in dramatizing the individual's struggle.

12. Classical psychodrama involves a group setting, is client-centered, and is a complex and intense method that requires at least two or more hours of group work. This approach entails an extended process of enacted exploration, which is an elegant process requiring considerable training and supervision on the part of the group leader. Group workers with diverse

theoretical orientations can use more limited forms of psychodrama (such as role playing) to foster self-awareness, improved communication, and problem solving. Psychodrama can use techniques such as enactment as a rehearsal for living.

13. Psychodrama has three phases: the warm-up process, which is designed to get the participants ready for the therapeutic experience; the action phase, which includes enacting and working through a past or present situation or an anticipated event; and the discussion phase, in which members are asked to share their reactions.

14. Psychodrama has many techniques designed both to intensify feelings and to bring about increased self-understanding by working through and integrating material that has surfaced in a psychodrama. Effective psychodrama consists of far more than the mere use of certain techniques. Practitioners must learn to know, and work with, the members' psychological worlds in an educated, trained, sensitive, caring, and creative manner.

15. A major contribution of psychodrama is that it supports the growing trend toward technical eclecticism and integration in psychotherapy. Although psychodrama can be usefully applied to various types of individual therapy, it is most powerful when used within the group context. Practitioners are challenged to draw on whatever tools will be useful in a given situation.

Glossary of Key Terms for Psychodrama

- **Action phase** The stage of psychodrama characterized by an enactment of a member's concern; this includes acting out and working through a past or present situation or an anticipated event.
- **Audience** Includes others in the group, before whom the problem is explored.
- **Auxiliary ego** Anyone in a psychodramatic enactment who helps the protagonist explore and understand a problem. Auxiliaries are supporting players who portray the roles of significant others in the life of the protagonist.
- **Behavioral practice** The process of replaying a scene until a member discovers a new response that is appropriate for dealing with a situation.
- **Catharsis** The expression of stored-up feelings that are released by verbal and physical acting out of an emotion-laden situation.
- **Classical psychodrama** An approach that requires specialized training on the director's part, adequate time for orientation and follow-up, a supportive group atmosphere, and members who are appropriate for these methods.
- **Closure** The phase in a psychodrama where members have an opportunity to talk about how they were affected and what they learned from a protagonist's work.
- **Director** The facilitator of an enactment in psychodrama.
- **Double technique** The use of an auxiliary ego who stands to the side and behind the protagonist and acts with or speaks for the protagonist. The double gives expression to the protagonist's thoughts and feelings about a situation.
- **Empty chair** Instead of another person (an auxiliary) playing the complementary figure in a protagonist's enactment, a chair represents this figure.
- **Encountering** A process at the very core of psychodrama through which people not only meet but understand one another on a deep and significant level.

- **Future projection** A technique designed to help members clarify and express concerns about a future situation. Members act out a version of the way they hope a given situation will unfold.
- **Insight** An increased awareness of a problem situation, which often allows for an emotional release.
- **Magic shop** A technique whereby group members bargain with each other by exchanging an imaginary quality.
- **Mirror technique** A method in which an auxiliary ego assumes the role of the protagonist by mirroring his or her postures, gestures, and words as they appeared in the enactment.
- **Multiple double** Two or more doubles help a protagonist express different parts of him- or herself.
- **Protagonist** The subject of a psychodramatic enactment; the member (a main player) who is the focus of therapeutic exploration.
- **Psychodrama** Primarily a group therapy approach in which clients explore their problems through role playing, enacting situations using various dramatic devices to gain insight, discover their own creativity, and develop behavioral skills.
- **Reality testing** Providing a relatively safe setting for trying out behaviors that may not be socially accepted in real-life situations.
- **Replay** A technique for repeating an action to refine it, play it with more expressiveness, or vary it in some other fashion.
- **Role playing** An offshoot of psychodrama that can be used in either a therapeutic or an educational context; the method does not aim at exploring a person's deepest feelings but generally deals with the less personal dimensions of a problem.
- **Role reversal** A technique whereby the protagonist changes parts with other personalities portrayed in his or her drama.
- **Role theory** J. L. Moreno's idea that people play multiple roles in everyday life; members are given the freedom to try out a diversity of roles, thereby getting a sharper focus on parts of themselves they would like to present to others.
- **Role training** As part of working through a problem, a systematic use of techniques such as replay, mirror, some role reversal, feedback, and modeling from the group to help clients develop more skill and confidence in dealing with situations that had previously felt awkward or threatening.
- **Self-presentation** A technique in which protagonists portray themselves and talk about their problem.
- **Sharing phase** The stage after an enactment by a protagonist; other members are asked to share their personal reactions to the protagonist's work.
- **Soliloquy** A technique in which protagonists imagine that they are alone and speak their thoughts and feelings out loud.
- **Spontaneity** An adequate response to a new situation or a novel response to an old situation.
- **Stage** The area where a psychodrama enactment takes place.
- **Surplus reality** The opportunity to replay an unfortunate or traumatic event with a more empowered and positive ending, or a chance to more fully express feelings in ways that might not be socially acceptable.

- **Tele** The two-way flow of feelings between people; a therapeutic factor related to change that promotes healing through a reciprocal empathic feeling.
- **Theater of Spontaneity** Playing out in a spontaneous manner events from the daily newspaper or topics suggested by an audience.
- **Unconscious** The source of wisdom and creativity as well as a repository of disowned emotions.
- **Warm-up phase** Initial activities designed to attain trust and involvement within a group.

Exercises and Activities for Psychodrama

Rationale

Psychodrama is based on the rationale that therapeutic work is enhanced by dealing with problems as though they are occurring in the present. The following exercises, activities, and problems are designed to give you some experience with psychodrama. Experiment with them as much as possible in your group. These exercises can help you directly experience your concerns. They can also help you increase your awareness of others' experiences and thus help you develop more sensitivity to others. As you work through these activities in small groups, think of imaginative ways to modify them.

Exercises

1. You are setting up a psychodrama for your group. What warm-up techniques will you use? Practice these techniques in your group, and get feedback on your effectiveness from fellow group members.
2. You encourage a member of the group you are leading to role-play a situation involving a conflict with her father. She says: "I won't role-play, because that seems phony. Role playing always makes me self-conscious. Is it OK if I just talk about my problem with my father instead?" How would you respond? (You might act this out in your own class group; have one person role-play the reluctant member, and another person the leader. Group members should take turns playing the roles, so that several ways of working with reluctance can be demonstrated.)
3. Imagine that a member with stored up angry feelings participates in a psychodrama without first voicing concerns that he might lose control of his emotions. During the psychodrama, his emotions escalate in intensity to the point that you (the leader) and the other members begin to feel concerned and threatened. How would you handle this situation? Discuss with your classmates the measures you might take to ensure that the participants of the psychodrama feel safe to do their work. Practice what you might say to members in the warm-up phase to establish ground rules to prevent the psychodrama from getting out of control.
4. A man in your group wants to explore his relationship with his daughter, which he describes as being strained. How would you proceed with him? What specific techniques might you suggest? What would you expect to accomplish with these procedures?
5. One of the women in the group describes her conflicts with her daughter as follows: "My daughter tells me that I simply don't understand what it's like to be 16. We fight continually, and the more I try to get her to do what I think is right, the more defiant she becomes.

STAGES OF DEVELOPMENT OF THE PSYCHODRAMA GROUP

Dimension	Initial Stage	Working Stage	Final Stage
Key developmental tasks and goals	The key task is the warm-up, which fosters spontaneity. This warm-up period develops a readiness to participate in the experience. Emphasis is on forming common bonds by identifying common experiences. Director suggests relationships that might be explored and scenes that might be enacted.	A major task of psychodrama is to facilitate expression of feelings in a spontaneous and expressive way through role playing. Full expression of conflicts leads to new awareness of problems. During this phase a corrective emotional experience occurs through enactment and catharsis leading to insight. Reality testing can follow using a variety of techniques.	Major tasks are working through conflict situations by behavioral practice and by getting feedback, developing a sense of mastery over certain problems, receiving support from the group, and integrating what is learned into life outside the group. Through a process of sharing reactions, increased cohesion is generated.
Role and tasks of group leader	Director introduces the nature and purpose of psychodrama and warms up the audience (group) by using techniques. Members are briefly interviewed and asked what kind of situation they would be willing to work on. A protagonist is selected. Director's main task is to create a climate of support and prepare the group drama. Director may select a theme (such as loneliness, dealing with intimacy) on which the group can focus. Main task is to create a safe and supportive climate.	During this phase the director's task is to encourage members to enact scenes involving conflicts. Emphasis is on action, keeping the members focused on the present, and helping them fully express feelings. Director facilitates and interprets the action and encourages spontaneity and expression. Director brings members forward to take the parts of other significant figures in the protagonist's drama. Director helps these auxiliary egos learn their roles.	After the main action, director helps protagonist integrate what has occurred. Director asks for feedback and support from other members; in this way all members get involved in the psychodrama. Care is taken so that those who participated in the psychodrama are not left without adequate closure. Director may summarize the session and help everyone integrate the psychodramatic events. Director encourages a personal sharing and consolidation of learnings.
Role of group members	Members discuss goals, get acquainted with one another, and participate in exercises to get them focused. They may decide on a theme of common interest, which in turn leads to the selection of a protagonist. Members decide what personal issues they will explore.	Members define in concrete terms a situation to be enacted; they reconstruct an anxiety-causing event from the past or one anticipated in the future. They express themselves as fully as possible both verbally and nonverbally. Members serve as auxiliary egos for the protagonist.	Members share with the protagonist feelings they had as the enactment took place. The sharing is done in a personal way, not an analytical way. Members give feedback to the protagonist and they offer support. They share the personal experiences that the psychodrama reminded them of.
Techniques	The warm-up period may be directed or undirected. Warm-up techniques may include the use of guided fantasy, dance, and music; the use of artistic materials; the sharing of drawings; and brief interviews of each member. Members share their here-and-now reactions as a way to create trust.	A wide range of action-oriented techniques is used. These include self-presentation, presentation of the other, role reversal, soliloquy, doubling, the mirror technique, dream work, and future projection.	After the action phase of a psychodrama, certain closure techniques may be used, such as sharing techniques, the magic shop, feedback, repeating the drama with new approaches, and discussing alternative behaviors and possible solutions.

114

Questions to consider

As a leader of a psychodrama, how can you tap into the creativity that exists within the group? Are you alert to connecting one person's work with others in the group as a way of promoting group cohesion?

What are some ways in which trust can be established, and how can members be encouraged to participate in role playing?

How can the members best be prepared for taking an active part in the group? How can you help them overcome their resistance to role playing?

What are some ways of finding themes and concerns that most members share? Once these common problems are identified, how can you facilitate the group so that members can work on these issues together?

How can cultural differences best be recognized and accepted?

As a leader, do you have the courage to experiment with methods even though you do not know the possible outcome?

Do you trust your clinical hunches to try out a technique and to flow with what the member produces?

Do you have control of the group without dominating it? Are the members able to express their spontaneity and get involved?

Are you able to orchestrate all the members so that everyone plays a vital part in the group process? Are some members working silently but not expressing their thoughts and feelings? How can they be encouraged to bring out their reactions?

What are you modeling by your behavior in the group?

After a psychodrama, does the member have an opportunity to put into words what he or she has experienced and learned? Is care taken so that the person is not left feeling unfinished? Are some steps taken to help the member translate what was learned in the group to situations in his or her everyday life?

After catharsis, how can the members be helped to give words to their emotional experience? How can a cognitive component be integrated with emotional work? How can members see a link between past emotional issues and options for change of current behavior?

As a leader, are you alert to ways in which others in the group might have been affected by a person's work?

How can you help members attain a vision of changes desired in the future? And how can this be practiced?

Reactions: Summarize your reactions to the psychodramatic perspective on group developmental stages. What do you like *most*? *least*? What aspects of this approach would you incorporate in your style of leadership?

I simply don't know where to begin. How can I reach her?" Act out the above situation in your class or small group. Assume you are the leader, and get another person in class to role-play the mother. Consider trying these techniques:

a. Role reversal (mother becomes the daughter)

b. Self-presentation (mother presents her side of this conflict)

c. Presentation of the other (mother presents the daughter's side)

d. Soliloquy (mother verbalizes uncensored feelings and thoughts)

e. What other techniques can you think of to practice in this situation?

6. Assume that the woman in the above case is role-playing with another member, who is playing the daughter. All of a sudden the mother stops and says: "I'm stuck; I just don't know what to say now. Whenever she gets that hurt look in her eyes and begins to cry, I feel rotten and guilty, and I freeze up. What can I do now?" In this instance try the *double technique.* (Another member becomes an auxiliary ego and stands behind the mother and speaks for her.) You could also use the *multiple double technique* (where two or more people represent different facets of the mother). One double might represent the guilty mother who attempts to placate her daughter, and the other double could be the firm mother who deals directly with the daughter's manipulation.

7. One of the women in your group wants to work on her relationship with her mother, but she is hesitant to role-play because in her culture family matters are not to be shared with strangers. How can you assist her in doing her work and at the same time work within the framework of her culture?

8. Think of a situation that you would like to change in an ideal way within a year. Experiment with applying the *future projection technique* to this life situation. If possible, set up a situation in your class or group and put this technique into action by playing it out the way you would like it to be in a year.

9. Select a personal problem that you are concerned about or a relationship that you'd like to understand better. Think of ways you could engage in a warm-up that would enable you to explore this relationship in a group. What would you need to feel safe in a group to do personal work on relationships?

Questions for Reflection and Discussion

1. What are some of the most striking differences, in terms of basic concepts and therapeutic techniques, between psychodramatic and psychodynamic groups? Do you see some ways of thinking in psychoanalytic terms while working with group members in a psychodramatic format?

2. What are some techniques you would consider using if you were leading a group with children or adolescents in a school setting? How might you incorporate action methods in working with problems that children or adolescents bring to group?

3. If you plan to rely heavily or exclusively on psychodrama in a group you are forming, how would you screen members to ensure that they are good candidates for the group? What questions might you ask them in the screening interview? Would you conduct group interviews or meet with prospective members individually?

4. What are your reactions to dealing with both the past and the future as though these events are happening in the present? What are some advantages you can see in this

present-centered focus? Do you see any problems with bringing all experiences into the "now" and asking group members to reenact a past event or act out some expected future event? How might you encourage members to stay in the present if they were reluctant to do so?

5. How might you respond to a group member who refuses to get involved in any type of role playing and says: "Why do you want me to go back and relive a painful period in my life? I've tried to forget about those difficult times. What good will it do me to go back there?"

6. What are some specific psychodramatic techniques that you find most interesting and potentially useful? To what degree are you likely to include various psychodrama techniques in the groups you are leading or might someday lead? What advantages can you see in incorporating psychodrama techniques in your group work? What are the disadvantages?

7. Role playing has many uses in many different kinds of groups and with populations of various ages. How inclined are you to introduce role-playing interventions when members struggle with interpersonal concerns? What kind of explanation would you give to members regarding the purposes and values of engaging in role playing?

8. Many forms of dramatic role playing can be done through the medium of play, art, movement, the use of puppets, and other nonverbal methods. How might you incorporate art, dance, music, and play into group work with children or adolescents? What value do you see in using these expressive approaches in conjunction with verbal communication?

9. Psychodrama consists of verbally and nonverbally releasing a variety of pent-up feelings. Do you feel able to deal with the release and expression of your own feelings? Have you already experienced a similar catharsis? Do you think you have the knowledge and the skills to deal effectively with a client who expresses intense emotions? Could you deal with the emotional effects that catharsis might trigger in other group members?

10. What are some possible psychological risks associated with psychodrama? What might you want to say to members before they participated in a psychodrama? What kind of orientation would you provide? How do you think the potential risks can be reduced? At the end of a psychodrama, what steps would you take to see that members were not left with unfinished business due to inadequate closure?

An Expert's Perspective on Psychodrama Groups: by Adam Blatner

ADAM BLATNER, MD, is a leading figure in contemporary psychodrama who has written several books on the approach. (See his biography at the beginning of Chapter 8 in the textbook.)

1. What attracted you to this particular theoretical orientation? How does this theory fit with the person you are?

I was a resident in a mildly psychoanalytically oriented psychiatric (MD) residency program in the 1960s when many other orientations were being considered (such as family therapy, transactional analysis, and Gestalt therapy). I found the potential of integrating activities that would involve improvisation, enactment, and creative collaboration among group members particularly empowering. As I learned more, I became impressed with the depth of insight and breadth of aspects that were involved: psychodrama includes elements that bridge over into transpersonal psychology, bioenergetic analysis (body therapies), psychosynthesis, and other imagery therapies.

As I now conceptualize it, psychodrama involves the integration and vitality of improvisation, enactment, and collaborative creativity—a type of group dynamics that is more actively supportive and encouraging. This is associated with a philosophy of creativity that fits with emerging trends in positive psychology.

2. What Key Concepts (1 to 3) of this theory are most applicable to the practice of group counseling?

Improvisation: Learning to improvise liberates people from the illusion that there are "right ways" and that the therapist knows "the answer."

Enactment: Acting something out requires that people cut through the evasive power of talk and commit themselves a bit more fully, yet they are still free to revise and replay a scene.

Creative collaboration: Working together in this way changes the group dynamics from several people and one "therapist" (who is expected to know "answers") to a group that works on a task together, unpacking a problem. One is the facilitator (usually the therapist), one is for the moment a main character, and others play roles as supporting actors or audience.

3. What Techniques (1 to 3) from this theory have the most practical value for group work practitioners?

Doubling: This "voice over" technique, or "thought bubble," helps people give voice to thoughts that were slightly repressed or ideas group members have never found words to express.

Role reversal: This is the key to empathic skill-building. This technique illuminates what it is like to be in the role of another person, and other group members also benefit from observing this enactment.

Replay: The techniques of psychodrama are basically action methods that offer participants the chance to try several different ways of acting or reacting. One of the dimensions that can be learned through action methods is the exploration of that aspect of social psychology that deals with how people choose each other. Moreno's concepts of "tele" and "sociometry" are being reworked in fields such as social network analysis.

4. How does this theory have particular relevance for addressing diversity and social justice issues in group work?

In sociodrama a group concern is addressed using psychodramatic techniques to challenge the collective group. Several techniques listed above can facilitate this process. Doubling helps bring to the surface hidden assumptions so they can be reevaluated in light of present consciousness. Role reversal can help participants warm up to the perspective of others because it requires an act of focused imagination. Giving the unspoken or not previously considered attitudes voice allows them to be discussed and negotiated, and this can be applied to cultural transitions we are all facing as well.

5. Raise a question from this theoretical framework that you consider especially important for group work practice?

What is the future of psychodrama in other pursuits? The term "psychodrama" has frequently been misused, but the principles embedded in this approach involve action explorations. These methods can be woven into many types of therapy, as well as into education, organizational development, business and professional training (through simulations), spiritual explorations, and everyday life in the home. I envision psychodramatic methods as informing and being enriched in turn by developments in coaching, applied improvisation, and the integration of experiential approaches in many fields.

Your Thoughts on Dr. Blatner's Perspective on Psychodrama

1. What value do you see in the technique of role reversal? When would you be inclined to suggest reversing roles in a group?
2. The techniques of psychodrama are basically action methods. What are the advantages of using action methods rather than having members simply talk about their problems or concerns?
3. What specific concepts and techniques of psychodrama do you find the most interesting and why? What aspects of this approach do you want to incorporate into your group work?

Quiz on Psychodrama: A Comprehension Check   Score ____%

Note: Please refer to Appendix I for the scoring key. Count 5 points for each error, and subtract the total from 100 to get your percentage score.

True/false items: Decide if the following statements are "more true" or "more false" as they apply to psychodrama.

T F 1. In a psychodrama participants are asked to enact their conflicts or crisis situations as if they are occurring in the present moment.

T F 2. Catharsis and insight are not considered important in psychodrama.

T F 3. Psychodrama is never appropriate in working with people who are emotionally inhibited.

T F 4. Psychodrama is considered to be an experiential and action-oriented method.

T F 5. In the soliloquy technique, the protagonist speaks directly to the audience by expressing some uncensored feelings or thoughts.

T F 6. Past events or traumatic childhood experiences are not generally explored in psychodrama because nothing can be done to change these events in the present.

T F 7. The concepts of *encounter* and *tele* are polar opposites.

T F 8. Psychodrama places importance on the past, present, and future.

T F 9. During the sharing phase, members are encouraged to offer interpretations and clinical hunches about the meaning of the protagonist's behavior.

T F 10. Dreams are generally not explored in a psychodrama format.

Multiple-choice items: Select the one best answer among the alternatives given. Consider each question within the framework of psychodrama.

_____11. Psychodrama emphasizes
   a. spontaneity and creativity.
   b. an intellectual understanding of the causes of conflicts.
   c. a way of challenging irrational beliefs.
   d. understanding of life scripts.
   e. working therapeutically with early recollections.

_____12. Psychodrama was developed by
   a. Alfred Adler.
   b. Rudolf Dreikurs.
   c. Rollo May.
   d. J. L. Moreno.
   e. Fritz Perls.

_____13. The technique whereby a protagonist (main player) speaks directly to the audience by expressing some uncensored feeling or thought is
   a. the mirror technique.
   b. soliloquy.
   c. projection.
   d. role reversal.
   e. self-presentation.

_____14. Through which technique can participants rehearse how they might approach someone with whom they would like to interact?
   a. mirror technique
   b. magic shop
   c. future projection
   d. double technique
   e. soliloquy

_____15. Which of the following techniques is the most useful for helping members clarify and prioritize their values?
   a. mirror technique
   b. magic shop
   c. future projection
   d. double technique
   e. soliloquy

_____16. According to psychodrama,
   a. unless a problem is solved, the enactment is a failure.
   b. members of the group can profit only if they are directly involved in reenacting an event.
   c. members of the group can benefit in vicarious ways by observing the work of others.
   d. members will change their behavior only if they develop a contract that specifies homework assignments.
   e. unless members resolve their transference relationship with the group leader, they will be fixated at an immature level of development.

_____17. Which of the following is *not* a key concept of psychodrama?

    a. encounter and tele

    b. catharsis

    c. dealing with the present

    d. exploring unexpressed emotions

    e. free association with the dreams of other members

_____18. In psychodrama, the past is dealt with by

    a. bringing it into the present.

    b. reenacting the event and reexperiencing earlier feelings.

    c. dwelling on causal factors of current problems.

    d. talking about possible reasons for hurts in the past.

    e. both (a) and (b).

_____19. The third phase of a psychodrama consists of

    a. some type of nonverbal exercise.

    b. encouraging a protagonist to act out a conflict.

    c. sharing by members of their personal reactions to what they observed during the action phase.

    d. an assessment by the members of the possible interpretations for the protagonist's behavior and difficulties.

    e. the leader giving an interpretation of the protagonist's behavioral dynamics and assigning homework to be carried out before the next meeting.

_____20. The ventilation of stored-up feelings is known as

    a. breaking out.

    b. breaking down.

    c. working through.

    d. acting out.

    e. catharsis.

CHAPTER NINE

The Existential Approach to Groups

Prechapter Self-Inventory for the Existential Approach

Directions: Refer to page 77 for general directions. Indicate your position on these statements using the following code:

5 = I *strongly agree* with this statement.
4 = I *agree,* in most respects, with this statement.
3 = I am *undecided* in my opinion about this statement.
2 = I *disagree,* in most respects, with this statement.
1 = I *strongly disagree* with this statement.

_____ 1. Group work best focuses on the subjective aspects of a member's experience; a group can help members to listen to themselves and pay attention to their subjective experience.

_____ 2. Central issues in an existential group are death, freedom, existential isolation, and meaninglessness.

_____ 3. Anxiety and guilt are not necessarily disorders to be cured, for they are part of the human condition.

_____ 4. Reflecting on the reality of death can help us to live fully.

_____ 5. The basic task of group therapy is to expand consciousness and thus extend freedom.

_____ 6. Over time, the interpersonal and existential problems of members become evident in the here-and-now interactions within the group.

_____ 7. A group leader's task is to encourage members to assume genuine responsibility for their functioning in the group and to carry these changes into daily life.

_____ 8. Authenticity involves claiming ownership, taking responsibility for our actions and the way we are living.

_____ 9. Existential group therapists are fellow travelers in the sense that they must come to terms with the ultimate existential concerns of life.

_____ 10. Group work is especially valuable for older persons as a way of assisting them in putting their life into perspective, in consolidating the meaning of their life experiences, and in finding new meaning.

Summary of Basic Assumptions and Key Concepts of the Existential Approach to Groups

1. People become what they choose to become; although there are factors that restrict choices, self-determination is ultimately the basis of their uniqueness as individuals.

The group leader focuses on choice and freedom, the potential within humans to find their own way, and the search for identity.

2. In the existential group basic human themes constitute the content of interactions. Existential crises are seen as a part of living and not something to be avoided or remedied. These crises frequently concern the meaning of life, anxiety and guilt, recognition of one's aloneness, the awareness of death and finality, and the fear of choosing and accepting responsibility for one's choices.

3. The leader's major tasks are to grasp the subjective world of members and to establish authentic relationships in which they can work on understanding themselves and their choices more fully. The leader's ultimate goal is to enable group members to be free and become responsible for the direction of their own lives. Therefore, group members are largely responsible for what occurs in therapy.

4. Group leaders do not behave in rigid or prescribed ways, for they can't predict the exact direction or content of any group. Leaders are not technical experts who carry out treatment plans with specialized techniques; rather, they establish real relationships with the members of the group.

5. Existential group leaders are free to adapt their interventions to their own personality and style, as well as pay attention to what each participant requires. Leaders are *not* bound by any prescribed procedures and can use techniques from other therapeutic orientations. Interventions are used in the service of broadening the ways in which group members live in their world. Techniques are tools to help members become aware of their choices and their potential for action.

6. The *presence* of the leader, or the leader's willingness to be there for others and to confront them when appropriate, is a major characteristic of the effective group. Group leaders must be willing to take responsibility for their own thinking, feeling, and judging. They are present as *persons* with the members and become active agents in the group.

7. Existential group leaders value being real and are willing to make themselves known through appropriate self-disclosure. Group leaders are fellow travelers, as they must address the ultimate existential concerns of life too.

8. Existential therapy is best considered as an invitation to members to recognize the ways in which they are not living fully authentic lives and to make choices that will lead them to become what they are capable of being. This approach does not focus on problem-solving techniques for the complexities of authentic existence.

9. Because the existential approach to groups is based on universal human themes, and because it does not dictate a particular way of viewing reality, it is highly applicable when working in a multicultural context. Themes such as relationships, finding meaning, anxiety, suffering, and death are concerns that transcend the boundaries that separate cultures. Members in an existential group are encouraged to examine the ways their present existence is being influenced by social and cultural factors.

10. The existential approach has something to offer group practitioners regardless of their theoretical orientation. It provides a perspective for understanding the value of anxiety and guilt, the role and meaning of death, and the creative aspects of being alone and choosing for oneself.

STAGES OF DEVELOPMENT OF THE EXISTENTIAL GROUP

Dimension	Initial Stage	Working Stage	Final Stage
Key developmental tasks and goals	Focus is on how members perceive and experience their world; thus, the approach is experiential and subjective. Main goal is to increase awareness of options to widen everyone's freedom. Initial task of a group is making a commitment to explore personally meaningful and significant issues concerning human struggles. Members decide how they want to use time in the group and what issues to explore.	Members explore a wide range of universal human concerns such as loneliness, the anxiety of recognizing that one is free to make choices and that freedom is always accompanied by responsibility, the meaning of life and death, and so on. Participants consider alternative ways of dealing with issues they are facing. Emphasis is on taking responsibility *now* for the way one chooses to be. Focus is on self-discovery, which often leads to giving up defenses and living authentically.	Group counseling or therapy is seen as an "invitation to change." Members are challenged to re-create themselves. In the group they have opportunities to evaluate their lives and to choose how they will change. Toward the end of a group, termination is another issue to face, for the ending of a group brings on anxiety. The termination of a group must be dealt with fully. Members are challenged with finding new ways of being.
Role and tasks of group leader	The leader's tasks are to confront members with the issue of dealing with freedom and responsibility and to challenge them to recognize that regardless of the limits there is always some element of choice in life. Leader helps members see the ways in which they are not living fully. Leader makes use of self as a way to create a safe climate for exploration. A key task is to create a safe climate that allows for taking risks.	Emphasis is on creating a quality relationship, which entails the leader's full presence. Leader's task is to be there as a person for the members; he or she embarks on an unknown journey with the members and is open to where they will go together. Leaders must understand and adopt the members' subjective world. They also engage in self-disclosure and model authentic behavior.	At the final stage of a group the leader challenges members to go into the world and be active. Leader helps members integrate and consolidate what they've learned in the group so that the maximum transfer can occur. Rather than "doing therapy," leader lives it through the openness of ongoing existential encounters with the members. Leader helps members see their contribution to the changes they've made.
Role of group members	Members always have a part in the group process. They look at *who* and *what* they are; they clarify their identity and make decisions concerning how they can achieve authenticity. Members decide what they will explore in the group, as well as how they want to change. They define their personal goals.	Members decide what struggles or existential concerns they will share. Typical concerns include changing roles, creating new identities when old identities are no longer meaningful, value conflicts, emptiness, dealing with loneliness, and working on the fear of freedom and responsibility.	To change, members must go out into the world and *act*. Members are responsible for their own lives, so they decide if and how they want to live differently. If a group is successful, members achieve an authentic identity and become aware of choices that can lead to action.

Techniques	There are no prescribed techniques, and therapeutic procedures can be borrowed from many approaches. More than a group leader's technique or skill, the leader's *attitude* and *behavior* are crucial for the group's results. Group leaders are not viewed as technical experts who apply therapeutic treatment plans. There is no assessment, nor is there a predetermined treatment plan for the group to follow. Emphasis is on understanding the members' world.	Emphasis is not so much on doing therapy by using techniques but rather is on being fully present. Thus, leaders may work with dreams; they may work with the current interaction in the group; they may explore the past with members; and they may be both supportive and challenging. Emphasis is on constructive confrontation so that members can learn how to confront themselves and evaluate their present behavior.	Because group counseling or therapy is seen as a spontaneous encounter between members (and between members and the leader), the leader is free to draw on a diverse range of techniques from many other therapies. Although the focus is on the *encounter* that occurs in the group, specific techniques can be developed to challenge members to recognize the choices they have and their decisions to make a new life.
Questions to consider	An existential group can be described as people making a commitment to begin and to continue a lifelong journey of self-exploration. Ask yourself the degree to which you are willing to embark on this journey. Are you willing to do in your own life what you ask your members to do? Are you able to experience the suffering and despair that is sometimes necessary? Are you able to tolerate the unknown yet still take action? Can you exercise your freedom without guarantees? How do you deal with anxiety in your own life? Do you face it, or do you try to avoid it? How might this affect the way you lead a group?	To what degree are you able to be present for those in your group? Are you willing to travel down whatever path a member might lead you? Can you adopt members' subjective views of the world? Do you model in the group those attitudes and behaviors you hope the members will develop? What do you model? Are you able to borrow techniques from other approaches and apply them to the struggles of members? Do you use techniques within the context of the relationship that you have established with members and in the climate of trust? Are you aware of ways that your techniques may or may not fit for a member's cultural background?	Are the members willing to take action? Are they able to act on what they have learned? Are they committed to making changes in their lives? How will they make certain changes? Are the members able to see that they do have choices? that there is a price to pay for acting on their choices? that they must choose for themselves in the face of uncertainty? Are they moving in the direction of trusting their decisions and relying less on others to decide for them? Are members more aware of the options for action available to them? Are members now better able to cope with the anxiety that comes with freedom than when they entered the group?

Reactions: Summarize your reactions to the existential perspective on group developmental stages. What do you like *most*? *least*? What aspects of this approach would you incorporate in your style of leadership?

Glossary of Key Terms for the Existential Approach

- **Anxiety** A condition that results from having to face choices without clear guidelines and without knowing what the outcome will be.
- **Authenticity** The process of creating, discovering, or maintaining the core deep within one's being; the process of becoming the person we are capable of becoming.
- **Death awareness** An awakening experience that can be a useful catalyst for making significant life changes. The confrontation with one's personal death can result in a massive shift in the way one lives in the world.
- **Existential anxiety** The feeling, viewed as a core characteristic of humans, resulting from having to make choices without clear guidelines and with no guarantees about the outcomes.
- **Existential group** People making a commitment to a lifelong journey of self-exploration.
- **Existential guilt** The result of, or the consciousness of, evading the commitment to choosing for ourselves; a condition that is rooted in the realization that we inevitably fall short of becoming what we could become.
- **Existential isolation** Our aloneness in the universe.
- **Existential neurosis** Feelings of despair and anxiety that result from inauthentic modes of living, the failure to make choices, and an avoidance of responsibility.
- **Existential tradition** Seeks a balance between recognition of the limits and tragic dimensions of human existence and the possibilities and opportunities of human life.
- **Existential vacuum** A condition of emptiness and hollowness that results from meaninglessness in life.
- **Freedom** An inescapable aspect of the human condition, making each of us the author of our life and, therefore, leaving us responsible for our destiny and accountable for our actions.
- **"Givens of existence"** Core themes in the therapeutic process: death, freedom, existential isolation, and meaninglessness.
- **Life-changing psychotherapy** An effort to help clients examine how they have answered life's existential questions and challenge them to revise their answers and begin to live authentically.
- **Logotherapy** Developed by Viktor Frankl, a brand of existential therapy that literally means "healing through reason"; focuses on challenging members to search for the meaning in life.
- **Phenomenology** A method of exploration that uses subjective human experiencing as its focus.
- **Restricted existence** The state of functioning with a limited degree of awareness of oneself and being vague about the nature of one's problems.
- **Search for meaning** The struggle for a sense of significance and purpose in life, a distinctively human characteristic.
- **Self-awareness** The capacity for consciousness that enables us to make choices.
- **Self-determination** The notion that we are free to choose among alternatives and therefore are responsible for directing our lives and shaping our destiny.
- **Solitude** A time we choose to make to be with ourselves, to discover who we are, and to renew ourselves.

Exercises and Activities for the Existential Approach

Rationale

The existential approach does not provide a ready-made set of techniques for group practitioners. It is more an orientation to group counseling than a system of therapeutic procedures. Practitioners can adhere to the existential perspective and at the same time use many other therapeutic techniques.

Here are examples of activities that are in some way related to existential themes. Use these exercises both on your own through self-reflection and journal writing, and in your group or class. Think about what you can learn about both yourself and group processes through these exercises.

Exercises

1. *Self-awareness*. Group members often say that they are afraid of learning too much about themselves. What is your position? Are you open to learning all that you can about yourself? What are some examples that illustrate your own struggles with becoming more self-aware? How do you see your willingness or unwillingness to increase your awareness as related to your potential effectiveness as a group leader? Discuss these questions in your class or group, or write about them in your journal.

2. *Freedom and responsibility*. Freedom of choice entails accepting the responsibility for influencing the direction of your life. Being free means that as long as you are alive you are making choices about who you are becoming. Do you believe you are who you are now largely as a result of your choices, or do you think that you are the product of circumstances? What are some *major choices* you've made that have been crucial to your present development? Discuss some of these crucial decisions in your group. How do you imagine your life would be different now if you had decided differently? What struggles have you had between desiring freedom and fearing it? To what degree do you see yourself as being ready to accept the responsibility that accompanies your freedom? Think of specific ways in which the answers to these questions have an effect on the way you lead groups. Discuss how your concerns about your choices might affect your group leading.

3. *Anxiety*. Anxiety is not only an impetus to change but also a result of recognizing that you are responsible for your choices. What kind of anxiety have you experienced in making key life decisions? In what situations do you experience the most anxiety? How do you deal with this anxiety? In your group or class discuss how your ways of dealing with anxiety in your own life will either help or hinder you in working with group members who are also dealing with their anxiety.

4. *Death*. Death awareness is an awakening experience that can be a useful catalyst for making significant life changes. How well are you able to accept the reality of your own death? Do you see any relationship between how you view death and the degree to which you are living fully now? This could be a useful topic for writing in your personal journal. To clarify your thoughts and feelings about death and to examine how it affects the way you live, try some of these exercises in your class or group:
   a. What do you think the significant people in your life would write on your tombstone? What would you like them to say?

b. Write the eulogy you'd like delivered at your funeral. Bring it to the group and share it with other members. (As an alternative, write your eulogy in your journal.)

c. Assume that you know you are going to die within 24 hours. What would you most like to do during these final hours? What does this say about your values?

d. Tell others in your group what you'd most like to accomplish before you die. What legacy would you like to leave?

e. What are your fears, if any, about your own death and dying or about the loss of those you love? How do you deal with these fears?

f. If you have lost someone close to you, consider sharing what this has been like for you. What did you learn about yourself through this experience?

g. As you reflect on your answers to the above questions, think about the implications for your ability as a group counselor to assist members in facing and dealing with the reality of their own death.

5. *Meaning in life.* Confronting our mortality makes us think about how meaningful our lives are. In your group let yourself imagine a typical day in your life 5 years ago. What was it like, and what were you like then? Are there any major differences between your life then and now? Share with others in your group some of the most significant changes you've made over the past 5 years. Then project yourself 5 years into the future. What do you *hope* you'll be like then? Explore in your group what you are experiencing in your life that contributes to or detracts from a meaningful existence. Again, how might your answers to these questions have implications for your ability to challenge clients to discover the meaning in their lives?

6. *Authenticity.* The existential perspective stresses that affirming ourselves is an ongoing process. We are authentic if we face the anxiety of choosing for ourselves and accept the consequences of our choices. Inauthentic people allow others to determine who and what they are. Discuss some crucial incidents in your own personal struggles to define yourself. Consider some of these questions as you construct your personal identity road map:

a. Who am I? What has contributed to the way I am?

b. What roles have I typically played? How have I seen myself?

c. What choices did I make? What choices did others make for me?

d. Have I lost contact with myself by looking to others for answers and direction? Do I trust others more than myself?

e. How has my life been shaped by past actions, people, and influences?

f. What more do I want from life?

g. If some of the aspects that are a part of my sense of identity were taken away, what would I be like?

7. *Loneliness.* Share in your group some ways in which each member has experienced loneliness. Can you recall the time in your life when you felt most alone? What was this like for you? Select a poem, a picture, or an excerpt from a book that captures the loneliness you have felt at some point in your life. Bring this to the group and share it. Think of some ways to help the members of a group you are leading deal with their own loneliness.

8. *Creative solitude.* Existentialists believe that unless we can enjoy solitude creatively we cannot develop genuine intimacy with others. Do you make time for yourself to be alone? When you are alone, what is this generally like for you? Select a song, poem, poster, or

picture that represents peaceful solitude to you. In what ways might you want to learn how to enjoy time alone? Do you have the quality of time alone that you would like?

9. *Role and functions of the group leader.* The existential approach emphasizes the role of the leader not so much as a doer of therapy but as a person to be fully present with the group members. Discuss in your group the degree to which you feel personally equipped to challenge others to look at the important issues in life. For instance, do you feel ready to challenge others to look at the choices they've made as well as the ones now open to them? Have you done this in your own life? Could you be psychologically present with another person who was exploring a life/death issue? Have you been willing to face such themes in your life?

10. *Personal evaluation and critique.* In your group or class discuss the concepts of the existential approach that you find most valuable. Consider some of these questions in your discussion:

    a. What key themes would you take from this approach and apply to groups you lead?

    b. What are the limitations of the approach? What disadvantages do you see in limiting yourself strictly to an existential orientation?

    c. Do you think this perspective has something to offer every client? For what client populations do you think it is the most appropriate approach?

    d. What do you see as both the strengths and limitations of the existential approach in working with groups composed of culturally diverse populations? What are some ways that you could link existential themes with certain cultural values of members?

    e. How are you able to relate in a personal way to the existential approach? What ways can you understand yourself better by reflecting on the key existential themes? How is your self-understanding related to your ability to encourage group members to explore their personal lives?

    f. An existential approach can form a philosophical foundation for group work. This approach allows for incorporating methods from various theoretical orientations. What therapeutic techniques from other models would you apply to existential concepts in the groups you lead or will lead?

    g. With what age populations and client populations might existential concepts best fit? Can you think of ways to apply existential themes in group work with children? adolescents? the elderly?

Questions for Reflection and Discussion

1. Which basic themes of the existential approach, if any, would you most want to include in your framework in approaching a group?

2. What one key point of this theory has the most meaning for you with respect to your way of facilitating a group?

3. What is the role of the existential group leader? How is the *leader as a person* vitally related to his or her functioning as a group counselor?

4. In this chapter the statement is made that anxiety results from having to make choices without clear guidelines and without knowing what the outcome will be. What implications are there for you as a group leader if you accept this view of anxiety? What are your thoughts on the role anxiety plays in a group?

5. According to Frankl, it is not the therapist's job to tell clients what their particular meaning in life should be but rather to encourage them to discover meaning for themselves. What are some ways you might challenge members to find meaning in their life? How might you deal with a member who continued to look to you for answers and direction?

6. Some existential therapists assume that the driving force behind many interpersonal relationships is existential isolation. If you accept this notion that humans are ultimately alone in the world, what are the implications for group counseling? How might a group help a person feel less isolated and less alienated?

7. In the existential view, therapy is a partnership and a shared venture between the therapist and the client. To develop this collaborative partnership, therapists focus on the person-to-person relationship. Existential therapists must bring their own subjectivity into their work, and it is essential that they demonstrate presence if they are to develop an effective working relationship with members. High priority is given to the quality of the therapeutic relationship as a healing force, with an emphasis on I/Thou encounters and dialogue. Techniques are secondary. Existential group leaders may incorporate techniques from other therapeutic approaches, but there are no set techniques associated with the theory. How comfortable do you feel as a group leader without have specific techniques to use? Do you think groups will engage in productive work without the use of techniques? What are your thoughts about incorporating techniques from other approaches?

8. According to Yalom, four ultimate concerns make up the core of existential therapy—freedom, isolation, death, and meaninglessness. From your vantage point, what meaning do these existential themes have for you personally? How are these human concerns related to your life and your struggles? Based on your experiences in life, what would you hope to be able to teach members of your groups? What meaning do these existential concerns have for the focus you might want to bring to a group you were leading?

9. In applying an existential approach to group work with culturally diverse individuals, what universal human concerns could link members? What value do you see in helping members come to an understanding of what they have in common with each other while respecting and valuing their differences?

10. How might you deal with those group members who spent a great deal of time trying to convince you that they are not responsible for their lives? If they attempted to hold others in their life responsible for their current problems, what might you be inclined to say or do in the group?

11. Consider the relevance of group work within an existential orientation in school counseling. If you were leading a crisis-oriented group in the schools, how might you use the crisis situation a member is experiencing as a way to understand existential concerns? In working with school-age students, can you think of ways to assist members in accepting personal responsibility for their choices? What are some ways you could assist children and adolescents in creating an internal locus of control and increasing their potential for choices in a group?

12. If you were leading a bereavement group with older persons, how could you draw upon existential notions in assisting members to make sense of their losses? What specific existential themes might you draw from in working with older persons in your group?

13. How could you incorporate movies or films into your groups as a way to promote discussion on existential themes? Brainstorm a list of movies that would be appropriate to use with various client and student populations that you might encounter. What existential themes would be highlighted in each of these films? As a group leader, what open-ended questions might you pose to group members to get them to reflect on the relevance of these themes to their own lives?

An Expert's Perspective on Existential Groups: by David N. Elkins

DAVID N. ELKINS, PhD, is Professor Emeritus in the Graduate School of Education and Psychology at Pepperdine University.

1. **What attracted you to this particular theoretical orientation? How does this theory fit with the person you are?**

I have always been filled with a sense of awe about the experience of human existence. When I was only 18, I remember walking through a country cemetery, reading the tombstones, and thinking about the meaning and limitations of life. When I attended graduate school to become a psychologist, I was naturally drawn to existential psychology because it addressed the issues that had always interested me. Existential psychology deals explicitly with life and death, isolation and loneliness, freedom and responsibility, and what it means to be "that self one truly is," as Kierkegaard put it. Existential psychology feeds my soul. Also, Viktor Frankl, who was a prisoner in Hitler's death camps and wrote *Man's Search for Meaning,* was one of my doctoral professors. He was an existential psychiatrist who left a lasting impression on me as a young psychologist.

2. **What Key Concepts (1 to 3) of this theory are most applicable to the practice of group counseling?**

Mortality and isolation: Although various existential issues can arise in group therapy, I have found that the issues of mortality and isolation are especially common. In regard to mortality, cohesive, effective groups often arrive at a point where they discuss grief over loss of a parent, sibling, or close friend. Also, it's not unusual for some group member to be dealing with a serious illness themselves. And of course some groups are specifically devoted to persons struggling with life-threatening medical problems such as cancer or AIDS. Perhaps more than any other therapeutic approach, existential therapy is particularly relevant in these situations.

Isolation and loneliness: These are not unusual issues in group work, and existential therapy can be very helpful for group members confronting such situations. Existential therapy cannot take away the fact that loved ones have died or that we, ourselves, will someday die. Nor can it take away the fact that isolation and loneliness are realities that we all face. Because existential therapists have the training and experience to address these issues directly, they are on "familiar terrain" and may be able to help the group find a sense of community and comfort in knowing that we all share these darker aspects of the human journey.

3. **What Techniques (1 to 3) from this theory have the most practical value for group work practitioners?**

Share an "existential moment: I have found that one of the most effective ways to begin a group is to ask each member to recall and share an "existential moment" that changed them forever. This helps set the tone for existential group therapy. The stories of events that changed members lives forever are often very moving. In my experience, this introductory exercise helps build a sense of connection and community in the first session.

Share something deeply meaningful: At the end of the first session, I usually give group members an "assignment" for the following meeting. I ask them to bring a poem, a painting, a piece of music, a short reading, or anything else that is deeply meaningful to them. At the beginning of the second meeting, I ask group members to explain what they brought, tell why it's meaningful to them, and then share it with the group.

Although I use very few techniques or group exercises in my group work, I have found that these two shared experiences help to establish connection and community among members in the early sessions.

4. **How does this theory have particular relevance for addressing diversity and social justice issues in group work?**

Because existential psychology addresses issues that are universal to human beings, the theory tends to transcend ethnic and racial boundaries. However, this does not mean that existential therapists should approach individual and cultural differences among group members by pretending that "we are all the same." The racial, ethnic, and cultural identities of group members often run deep and may be vitally important to a group member's sense of self. I try to respect, and even prize, individual and cultural differences, knowing that they can contribute immeasurably to personal growth and to the group "community." Although existential psychology focuses on universal human themes, these themes are expressed in uniquely individual and cultural ways.

5. **Raise a question from this theoretical framework that you consider especially important for group work practice.**

As an existential therapist, what criticisms or concerns regarding existential psychology do you have? The existential literature focuses largely on existential issues as they affect the individual and does not adequately address, in my view, social issues such as racism, prejudice, poverty, violence, war, genocide, and extreme materialism. Yet these are major "existential issues" that have devastating effects on human life. Existential scholars could bring a unique and needed perspective to these issues.

Your Thoughts on Dr. Elkins's Perspective

1. What do you think of the technique of recalling and sharing an "existential moment" as a way to begin a group experience, as described by Dr. Elkins?
2. Most existential group leaders do not rely on group techniques or exercises. What possibilities do you see for incorporating techniques from other therapeutic approaches if existential therapy appeals to you as a foundational theory?
3. What are your reactions to why Dr. Elkins was drawn to existential therapy?

Quiz on the Existential Approach to Groups: A Comprehension Check

Score ____%

Note: Please refer to Appendix I for the scoring key. Count 5 points for each error, and subtract the total from 100 to get your percentage score.

True/false items: Decide if the following statements are "more true" or "more false" as they apply to the existential approach to groups.

T   F   1. The existential group focuses on techniques designed to assist members in experiencing catharsis.

T   F   2. Anxiety can be an impetus to change and thus can be a positive characteristic.

T   F   3. The fact that we will die can motivate us to create a meaningful existence.

T   F   4. Existentialists believe we are not ultimately alone if we establish intimate ties with others.

T   F   5. An existential group might be described as people making a commitment to begin and complete a lifelong journey of self-exploration.

T   F   6. The existential approach to group work fits in well with managed care programs.

T   F   7. The basic goal of an existential group is to treat symptoms so that members can be free of existential anxiety.

T   F   8. The existential group leader sets the tone for the group by introducing techniques and doing something to get people talking openly.

T   F   9. Existential group work is especially valuable for older persons as a way of assisting them in putting their lives into perspective, in consolidating meaning of their life experiences, and in finding new meaning in life.

T   F   10. Existential group work aims at curing people in the traditional medical sense.

Multiple-choice items: Select the *one best answer* among the alternatives given. Consider each question within the framework of existential therapy.

_____11. Existential therapy is best described as a
   a. systematic approach to behavior modification.
   b. philosophy with which a therapist operates.
   c. set of techniques designed to change behavior.
   d. form of psychoanalytic therapy.
   e. separate school of therapy.

_____12. An existential group works toward all of the following goals except
   a. enabling people to become truthful with themselves.
   b. widening clients' perspectives on themselves and the world around them.
   c. helping people adjust to the dominant norms in society.
   d. finding clarity on what gives meaning to present and future living.

_____13. Two of the most significant spokespeople for the existential approach in the United States are
   a. Heinz Kohut and Otto Kernberg.
   b. Medard Boss and Ludwig Binswanger.
   c. Rollo May and Irvin Yalom.
   d. Martin Buber and Jean-Paul Sartre.
   e. Erik Erikson and Margaret Mahler.

_____14. The existential group focuses on
    a. unresolved conflicts that were repressed in childhood.
    b. here-and-now forces within the group.
    c. techniques designed to assist members in gaining catharsis.
    d. measuring the observable outcomes of a group.
    e. working through the transference relationship with the leader.

_____15. According to the existential view, we can turn our fear of death into a positive force when we
    a. accept the reality of our mortality.
    b. educate ourselves about medical advances that can help people live longer lives.
    c. seek the support of religious leaders in our communities.
    d. dwell on it.
    e. take antianxiety medication to manage our death anxiety.

_____16. Existential therapy places emphasis on
    a. a systematic approach to changing behavior.
    b. the quality of the relationship between the leader and members.
    c. teaching clients cognitive and behavioral coping skills.
    d. uncovering early childhood traumatic events.
    e. working through the transference relationship.

_____17. All of the following are considered key concepts guiding the functioning of an existential group except
    a. the search for authenticity.
    b. discovering the patterns of one's lifestyle.
    c. death and nonbeing.
    d. the search for meaning.
    e. aloneness and relatedness.

_____18. The existential view of death is that it
    a. renders us hopeless.
    b. makes life less meaningful.
    c. gives meaning to every moment.
    d. creates an existential vacuum.
    e. motivates us to seek organized religion as a source of values.

_____19. In an existential group the leader would tend to
    a. challenge members to become aware of their freedom and responsibility.
    b. urge members to free themselves of guilt and anxiety.
    c. aim for a deep catharsis for each member.
    d. encourage a regression to one's early past.
    e. help each member see how his or her lifestyle has a bearing on present interactions with others in the group.

_____20. The view in existential groups is that techniques
    a. should be secondary to understanding members.
    b. are specified to bringing about change.
    c. always interfere with the therapeutic process.
    d. imply a loss of faith in the client's ability to find his or her own way.
    e. lead to inauthenticity on the part of members.

CHAPTER TEN

The Person-Centered Approach to Groups

Prechapter Self-Inventory for the Person-Centered Approach

Directions: Refer to page 77 for general directions. Indicate your position on these statements using the following code:

5 = I *strongly agree* with this statement.
4 = I *agree,* in most respects, with this statement.
3 = I am *undecided* in my opinion about this statement.
2 = I *disagree,* in most respects, with this statement.
1 = I *strongly disagree* with this statement.

_____ 1. The group members, not the leader, have the primary responsibility for the direction the group takes.

_____ 2. The therapist's attitudes of genuineness, positive regard, and accurate empathy are both necessary *and* sufficient for therapeutic change to occur.

_____ 3. A leader's structuring and active intervention are not necessary for a group to move in a constructive direction.

_____ 4. A major function of the group facilitator is to establish a climate of trust in the group.

_____ 5. A group leader can be effective without attending to transference.

_____ 6. Self-disclosure by the leader tends to increase trust and self-disclosure on the part of the members.

_____ 7. Effective group facilitation is best considered as a "way of being" rather than a "way of doing."

_____ 8. The group counselor is more a facilitator than a director or a coach.

_____ 9. Directive intervention by the leader can interfere with the group process.

_____10. It is well for group leaders to avoid giving advice to members.

Summary of Basic Assumptions and Key Concepts of the Person-Centered Approach

1. Individuals are basically trustworthy and have the potential for self-direction. The group can become aware of problems and the means to resolve them if the facilitator encourages members to explore present feelings and thoughts. Person-centered therapy is based on a deep sense of trust in the group's ability to develop its own potential by moving in a constructive direction. Group leaders provide a minimum of direction; members make their own choices and bring about change for themselves.

2. The person-centered approach emphasizes the personal qualities of the group leader rather than techniques of leading because the primary function of the group facilitator is to create a climate in which healing can occur. Congruent group leaders avoid using their professional role to keep themselves hidden. Person-centered group facilitators use themselves as instruments of change in a group. Their central function is to establish a therapeutic climate in which group members will interact in increasingly authentic ways. The therapeutic relationship between the facilitator and members helps the members heal and change.

3. The therapeutic core conditions for growth are genuineness, unconditional positive regard, and empathic understanding of the members' subjective world. To the extent that facilitators experience and demonstrate these attitudes and behaviors toward the members, therapeutic change and growth will occur.

4. Accurate empathy is central to the practice of person-centered group work. It is a way for facilitators to hear the meanings expressed by members that often lie at the edge of their awareness. Empathy is essentially the facilitator's capacity to imagine what it is like to be the group member and to communicate that clearly to the person.

5. External measures such as diagnosis, testing, interpretation, advice giving, and probing for information are not useful in group work. Instead, group counseling comprises active listening, reflection and clarification, and understanding the inner world of the members.

6. The group member's active involvement is critical to successful therapeutic outcomes. This involvement encompasses openness and a willingness to engage in the tasks of therapy, cooperative participation, and a collaborative stance. Group facilitators encourage members from the outset to assume responsibility for determining their level of investment in the group and for deciding what personal concerns they will raise.

7. A main strength of this approach is the emphasis on truly listening to and deeply understanding the internal frame of reference of the group member's world. It is essential for leaders to attend closely to the moment-to-moment happenings in a group session. Paying attention to what members want to talk about enables the group to move forward.

8. The group facilitator is a fellow explorer who strives to deeply understand the experiential world of the members in an interested and open way.

9. A basic characteristic of this approach to group work is the focus on the members as the center of the group. Members of a person-centered group are often as facilitative as the group leader.

10. Today there are relatively few practitioners who adhere to a classical client-centered model. Most person-centered practitioners use an integrative model that allows them to adapt the approach to their personal convictions and personal style. Integrative person-centered group facilitators subscribe to the fundamental philosophy of the approach but also integrate their own life experiences and ideas into their work with groups.

11. There is no one version of person-centered therapy today, but a number of continuously evolving person-centered psychotherapies. Person-centered therapy has evolved through diversity, inventiveness, creativity, and individualization in practice.

12. As the group movement developed, the person-centered approach became increasingly concerned with reducing human suffering, with cross-cultural awareness, and with conflict resolution on an international scale. This approach has been applied to bringing people of diverse cultures together for the purpose of developing mutual understanding.

Glossary of Key Terms for Person-Centered Therapy

- **Accurate empathic understanding** The act of perceiving the internal frame of reference of another, of grasping the person's subjective world, without losing one's own identity.
- **Actualization tendency** An intrinsic source of growth or a tendency toward self-realization, which means that the individual moves inherently toward self-regulation, self-determination, and inner freedom.
- **Collective resonance** This occurs when a group of diverse people is deeply in tune with their own feelings and thoughts as well as with what others are experiencing.
- **Congruence** The state in which self-experiences are accurately symbolized in the self-concept. As applied to the therapist, congruence is matching inner experiencing with one's external expressions; genuineness.
- **Empathic understanding** The ability to sense accurately the personal meanings others are experiencing, and being able to convey that to others.
- **Expressive arts therapy** An approach that makes use of various arts (such as movement, drawing, painting, sculpting, music, and improvisation) in a supportive setting for the purpose of growth and healing.
- **Formative tendency** A central source of energy that seeks fulfillment and actualization, involving both maintenance and enhancement of the organism.
- **Genuineness** The quality of realness of the group leader; being without pretenses; congruence.
- **Humanistic psychology** A movement, often referred to as the "third force," that emphasizes freedom, choice, creativity, spontaneity, values, growth, self-actualization, humor, and peak experiences.
- **Internal locus of evaluation** The ability to give oneself credit and appreciation when it is due and to be guided by one's own beliefs and standards.
- **Nondirective counseling** Introduced by Carl Rogers in the 1940s, this was a powerful and revolutionary alternative to the directive and interpretative approaches to therapy then being practiced.
- **Openness to experience** Involves a lack of defensiveness and an ability to perceive the present moment as it is without prejudgment; includes a lack of rigidity, openness to new concepts and beliefs, and a tolerance for ambiguity.
- **Personal power** A state in which individuals are aware of and can act on their own feelings, needs, and values rather than looking outside of themselves for direction.
- **Presence** The ability to "be with" someone fully in the present moment.
- **Self-actualizing tendency** A growth force within us, leading to the full development of one's potential; the basis on which people can be trusted to identify and resolve their own problems in a therapeutic relationship.
- **Therapeutic conditions** The characteristics of the client–therapist relationship necessary and sufficient for change to occur. These core conditions are therapist genuineness, unconditional positive regard, and accurate empathic understanding.
- **Unconditional positive regard** The nonjudgmental expression of a fundamental respect for the person; acceptance of a person's right to his or her feelings.

Stages of Development of the Person-Centered Group

Dimension	Initial Stage	Working Stage	Final Stage
Key developmental tasks and goals	Characterized by some floundering and a search for direction. Typically, members present a socially acceptable facade or reveal the "safe" sides of themselves; they describe themselves in a "there-and-then" manner. There is a milling around and a sense of confusion concerning the purpose and the function of the group. A key task is to build trust and a supportive climate that will allow for genuine encounters.	Negative feelings often surface over the lack of leadership. Then, a more accepting and trusting climate may prevail. Members show more of themselves, cohesion develops, and members find support in the group. Some confrontation may occur, especially when members sense that others are not being genuine. False fronts give way to a real expression of self. There is a willingness to explore significant personal concerns.	The group develops a healing capacity, and members are able to move forward based on the support offered. Members develop self-acceptance; they offer feedback to one another in a climate of honesty, and a sense of community develops. Behavior changes are noticed in the group. Members show increased ease in expressing their feelings, and they gain insight into how they relate to others.
Role and tasks of group leader	Facilitator's main role is to grant freedom to members to develop a structure of their own. Leader places responsibility on members for the direction they will take and follows that lead. Leader is concerned with creating a climate that is psychologically safe for the members. Leader's role is to be without a role. Central function is to help members interact honestly. Leader encourages members to state and explore all reactions.	A central task of the leader is to adopt an empathic viewpoint; it is important that members feel deeply understood and cared for. Leader needs to accept and understand a wide range of feelings that members express. Leader needs to share ongoing feelings and reactions with the group. Leader listens actively, reflects, clarifies, summarizes, links members' statements, demonstrates respect, and shows acceptance and caring for members.	Central job of leader is to help members express how they have experienced this group and to encourage honest feedback. Leader helps members apply what they have learned in the group to life outside of it. Leader provides support for members in making significant changes. Leader helps members accept responsibility for these changes. Leader is mainly interested in empowering members to develop their direction.
Role of group members	Members are expected to develop their own goals and decide for themselves how they will spend their time together. At first members are rather confused and search for a structure. They are hesitant in sharing personally significant material. They are encouraged to express whatever they are feeling or experiencing.	Members decide what they will reveal about themselves; they express feelings to others in the group. They offer both support and challenge to others; they give and receive feedback. Members at this stage are usually willing to express immediate interpersonal feelings of both a positive and a negative nature. Self- exploration occurs on a deeper level.	Members move from playing roles to being real, from being relatively closed to being open and able to tolerate some ambiguity, from being out of contact with internal and subjective experience to being aware of the ongoing subjective process, from looking for external answers to looking inward for direction.

Techniques	Person-centered leaders tend to avoid using planned exercises and techniques to "get a group moving." They rely on the capacity of the group to decide how time will be spent. Leader's attitudes and personal characteristics are far more important than the techniques used.	Key techniques include active listening, reflection, clarification, self-disclosure, respect, and congruence. Members are encouraged to speak in an open way about whatever they are feeling at the moment. These tools do not represent techniques so much as basic attitudes/behaviors.	Leader is really not necessary at this stage if the group has been effective, for now the group is fairly self-directive and can draw on its own resources for direction. Leader may help members summarize what they have learned and encourage them to apply it to life outside the group.
Questions to consider	Active listening is a basis of this approach. Ask yourself how your ability to hear and to understand might be hampered. What are some barriers in yourself to hearing others?

Are you talking too much and too soon?

Are you too concerned with answers and not allowing members to explore feelings?

Are you too quick to give advice or to look for an easy solution?

Are you asking too many closed questions?

Are you being overly directive and doing too much for the group?

Are you selectively listening or looking for ways to confirm your preconceived notions about members?

Are you paying too much attention to the content and to words and failing to hear subtle meanings? | Are you able to tolerate the expression of negative feelings within a group? Can you accept in a nondefensive manner reactions that are directed toward you?

Are you able and willing to share your own reactions in an appropriate manner with the members?

Are you able to be yourself in the group, or do you hide behind professional roles?

Do you trust the members with your feelings? Are you able to let them know how they are affecting you?

How do you demonstrate respect for the members by your behavior in the group? Does your behavior indicate understanding and acceptance?

Do you trust the group to develop in a positive direction? | Are you able to facilitate a group rather than direct it? Can you let the members lead the way, helping them look at their process when necessary?

As a person and as a group facilitator, have you allowed yourself to be changed by a group? Are you open to growth yourself? What changes do you detect in yourself?

Are you able to be both supportive and confrontive? Can you provide nurturing and challenge at the same time?

Have you facilitated the group in such a manner that the members no longer look to you for direction or answers? Is the group able to function largely independently of you?

Do you assist members in taking credit for the changes they have made? |

Reactions: Summarize your reactions to the person-centered perspective or group developmental stages. What do you like *most? least?* What aspects of this approach would you incorporate in your style of leadership?

Exercises and Activities for the Person-Centered Approach

Rationale

As is true for the existential approach, the person-centered approach emphasizes the group leader's attitudes far more than the techniques employed to facilitate a group. The most important consideration is the quality of the relationship you are able to create among the members and between yourself and the members. As you practice the exercises, do your best to keep within a person-centered framework. Attempt to attend to, listen to, and clarify what you hear, and *facilitate* more than *direct* the group process in these exercises.

Exercises

1. *Your personal effectiveness.* Think about what you have learned about yourself to this point that will either enhance or restrict your effectiveness as a group facilitator. What do you see as your single most important personal quality or strength? Can you identify at least one specific personal characteristic that is likely to get in the way of your effectiveness? If you are exploring these issues in a group, it would be a good idea for everyone to assume responsibility for the direction of the group. This could be an interesting exercise in itself to see what occurs in the absence of structured leadership for a session. As an alternative exercise, one or two members can assume responsibility for being the facilitator of the group. In this facilitation do your best to keep within the framework of the person-centered approach. Allow some time before the end of the exercise to share your reactions to being a member and a facilitator during the session.

2. *Empathic understanding.* One of the cornerstones of the person-centered approach is accurate empathy. Use the following questions as catalysts for discussion in your class or group: What is your understanding of empathy? How can you improve your ability to develop appropriate empathy for others? Do you expect to have the problem of overidentification, or losing your own identity by immersing yourself in another's world? What part does leader self-disclosure play in the expression of this empathy? What kind of person do you have a hard time empathizing with, and what does this tell you about yourself?

3. *Increasing empathy for difficult group members.* This exercise is designed to help you increase your empathy for people you might identify as "problem group members." Think about a particular kind of person (especially a group member) you are likely to have the most difficulty understanding or accepting. Think about the kind of group member you hope would drop out of the group or, better, who would not have joined in the first place. In your class or group, each member can talk about the specific behaviors of clients that present the greatest challenge. As an alternative exercise, instead of merely talking about these difficult group members, assume the identity of one of these clients, and role-play that person. Each person in the group should challenge him- or herself to stay in the role of a problem member for most of the session. Two members should assume the role of cofacilitators of the group and stay within the person-centered framework. Leave enough time to discuss these questions:
   a. What was it like for you to assume a particular role of a difficult member? What did you learn about this kind of member?
   b. What did you recognize about yourself in relation to this person?
   c. What was it like to be part of a group that was facilitated in a person-centered way?

　　d. What was the experience like as a group participant?

　　e. What was it like for the facilitators?

4. *Identifying personal goals.* Assume that you have joined a person-centered group. This is the first session, and each member has been asked to say what he or she wants from this group experience. Spend some time identifying the personal goals that would guide your participation in this group. If you were to talk about your hopes and expectations as a member, what might you say? After you have completed this exercise, spend some time as a group discussing these questions:

　　a. Do you agree with Rogers's contention that the group has the capacity to move in constructive directions without structure, direction, and active intervention on the leader's part? Why or why not? What are the implications for practice if you accept this assumption?

　　b. Do you agree that group members are the ones to formulate specific goals? What is the leader's role in assisting members with this task?

　　c. What is it like for you to identify what you want from a group and talk about it in a session?

5. *An unstructured group.* Form small groups in your class and participate in an unstructured group session for about one hour. The rules for this particular group are that there would be no planned agenda, no structured group exercises, no opening or closing techniques, and no probing questions. The aim of the session is to allow the group to unfold naturally. After the exercise, ask each participant to share what it was like to be in an unstructured group situation. If you were a member of this group, what was it like for you? If you were the facilitator of this group, how was it for you to function without an agenda or a preconceived structure? What possible advantages and disadvantages are there to an unstructured group? With which client or student populations would an unstructured approach work best? Which populations might have difficulty with this approach?

6. *Receiving feedback on how we come across.* Sometimes we need feedback from others on how well we listen, how accepting we appear to be, how genuine we come across, and the degree to which we demonstrate respect for others. After you have had a chance to try out at least one of the exercises in this section, discuss these questions in your class or group:

　　a. *Attending and listening.* How well do you listen? What gets in your way of fully attending to others? How can you improve your attending skills?

　　b. *Unconditional positive regard and acceptance.* To what degree do you have these qualities? What prejudices or assumptions might you have that could make it difficult for you to accept some people? Would you put certain conditions on your acceptance of people? If so, what might some of these conditions be?

　　c. *Respect.* What are some specific ways you are able to demonstrate respect for group members? Do you think it's possible to work effectively with members if you don't respect them? Why or why not? Can you think of an example of when you did not show respect for a group member?

　　d. *Genuineness.* What criteria can you employ to determine your level of genuineness? Is it possible to be an effective group leader and not be genuine? What problems do you think you might have in "being yourself" as a group leader?

7. *Evaluation and research.* Rogers stresses subjective research on group processes and outcomes, consisting mainly of self-reports by the participants. What do you think of

subjective measures to determine the outcomes of a group? What are some of your ideas regarding ways of finding out whether a group is successful? How would you evaluate the outcome of your groups?

8. *Expressive arts therapy.* Any art form generated from deep emotions aids in the process of self-discovery, and the raw and spontaneous product—as is—is part of the therapeutic process. Consider the ways in which you could incorporate expressive arts therapy into the groups you lead. In a small group or classroom setting, use your creativity to experiment with an exercise that might involve movement, drawing, painting, sculpting, writing, music, or improvisation. Afterward, get feedback from all participants on how useful the exercise was in helping them to tap into their emotions and deepen their self-awareness. What did they learn about themselves through the exercise? Were they surprised at what they discovered about themselves?

9. *Critique of the person-centered approach.* Give your personal evaluation of this model using some of these questions as a guide.
    a. What would it be like for you to facilitate this type of group?
    b. In what ways could you use many of the concepts of the person-centered approach in creating a therapeutic relationship and as a foundation for other approaches?
    c. What do you consider to be the major contribution and major limitation of the person-centered approach to groups?
    d. What are your thoughts about the contributions of Natalie Rogers with her methods and approaches based on the expressive arts?

Questions for Reflection and Discussion

1. What specific attitudes of person-centered leaders would assist you in understanding and working with culturally diverse populations?
2. What implications do you see in using a person-centered approach in working with a mandatory group? Can you think of ways to apply the key concepts of this approach to counseling reluctant and involuntary clients?
3. What are your thoughts on the matter of selecting members to participate in a group? Can you think of both advantages and disadvantages to the absence of screening and selection procedures?
4. What are the advantages of having group facilitators who are not professional psychotherapists? What are the disadvantages?
5. What are some key concepts and basic attitudes of the person-centered approach that you think could be effectively integrated into any other theory of groups? In what ways can the person-centered approach be a foundation for group practitioners, regardless of their theoretical orientation?
6. What one key point of this theory has the most meaning for you with respect to your way of facilitating a group?
7. Do you think you can adopt a person-centered philosophy and still incorporate techniques from some of the directive therapies in your group leading? Can you view people from a person-centered perspective yet assume a more active and central role in leadership? Explain.

8. According to Natalie Rogers, what are some of the basic principles of expressive arts therapy? What are the basic conditions upon which the various methods are based? How can the various art forms supply some structure and direction to the work of members in groups?

9. What aspects of the expressive arts would you be interesting in incorporating into your group practice? What kinds of groups do you think would be most appropriate for the expressive arts?

10. What are your thoughts about the role of the person-centered facilitator of groups? Would you feel comfortable participating as a member in a group you were facilitating?

11. Using a scale of 0 to 10 (0 = almost never and 10 = almost always), rate yourself on how often you convey each of the basic attitudes of the person-centered group leader (genuineness, unconditional positive regard, and empathy). In your future practice as a group leader, what can you do to increase or improve these attitudes? What barriers might prevent you from doing so? What other leader and member attitudes or qualities do you think might contribute to effective outcomes in a person-centered group?

12. With what populations, and with what types of groups, do you think the person-centered approach would be most effective? In what cases, if any, do you think this approach would be inappropriate and ineffective?

An Expert's Perspective on the Person-Centered Expressive Arts Approach to Group Work: by Natalie Rogers

NATALIE ROGERS, PhD, is the originator of person-centered expressive arts has conducted workshops in many parts of the world on this approach. (See her biography at the beginning of Chapter 10 in the textbook.)

1. What attracted you to this particular theoretical orientation? How does this theory fit with the person you are?

I remember as a 15-year-old high school student going into my father's (Carl Rogers) study and reading his book, *Counseling and Psychotherapy*. I was inspired! The funny part is that I said to myself, "I am glad he has the same values that I do." Obviously, some sort of osmosis of values had occurred because my dad did not discuss his work at home.

Carl Rogers's person-centered approach is the foundation for all of my work, both as a psychotherapist and as a group facilitator. I studied with him on various occasions and during his later years my father and I, with other staff, cocreated and facilitated large encounter-type groups over seven summers (1974–1981). It was during these large 10-day encounter groups with more than a hundred people in each group that I had the opportunity to explore and experiment with nonverbal methods to help people gain self-insight. I got tired of sitting in verbal sessions morning, afternoon, and evening, so I invited people to explore their emotional issues by using the arts in a separate room where I had art supplies. Two other staff members and I spontaneously created ways that people could delve deeply into their problems using art, movement, and psychodrama. There was no such thing as expressive arts in those days, so my theories and ideas sprang from these explorations.

My mother, Helen Rogers, was an artist and encouraged my creativity. I loved to dance expressively to music. So the expressive arts (which I helped to develop) fit exactly the person that I am. Person-centered expressive arts integrates the person-centered philosophy and methods along with expressive movement, art, journal writing, and psychodrama for self-healing and social change.

Also, Abraham Maslow suggested I return to school (as a married woman with two children) at Brandeis University where my husband was a faculty member. This lit my intellectual fire as I studied with him focusing on the experiences of creativity.

Thus, it was a natural evolution that I expanded and extended these notions of creativity with my own sense of the arts as healing. Person-centered expressive arts for counseling and groups emerged. My theories and practice have evolved over 35 years of exploration with clients and groups around the world. My passion has been to use the arts to bring forth creativity as our life force energy.

2. What Key Concepts (1 to 3) of this theory are most applicable to the practice of group counseling?

Building trust: Each person has the capacity for self-understanding and growth if given a safe environment. I believe the most important concept in group counseling or group workshops for personal growth is for the facilitator to build trust. This is true if it is a verbal group or a group integrating the nonverbal methods of expressive arts. As a participant I need to know that I can feel free to reveal my darker sides and my spiritual experiences. This can happen if the facilitator accepts all aspects of me whether I am grieving, angry, disappointed, or frustrated, or if I wish to share my numinous experiences of ecstasy.

A facilitator who is person-centered will listen carefully to each group member in an empathic way giving him or her the sense of being deeply understood. This applies to whether members are *talking* about their issues or *sharing their art experiences*. We do not interpret or give suggestions as to the meaning of sculpture, painting, movement, or journal writing of group members. We help them explore the meaning that the art has for them. This allows the participants to find their own answers and to create their own path. This way of being as a facilitator is based on Carl Rogers's theory that each person has the capacity for self-understanding and growth if given a safe environment in which to explore one's self.

Being fully present: It is not only what we do as facilitators; it is also the qualities that we manifest as human beings that elicit trust. A second important concept is for the facilitator to be fully present in a way that evokes trust and safety. Being an empathic listener is certainly one way. However, there are other qualities that make for an effective facilitator. Being nonjudgmental comes to mind as a priority. Many participants have said that never before have they been in a group where judgment by the facilitator (and therefore most of the group members) is absent. They have been graded and judged in every aspect of their lives: in school, in relationships, and in their creative endeavors. As a facilitator, leaving judgment at the door as you walk into the group room is not always easy. But the results are enormous and transformative for group members. Being judged can halt a group member's budding endeavor to explore through expressive arts media.

In one of our groups we brainstormed the personal qualities that are useful as a facilitator. Here are a few of the group members' thoughts to add to the above mentioned qualities: being transparent or real, genuine, warm hearted, egalitarian, sensitive to other cultures and races, curious, nonintrusive, permission-giving, setting clear limits, and being vulnerable. As facilitators, it is not just what we do that counts, but who we are as a person that brings about trust and safety.

The Creative Connection® concept: As I developed my own version of the expressive arts, I discovered that using the arts in sequence before using words allowed participants to go inward, discovering aspects of their unconscious and bringing them to consciousness. For instance, I can suggest that people use movement to explore what they are feeling at the moment. Although they do this in the group, each person is in his or her own private world. This can take 10 minutes or more. This type of moving with awareness opens individuals to profound feelings that can then be expressed in color, line, or form, which offers them another view of themselves. When they write immediately after the art expression, a free flow emerges sometimes resulting in poetry. This Creative Connection process can take up to 2 hours. Only then do the participants talk about this process, sharing what they are learning about themselves. During these 2 hours there is a special aura in the room as each individual goes on his or her own journey in silence in the presence of others. It feels like a sacred space. An important *connection* exists between using one art media to unleash creativity in another.

3. **What Techniques (1 to 3) from this theory have the most practical value for group work practitioners?**

Nonverbal introductions: Using the person-centered expressive arts is very helpful in opening a group. Rather than starting out by asking people to introduce themselves verbally, we invite them to engage in a Creative Connection experience that will help them to share who they are in a nonverbal way. We offer some "ice breaking" methods to release nervousness and anxiety by moving around the room, touching elbows, then touching shoulders as they keep moving and possibly continue by touching knees or backs. As participants move around the room bumping into each other in these ways, laughter arises and the energy shifts from anxious to playful.

Then we introduce an exercise that helps them express "Who Are You Now, and Who Would You Like to Be?" We give some guidelines on how to move to find out what they are feeling now, then invite them to take a pose to express that feeling. Then we suggest they take a pose as to who they would like to be. They are asked to take some time moving from one pose to the other to see what it takes, kinesthetically, to make this change. Using art materials, then journal writing, brings them new insights. Finally, they share their process with one or two others. The whole group reconvenes in a circle and those who wish to share their experience with everyone. This process ensures that all the group members have talked in depth about who they are to at least one other group member within the first session. This begins the sense of group trust and community.

Group wood-chopping: In the midlife of any ongoing group I am usually aware that there are some strong emotions that are not being shared. This is where the expressive arts are helpful. One method I offer is what I call "wood-chopping." In this exercise I invite people to stand in a circle, and I explain to them that we will be creating a lot of sound for the next 10 or 15 minutes. I remind them that they can participate or not—that they can observe and experience this process vicariously, or leave the room if they wish. There is no judgment about what they choose. I demonstrate the process of chopping wood by raising my arms as though I have an axe in my hand and a piece of wood below. As I chop the wood, I let out a loud guttural sound. People can use any words or sounds they wish. Often the word "NO" comes out as they chop.

We do this as a group three or four times and then stop to get feedback as to what this is stirring up in people. For some people this is a delightful release of their anger or frustration, for others it brings up times of severe conflict or violence they have experienced, for others it allows for grief to be expressed. I listen carefully to each person and respond empathically. I ask if they would like to do it again. Some say yes, others drop out and go on to use the art materials to further explore their feelings. After this process has exhausted itself, I suggest they use paint or clay or journal writing to explore the feelings that have arisen. Each person has the opportunity to use the arts and then share their process with one or two others. Thus, some of the strong emotions that have been covered over have a chance to emerge in a safe environment.

Bridging from here to home: Separation is difficult for some people. If the group has been caring, enriching, and empowering, it can be difficult to say good-bye. Here they have experienced acceptance and have been encouraged to be authentic. We offer exercises that help people face both the separation and look realistically about going home. For some, going home is great; for others, it may stir a sense of loneliness or conflict. We ask participants to start by using their left brain more actively—by brainstorming and reviewing the concepts they have learned. Most important is the exercise Bridging from Here to Home. Weather permitting we ask people to go outside and find a beginning point that will be the marker for being here at the group. Then we ask that they start walking slowly to a point in the distance that they imagine is home. "As you walk, be aware of what you are leaving behind and what you are going toward. Notice your thoughts and feelings. There is no right or wrong to what you are feeling. Take 10 minutes for this."

Participants return to the room to create art and write in their journal and finally choose two or three people with whom to share their experience. This simple walk and the art that is evoked is a profound experience. Facing the reality of separation and rejoining the home situation can have deep personal meaning.

4. How does this theory have particular relevance for addressing diversity and social justice issues in group work?

Honoring diversity and finding ways to support social justice have been my deepest passion as I explore ways to facilitate groups at home with people of many cultures and backgrounds and with groups around the world. The expressive arts allows people of all cultures to relate to each other in meaningful ways without words. Words are important, but the arts can help people express what they might be afraid to say.

When my colleagues and I created a weekend workshop in Israel, we invited Palestinian Muslims and Israeli Jewish women to come together to work toward a peaceful future. At one point, we asked each person to partner with someone of the "other" culture. As an Arab woman sat down with a Jewish woman, we placed a large piece of paper between them and gave each of them a pile of clay. They were asked to have a nonverbal conversation; one of them would place a piece of clay of any shape on the paper, then the partner would respond by placing her piece of clay where she wished on the paper. No words were spoken. Some partners created battles and conflict situations. Others worked to create something collaboratively. Whatever happened, it brought forth very interesting and sometimes painful discussions. With empathic listening to each view of each situation, insights were gained. We were facilitating mutual understanding. We were not asking for solutions.

My colleagues and I have found amazing results using the arts to share cross-cultural experiences as we have worked around the globe. We often have people from many countries in our extensive training programs. One simple but beautiful experience is to ask the foreigner to say what she is feeling in her own language. We tell her it is a beautiful experience for us to hear the music of her language and that her heartfelt expression comes through to us as she speaks. We all benefit from this. Often it is not even necessary that she translate what she has said. We get the essence of her meaning by the authenticity with which she has spoken.

Because the person-centered approach creates a safe environment, gay and lesbian people quite quickly feel at home sharing their sexual orientation. This is honored and respected. We also invite Asian Americans, Blacks, and Hispanic participants to offer their life experiences. When facilitators listen to each person's life story with respect and appreciation, this is role modeling for all of the group members. Community builds as individuals become grateful for the diversity present.

5. Raise a question from this theoretical framework that you consider especially important for group work practice.

Why is it that 98% of participants in expressive arts training and workshops are women? Although some of the major authors in the field of expressive arts are men, most of the participants in training programs and workshops and in the membership of the International Expressive Arts Therapy Association (IEATA) are women. In the early days I made a concerted effort to find male cofacilitators (which I enjoyed) with the hope it would attract male participants. Many times I have had wonderful conversations with men who seemed really interested in our work. At the end of the conversation the man would say, "I'll tell my wife about this, I think she would like to join your training program." CLUNK.

My own theory is that most men are not ready to open to their right brain and heart-felt functions—those aspects of our brain that bring us creativity, intuition, and feelings. For most men being vulnerable is unfamiliar territory or is even uncomfortable. It is much easier for them to use their very creative processes in developing computer programs or other high-tech development. I think it is a pity, both for them and for women, to be separated in this way. In my opinion, men need to develop their *Anima,* their feminine side, just as women are now developing their *Animus,* or masculine side. When we find a way to balance ourselves, it will be a more peaceful world.

Your Thoughts on Dr. Natalie Rogers's Expressive Arts Perspective

1. What do you think about using expressive arts techniques within the framework of the person-centered philosophy?
2. Dr. Rogers's believes that the expressive arts allows people of all cultures to relate to each other in meaningful ways without words. How can participation in expressive arts bring a diverse group of people together and create a community spirit?
3. How do you imagine it would be like for you to be a participant in a person-centered expressive arts group?

Quiz on the Person-Centered Approach to Groups: A Comprehension Check   Score ____%

Note: Please refer to Appendix I for the scoring key. Count 5 points for each error, and subtract the total from 100 to get your percentage score.

True/false items: Decide if the following statements are "more true" or "more false" as they apply to the person-centered approach to groups.

T   F   1. Carl Rogers based some of his notions of therapeutic practice on existential principles about what it means to be human.

T   F   2. The group leader's personal qualities and attitudes are more important than the techniques he or she uses in a group.

T   F   3. The role of a person-centered group leader is to be without a role.

T   F   4. The person-centered view of group therapy places emphasis on diagnosis and interpretation.

T   F   5. The phrase *formative tendency* refers to conditioning during the early years of development.

T   F   6. A primary means of determining whether members experience a facilitator's empathy is to secure feedback from them.

T   F   7. Rogers's original conviction was that the core conditions operated independently rather than worked together.

T   F   8. During the creative connection process in the expressive arts, one art form stimulates and nurtures the other.

T   F   9. A deep faith in the individual's innate drive to become fully oneself is basic to the work in person-centered expressive arts.

T   F   10. Natalie Rogers's group work differs from Carl Rogers's approach in that she offers group guidelines at the beginning of an experiential workshop so participants understand the concepts of creative expression and the basic guidelines for group behavior.

Multiple-choice items: Select the *one best answer* among the alternatives given. Consider each question within the framework of person-centered therapy.

_____11. One of the strengths of the person-centered approach is that

    a. it offers a wide range of cognitive techniques to change behavior.

    b. it teaches clients ways to explore the meaning of dreams.

    c. it places emphasis on reliving one's early childhood memories.

    d. therapists have the latitude to develop their own counseling style.

    e. clients are given a concrete plan to follow.

_____12. A limitation of the person-centered approach is the

    a. lack of research conducted on key concepts.

    b. tendency for practitioners to give support without challenging clients enough.

    c. lack of attention to the therapeutic relationship.

    d. failure to allow clients to choose for themselves.

    e. lack of any applicability in working with culturally diverse client groups.

_____13. Carl Rogers made a contribution to

    a. developing the humanistic movement in psychotherapy.

    b. pioneering research in the process and outcomes of therapy.

    c. fostering world peace.

    d. pioneering the encounter group movement.

    e. all of the above.

_____14. As a result of experiencing person-centered therapy, it is hypothesized, the client will move toward

    a. self-trust.

    b. an internal source of evaluation.

    c. being more open to experience.

    d. a willingness to continue growing.

    e. all of the above.

_____15. Unconditional positive regard refers to

    a. liking clients.

    b. accepting clients as worthy persons.

    c. approving of clients' behavior.

    d. agreeing with clients' values.

    e. accepting clients if they meet the therapist's expectations.

_____16. The crucial factor that determines the outcome of the person-centered group is the

    a. leader's technical skills.

    b. leader's relationship with the members in the group.

    c. leader's knowledge of group dynamics.

    d. members' willingness to think rationally.

    e. accurate assessment of the members' lifestyles.

_____17. All of the following are considered to be key concepts of the person-centered approach except for the notion of

    a. social interest.

    b. congruence.

    c. unconditional positive regard.

    d. empathic understanding.

    e. nonpossessive warmth.

_____18. Empathy refers to the group leader's ability to
   a. feel exactly what the members are experiencing.
   b. sense accurately the inner world of a member's subjective experience.
   c. objectively understand the dynamics of a member.
   d. accurately diagnose the core problem of a member.
   e. approve of a member's behavior.

_____19. Research suggests that when therapists engage in self-disclosure it should be done to
   a. validate a client's reality.
   b. normalize experiences.
   c. strengthen the alliance.
   d. present alternative ways of thinking or acting.
   e. all of the above.

_____20. All of the following are true of Natalie Rogers's person-centered expressive arts
   except which statement?
   a. Any art form generated from deep emotions aids in the process of self-discovery.
   b. The expressive arts lead us into the unconscious, which allows us to express
      previously unknown facets of ourselves.
   c. Our society tends to promote creativity and original thinking in young people.
   d. Expressive arts methods require a safe, supportive environment created by group
      facilitators.
   e. This approach offers structured experiences to group members by encouraging
      them to use movement, visual arts, music, and journal writing to go on their inner
      journey.

CHAPTER ELEVEN

Gestalt Therapy in Groups

Prechapter Self-Inventory for Gestalt Therapy

Directions: Refer to page 77 for general directions. Indicate your position on these statements using the following code:

5 = I *strongly agree* with this statement.
4 = I *agree,* in most respects, with this statement.
3 = I am *undecided* in my opinion about this statement.
2 = I *disagree,* in most respects, with this statement.
1 = I *strongly disagree* with this statement.

_____ 1. The goal of group counseling is to help members integrate the fragmented parts of their personality enough that they can carry on the process of development alone.

_____ 2. Group work should focus on here-and-now experiencing in order to increase members' awareness.

_____ 3. Past conflicts or events are best understood by reexperiencing them in the here-and-now.

_____ 4. It is generally more productive to ask "what" and "how" questions than to ask "why" questions.

_____ 5. Unfinished business from the past tends to manifest itself in one's current behavior.

_____ 6. In a group setting it is important to explore the members' nonverbal messages and blocks to awareness.

_____ 7. With awareness, group members have the capacity to find within themselves the resources necessary to solve their problems and to discover the conditions that will make change possible.

_____ 8. The most creative and effective experiments grow out of what is happening in the group.

_____ 9. The best way to deal with future concerns is to bring them into the here-and-now.

_____ 10. Effective contact means fully interacting with nature and with other people without losing one's sense of individuality.

Summary of Basic Assumptions and Key Concepts of the Gestalt Approach to Groups

1. A basic assumption of Gestalt therapy is that the focus on the here-and-now encompasses the past and helps influence the future. The past, which has a significant role in shaping current behavior, is brought into the present by reenacting earlier situations that are still

unfinished. In Gestalt groups the participants bring past problem situations into the present by reenacting the situations as if they were occurring now.

2. The Gestalt approach puts awareness, choice, and responsibility as cornerstones of practice. People are essentially responsible for their own conflicts, and they have the capacity to deal with their life problems. Therefore, group members tend to make their own interpretations and to discover for themselves the meaning of their experiences.

3. Gestalt therapists use experiments when assisting group members to increase their awareness. Through group interaction, members will become more aware of conflicts and places where they "get stuck" (arrive at an impasse). In the group, members can experiment with a variety of ways to work through the impasse and move to a new level of integration. Experiments can be applied to future events as well as to present conflicts and unfinished situations from the past.

4. As compared with individual therapy, Gestalt group process offers a greater chance to awaken some unfinished business in members because of the present-centered interactions among the members.

5. One of the group leader's tasks is to help members locate the ways in which they are blocking energy and expressing their resistance in their body. Through body-awareness work, members are mobilized and can take active responsibility for their therapy. They can then be encouraged to try more adaptive behaviors.

6. Gestalt group therapists do not assume that they know better than the participants of their group, nor do they explain or tell members why they do things, nor do they interpret the true meaning of a member's experience.

7. Although the Gestalt leader encourages members to assume responsibility for expanding their awareness, the leader also takes an active role in creating experiments designed to help members tap their resources. The essence of creative therapy is designing experiments that grow out of the existential situation of the therapy encounter. Through these experiments, members are able to confront the crises of their lives by playing out their troubled relationships in the safety of the therapeutic setting.

8. Contemporary Gestalt therapists make use of facilitative interventions that highlight interpersonal processes rather than using a coercive and confrontational style.

9. There are different styles of practicing Gestalt therapy, but all styles share common elements: direct experiencing and experimenting, the use of direct contact and personal presence, attention to *what* and *how*, and *here-and-now*. Gestalt therapy is a humanistic, existential, and holistic model that brings a fresh and creative perspective to the practice of group work.

10. Gestalt experiments are powerful and often lead to the expression of immediate emotions and the reexperiencing of old feelings. The Gestalt present-centered methods of reenacting early life experiences bring vitality both to an individual's work and to the participants of the group. Before Gestalt procedures are introduced, it is essential that the members have been adequately prepared and that the cultural context is taken into consideration.

Glossary of Key Terms for Gestalt Therapy

- **Awareness** The process of attending to and observing one's own senses, thoughts, feelings, and actions; paying attention to the flow of one's experiences in the moment.

- **Blocks to energy** Paying attention to where energy is located, how it is used, and how it can be blocked.
- **Confluence** A disturbance in which the sense of the boundary between self and environment is lost.
- **Confrontation** An invitation for the client to become aware of discrepancies between verbal and nonverbal expressions, between feelings and actions, or between thoughts and feelings.
- **Contact** A process of interacting with nature and other people without losing one's sense of individuality.
- **Continuum of awareness** Staying with the moment-to-moment flow of experiencing, which leads individuals to discover how they are functioning in the world.
- **Deflection** A way of avoiding contact and awareness by being vague and indirect.
- **Dialogue experiments** These experiments are typically used to heighten awareness of introjections and projections. Through dialogues with the different facets of oneself, a person may be able to reclaim disowned parts.
- **Dichotomy** A split by which a person experiences or sees opposing forces; a polarity (tough/tender, open/closed).
- **Disturbances to contact** Contact with the environment is diminished in ways that prevent us from experiencing and staying with the present in a full and real way.
- **Dream work in groups** Using a Gestalt approach, group members do not report their dreams or talk about them in the past tense. Instead, they are asked to tell the dream as if it were happening in the present. By avoiding analyzing and interpreting the dream and focusing instead on becoming and experiencing it in all its aspects, group members get closer to the existential message of the dream.
- **Experiments** Interventions designed to enhance here-and-now awareness; activities members try out in a group as a way of testing new ways of thinking, feeling, and behaving.
- **Field theory** The notion of the individual being viewed in his or her environment, or in the context of a constantly changing field.
- **Figure-formation process** Describes how the individual organizes the environment from moment to moment and how the emerging focus of attention is on what is figural.
- **Group exercises** Leaders prepare some kind of structured technique before the group meets as a way to promote interaction.
- **Group experiments** A creative happening that grows out of the group experience; experiments are not predetermined, and the outcome cannot be predicted.
- **Holism** A core concept in Gestalt theory that implies that all nature is a unified and coherent whole.
- **Introjection** The uncritical acceptance of others' beliefs and standards without assimilating them into one's own personality.
- **Nonverbal language** The exploration of nonverbal expressions can increase members' awareness of what they are experiencing in the moment.
- **Organismic self-regulation** Pertains to the relationship between the individual and the environment and the tendency to restore equilibrium and contribute to change.
- **Paradoxical theory of change** A concept that implies that individuals change when they become aware of what they are, as opposed to attempting to become what they are not.

Dimension	Initial Stage	Working Stage	Final Stage
Key developmental tasks and goals	A central goal is to gain here-and-now awareness of what is being felt, sensed, and thought; group members must experiment and experience. Personal goals include achieving contact with self and others and defining one's boundaries with clarity.	Members deal with unfinished business from the past that is impeding full functioning now. The task is to integrate polarities. Group therapy is aimed at helping members give expression to the side of themselves they tend to repress.	Members assume personal responsibility, which means that they integrate the fragmented aspects of their personalities. By achieving a moment-to-moment awareness of whatever is being experienced, members have the means within themselves to make changes.
Role and tasks of group leader	It is the leader's task to follow whatever leads are provided by group members; in this way members are able to become aware of the "what" and the "how" of their experiencing. The leader functions much like an artist inventing techniques that arise from the material in the group. The emphasis is on creating effective personal relationships.	The leader's task is to pay close attention to both the verbal and nonverbal messages of members and to pay attention to the here-and-now. Leader suggests experiments designed to enhance and intensify the experiences of the members. Leader pays attention to energy and helps members recognize their patterns of avoidance.	After a piece of work is completed, the leader may ask members to state what they are aware of. There is not much emphasis on cognitive structuring or behavior modification. It is assumed that once members gain an awareness of what they are doing to prevent themselves from fully experiencing the moment, they are capable of changing.
Role of group members	Members are expected to focus on the here-and-now and to reexperience past conflicts as though they were going on now. Members decide what they will explore in the group. Members are challenged to accept responsibility for whatever they are experiencing and doing. They learn to live up to their own expectations, and they make decisions.	Members are expected to directly communicate to one another and to make "I" statements. They are discouraged from asking "why" questions. The focus is on exploration of feelings. To experience these feelings fully, members take part in a variety of action-oriented activities. They don't talk about problems; rather, they act out their various roles and conflicts.	Members give and receive feedback. They have the opportunity to identify unfinished business from their past that impedes present functioning and to work through impasses. By gaining awareness of areas that were out of consciousness, they become more integrated. They are increasingly able to live with their own polarities and to be more self-directed.

Techniques	Leader uses "what" and "how" questions, not "why" questions, to help members focus on themselves and what they are experiencing. Leaders may use many experiments including fantasy approaches, asking people to pay attention to what they are experiencing physically, thinking out loud, and so on. The skilled leader avoids using techniques in a mechanical way. Rather, the leader creates experiments that express what is going on in the group now. A wide range of experiments all have the general goal of helping members intensify their experiencing in the present moment. Members may explore dreams by becoming all parts of their dreams; they may engage in role playing in which they act out all the parts; or they may exaggerate a particular gesture or mannerism. Symbolic encounters are used to help members deal with unfinished situations. Members can be asked to enact a situation the way they'd like it to be; they play all the parts. Members are often asked to give a new ending to an old and unfinished situation. Experiments help members see how past unfinished situations get in the way of effective living in the present. Members are asked to practice and experiment with new ways outside of the group. Action follows experiencing.
Questions to consider	Are you able to create a climate within the group that encourages members to try out creative experiments? Have you prepared them for Gestalt techniques? Have you earned their respect and trust? Do they see benefits in participating in a variety of experiments aimed at enhancing their awareness? Do you avoid using planned techniques to make something happen in a group? Can you follow the process and invent a technique that will highlight members' concerns? Do you take care to avoid being mechanical in using techniques? Are the methods you employ an extension of what is happening within the members at a given time in the group? Do you invite members to take part in an experiment as opposed to commanding them? Can you respect resistance in a group member? Are you able to work therapeutically with resistance? Do you focus on what is going on within the group now? Are you able to pay attention to the subtle nonverbal messages and work with them? Do you help members stay with their present experience and not talk about what they are thinking or feeling? Do you bring yourself in as a person, and do you respond to others in personal ways? How can you create experiments that will help members gain awareness of what they are doing to prevent themselves from being fully in the present? How can members be helped to work through unfinished business that interferes with living now in a vital way? How can any unfinished business within the group be addressed? Have the members recognized ways in which they block their strengths and keep themselves from living the way they want? Are you able to help members deal with their feelings about termination? Do you encourage them to express feelings about separation?
Reactions:	Summarize your reactions to the Gestalt perspective on group developmental stages. What do you like *most? least?* What aspects of this approach would you incorporate in your style of leadership?

- **Projection** The process by which we disown certain aspects of ourselves by ascribing them to the environment; the opposite of introjection.
- **Rehearsal** Internal processing about the roles we think we are expected to play. As a technique, members are asked to "rehearse out loud" so that others can experience the internal process of thinking and censoring.
- **Relational Gestalt therapy** A supportive and compassionate style that emphasizes dialogue in the therapeutic relationship.
- **Retroflection** The act of turning back onto ourselves something we would like to do (or have done) to someone else.
- **Techniques** Exercises or procedures that are often used to bring about action or interaction, sometimes with a prescribed outcome in mind.
- **Unfinished business** Unexpressed feelings (such as resentment, guilt, anger, grief) dating back to childhood that now interfere with effective psychological functioning; needless emotional debris that clutters present-centered awareness.

Exercises and Activities for Gestalt Groups

Rationale

Gestalt therapy makes use of a variety of action-oriented methods that are designed to intensify what members are experiencing. Instead of discussing conflicts, for example, members are encouraged to "become the conflict." The idea is to fully experience every dimension of oneself (to be authentic). The Gestalt therapist will suggest experiments to help members try some new behavior and thus experience everything fully.

It is important that the following exercises *not* be done mechanically. Each exercise is best if it is tailored to the unique needs of the members in your class/group. Further, it is a good idea to give members some preparation before springing an experiment on them. Enlist the cooperation of group members by giving a brief explanation of the basic purpose of each exercise. By trying many of the exercises in your own small group, you will be in a better position to know which of these techniques you might want to use when you are a group leader.

Exercises

1. *Here-and-now versus there-and-then.* Talk about a personal experience in the past tense for about 3 minutes. Then, relive the same experience as though it were happening in the present. What difference do you notice between these 3-minute exercises? What value do you see in encouraging people in groups to make past experiences into present-centered ones?

2. *Bringing the future into the now.* Are you anticipating any future confrontations? This exercise can be a form of rehearsal. Using the two-chair technique, take turns being yourself and then becoming the person you expect to confront, then be yourself, and so on for a brief period of time. Make this future event happen in the here-and-now. When you are finished, discuss what this experience was like. What did you learn through the experiment? What are your fears and hopes regarding this future event?

3. *Identifying unfinished business.* Gestalt therapy emphasizes the role of unfinished business, which can get in the way of our being effective in the present. Can you identify any

unfinished business that might limit your effectiveness in working with members' concerns? What are some ways to explore your own unfinished business that could allow you to be more fully present for others?

4. *Avoidance.* The concept of avoidance is central in Gestalt therapy. How many ways can you think of in which you sometimes avoid aspects of living? What do your avoidance patterns tell you about yourself?

5. *Nonverbal language in the group.* Exaggerate some of your typical body language. If you often frown, let yourself really get into that frown. If you have a certain mannerism, develop it fully. What can you learn from this exercise about your nonverbal language? Pay attention to others as they speak, and note their tone of voice, manner of speech, quality of voice, posture, facial expressions, gestures, speed and rate of speech, and so on. What do people tell you about themselves nonverbally?

6. *Experimenting with dialogues.* Have each person in a small group experiment with the dialogue technique. You can also do this at home alone. Place two chairs facing each other. Next, choose one of your conflicts (that you are willing to share in a group) and become one side of this conflict. Talk to the other side, which is in the other chair. Now get up and sit in the other chair, becoming that other side. Carry on this dialogue for a time. If you're doing this in a group, discuss what you learned. What is it like for you to do the experiment? Which side felt dominant? Here are some examples of typical conflicts that often keep us fragmented:
   a. Part of me wants to open up; the other part of me wants to keep closed.
   b. I have a serious side; then there is the fun side.
   c. I want to love, yet I don't dare let myself.
   d. Part of me wants to take a risk; the other part wants to play it safe.

List all the conflicts or fragmentations that exist inside of you. Do you have trouble integrating dichotomies such as tough/tender, masculine/feminine, worthwhile/worthless?

7. *Gestalt dream work.* Try some Gestalt dream experiments in your group. Have a volunteer recount a dream as though it were happening now. After telling the dream in the present tense, others in the group can ask:
   • What part of the dream most interests you? Why?
   • What aspects of the dream most stand out for you?
   • What is the general mood surrounding the dream?

After recounting the dream, make up a dialogue between one or more parts of the dream. Act them out in the present tense, and let yourself really experience the dream. Carry on a dialogue between various parts of the dream, making sure to have several interchanges between the aspects of the dream. What does your dream teach you about yourself? Ask for feedback from others in your group. Others in the group can explore the question, "What idea does the dream give each of you about the dreamer?"

If you are keeping a journal, I recommend that you begin to record your dreams if you are not already doing so. Simply writing down your dreams and reviewing them can give you clues about your struggles. Look for patterns in your dreams, and speculate on the meaning of these patterns. What can you learn from your dreams?

8. *Making the rounds.* In this exercise a member goes around to everyone in the group and says something to each person, usually something that he or she struggles with

in expressing. Make up some incomplete sentences, and experiment with making the rounds and completing these sentences. Here are some examples of incomplete sentences:

a. "If I were to depend on you, then _____."
b. "I keep my distance from you by _____."
c. "If I were to get close to you, then _____."
d. "If I would not smile when I'm in pain, I _____."
e. "When I look at you, _____."
f. "One thing I want you to know about me is _____."
g. "I am like you in that I _____."

Any of these sentences can be selected and completed for every person in the room. It is important that you respond quickly and give your uncensored and initial reaction. After you've experienced a go-around, talk about what you learned from it and what it was like for you to do this.

9. *Rehearsal.* Internal rehearsal saps much of our vitality. We often think so carefully about the appropriate way to be that any spontaneity is squelched. The rehearsal technique consists of saying out loud what you are thinking silently. In this exercise select a situation in which you would typically rehash all the pros and cons to yourself before deciding what to do or say, but this time allow yourself to think out loud. For example, let yourself play out in a group what you go through before you ask a person for a date, or go on a job interview, or give a speech. What are all the things you say to yourself? (The exercise can make you more acutely aware of how you are striving for approval or how you fear rejection.)

Questions for Reflection and Discussion

1. Both Gestalt therapy and person-centered therapy share some features with the existential approach, yet they employ very different methods in a group. Although they have some common philosophical views of human nature, Gestalt therapy relies on therapist direction and interventions, whereas person-centered therapy de-emphasizes techniques and therapist direction. Do you see any basis for the typically active Gestalt leader to incorporate some person-centered concepts? What are some person-centered assumptions and concepts that could fruitfully be incorporated in Gestalt practice?

2. Do you see a possibility of thinking in psychoanalytic terms and using Gestalt experiments? How might you integrate psychoanalytic concepts with Gestalt concepts and methods as part of your leadership style?

3. Gestalt therapy focuses on what people are *experiencing* and *feeling* moment to moment. The focus is on highlighting awareness. It is important for the leader to follow whatever is in the client's awareness and to introduce experiments that grow out of this awareness and the existential situation. Using the principle of following whatever is in the client's awareness, how might you decide what kind of experiments to suggest?

4. What are the major ethical considerations that need to be addressed in Gestalt group work? What safeguards can you think of against some potential risks associated with Gestalt groups?

5. What are some key Gestalt concepts and experiments you can apply to the process of understanding yourself? How might you use some Gestalt methods to increase your own level of awareness? What do you think it would be like for you to be in a Gestalt group?

6. If you were to make use of Gestalt experiments in your group, in what ways might you prepare your members to increase their readiness to get involved in these experiments? What might you say to a member who asked what good it does to relive an event in the here-and-now rather than telling about a problem in the past? If you suggested to a member that she enact her dream and have dialogue with the different parts, how would you react if she thought doing so would be silly or pointless?

7. What are some ways you might work with the body in therapy? What kind of training would you want to have before you introduced body-oriented techniques? What advantages, if any, do you see in incorporating body work, as opposed to limiting the group strictly to verbal methods? What risks, if any, do you see in working with the body?

8. What are your reactions to the Gestalt approach of working with dreams in a group setting? How could you encourage members to share a dream and explore its meaning with them?

9. You are asked to design a counseling group for either children or adolescents in the school setting. What are some specific key concepts from Gestalt therapy that could be applied in this setting? What are some Gestalt techniques you might incorporate in your group with either children or adolescents? How would you prepare the members for participating in Gestalt experiments?

10. What are some advantages and potential disadvantages of using a Gestalt approach with culturally diverse client populations? How would you take into account the group members' cultural background using this approach?

An Expert's Perspective on Gestalt Group Therapy: by Jon Frew

JON FREW, PhD, is Professor of Psychology at Pacific University's School of Professional Psychology and is in private practice in Vancouver, Washington.

1. What attracted you to this particular theoretical orientation? How does this theory fit with the person you are?

My first encounters with Gestalt therapy were with Fritz Perls, or, more accurately, with how he practiced and personified his theory. I was impressed by his style and the power and energy he could generate in minutes with workshop volunteers he had never met before. It was clear to me, this was in 1972, that Gestalt therapy *did not fit* the person I was. Three years later, I had a more balanced experience/encounter with Gestalt therapy in Cleveland, Ohio, and that is when the fit was obvious and my training began.

The fundamentals of Gestalt therapy have always lined up well to the way I conceptualize individuals and our complex relationship with the environment that surrounds and sustains us. Gestalt therapy is a theory of health, not pathology. Individuals must be understood in context, not isolated from their field conditions. Individuals are fully capable of self-regulating in the environment. The nature of our relationship with the environment is one of interdependence. Gestalt therapists have no interest in having our clients adjust to any particular majority ideology or set of values. All aspects of the individuals' feelings, thoughts, behaviors, dreams, spirituality, are equally salient—the client chooses which aspect is most important, not the therapist's theoretical orientation. These are some of the basics of Gestalt therapy that attracted me to the field more than 40 years ago and continue to excite me today.

2. What Key Concepts (1 to 3) of this theory are most applicable to the practice of group counseling?

Field theory: This concept was adapted from Kurt Lewin and is one of the philosophical underpinnings of Gestalt therapy. Gestalt therapists always view the individual as in continuous contact with the field, or environment. Applied to group work, the group itself is the environment of most relevance. Group leaders attend to how each member both contributes to the development and evolution of the community over time and how they utilize the group to satisfy needs, and to attend to wants and curiosities. Contact with the environment requires both individual support and environmental support.

Environmental support: Gestalt group leaders cultivate environmental support by attending to a group's phases of development and encouraging members to make contact with others with an eye to the group's current level of safety and cohesion.

Individual support: Individual group members are encouraged to support themselves by being physically grounded, by paying attention to their breathing, and by making group-by-group decisions about how much to disclose and ask for from the group.

3. What Techniques (1 to 3) from this theory have the most practical value for group work practitioners?

Group process levels: The majority of Gestalt therapists who do group work have moved beyond the "hot seat" method that Fritz Perls used in his demonstration workshops. Gestalt group leaders attend to processes at three levels: intrapersonal, interpersonal, and group or system. All these levels exist at every moment in a group, and leaders try to make interventions that include all three. *Intrapersonal interventions* are directed to individual members and often address a member's current awareness level. *Interpersonal interventions* allow the group leader to work with how group members are making contact with other members. Finally, *group level interventions* are used to attend to a group as a community and to assess group norms, safety, or accomplishments.

4. How does this theory have particular relevance for addressing diversity and social justice issues in group work?

As a field theory, Gestalt therapists always consider each individual contextually. We are keenly interested in learning about "field conditions" that have in the past and are in the present affecting our clients. All the diversity factors discussed in multicultural counseling literature would be embedded in those field conditions.

Gestalt therapists utilize *phenomenological inquiry* as a basic method of working with clients, individually and in groups. We bracket off (as much as possible) our preexisting beliefs and experiences and work to understand each individual based on his or her subjective reality. We observe and describe and limit the use of interpretation or explanation. Proceeding from a phenomenological stance is especially crucial in working with clients from diverse backgrounds.

In terms of social justice, we are interested in how our clients have creatively adjusted to their circumstances, not in having our clients adjust to the majority culture.

5. Raise a question from this theoretical framework that you consider especially important for group work practice.

How do group leaders characterize resistance? Words like "resistant," "challenging," and "avoidant" are commonly used in the counseling profession. From a Gestalt therapy perspective, they are often used when group leaders are frustrated because a group member is not doing what is expected. Gestalt therapists are not "trying to get" our clients anywhere, therefore *there can be no resistance*! Individuals do the best they can in the moment to self-regulate in their current environment. Group members are doing the best they can to support themselves in the group. Rejecting the notion that group members are, in some way, not cooperating allows group leaders to avoid power struggles. Instead, the leader seeks out a clearer understanding of each member's ongoing experience.

Your Thoughts on Dr. Frew's Perspective on Gestalt Therapy Groups

1. What do you think about Dr. Frew's belief that there can be no resistance in Gestalt therapy because the group practitioner does not have a preconceived notion of what the client should move toward?
2. What aspects of Gestalt therapy most interest you and why?
3. How do you imagine it would be for you to be a participant in a Gestalt therapy group?

Quiz on the Gestalt Approach to Groups: A Comprehension Check   Score _____ %

Note: Please refer to Appendix I for the scoring key. Count 5 points for each error, and subtract the total from 100 to get your percentage score.

True/false items: Decide if the following statements are "more true" or "more false" as they apply to Gestalt therapy.

T   F   1. Therapist interpretation is a necessary condition for change to occur.
T   F   2. The basic methodological tool in Gestalt therapy is the experiment.
T   F   3. Gestalt leaders use a wide range of cognitive behavioral techniques designed to get members to think about the origin of their problems.
T   F   4. Gestalt therapy, being concerned with the here-and-now, is not interested in and does not deal with one's past.
T   F   5. In a Gestalt framework, blocked energy can be thought of as resistance.
T   F   6. Typically, the Gestalt leader is highly active and directive.

T F 7. In Gestalt dream work, the leader interprets the hidden and symbolic meanings of the dream for the member.

T F 8. The main goal of the Gestalt group is to assist members in resolving their dichotomies or polarities through problem-solving methods.

T F 9. Methods of working with the body can be fruitfully combined with other techniques in Gestalt therapy.

T F 10. Overuse of techniques in a Gestalt group can serve the function of keeping the leader hidden.

Multiple-choice items: Select the *one best answer* among the alternatives given. Consider each question within the framework of Gestalt therapy.

_____11. The process of distraction, or interruption of awareness, which makes it difficult to maintain sustained contact, is
   a. introjection.
   b. projection.
   c. retroflection.
   d. confluence.
   e. deflection.

_____12. The process of turning back to ourselves what we would like to do to someone else is
   a. introjection.
   b. projection.
   c. retroflection.
   d. confluence.
   e. deflection.

_____13. The tendency to uncritically accept others' beliefs without assimilating or internalizing them is
   a. introjection.
   b. projection.
   c. retroflection.
   d. confluence.
   e. deflection.

_____14. The process of blurring the awareness of differentiation between the self and the environment is
   f. introjection.
   g. projection.
   h. retroflection.
   i. confluence.
   j. deflection.

_____15. Which of the following is a limitation of Gestalt therapy as it is applied to working with culturally diverse populations?
   a. Clients who have been culturally conditioned to be emotionally reserved may not see any value in experiential techniques.
   b. Clients may be "put off" by a focus on catharsis.
   c. Clients may be looking for specific advice on solving practical problems.
   d. Clients may believe that to show one's vulnerability is to be weak.
   e. All of the above are limitations.

_____16. A primary function of the Gestalt group leader is to
   a. make interpretations for the members.
   b. serve as a blank screen to foster transference.
   c. suggest experiments that will lead to heightening awareness.
   d. confront clients' irrational thoughts and mistaken beliefs.
   e. help clients understand their unique style of life.

_____17. In Gestalt therapy, awareness is best described as
   a. introspection.
   b. insight.
   c. recognition of why one struggles with a certain problem.
   d. understanding the root cause of dysfunctional behavior.
   e. recognition of current feelings, actions, and sensations.

_____18. There are different styles of practicing Gestalt therapy, but all styles share which of the following common elements?
   a. direct experiencing and experimenting
   b. the use of direct contact and personal presence
   c. attention to what and how
   d. attention to the here-and-now
   e. all of the above

_____19. Gestalt techniques are aimed at
   a. teaching members how to think rationally.
   b. integrating conflicting sides within members.
   c. teaching clients how to discover the causes of their problems.
   d. helping members understand unconscious dynamics.
   e. rewriting members' life scripts.

_____20. Gestalt therapy focuses most on
   a. exploration of the past.
   b. the here-and-now.
   c. the future.
   d. both the past and the future.
   e. getting members to talk about their basic problems.

CHAPTER TWELVE

Transactional Analysis in Groups

Prechapter Self-Inventory for Transactional Analysis (TA)

Directions: Refer to page 77 for general directions. Indicate your position on these statements using the following code:

5 = I *strongly agree* with this statement.
4 = I *agree,* in most respects, with this statement.
3 = I am *undecided* in my opinion about this statement.
2 = I *disagree,* in most respects, with this statement.
1 = I *strongly disagree* with this statement.

_____ 1. In achieving autonomy, people have the capacity to make new decisions (redecide), thereby empowering themselves and altering the course of their lives.

_____ 2. Once we decide on a life position, as a rule, there is a tendency for it to remain fixed unless there is some therapeutic intervention to change the underlying decisions.

_____ 3. Contracts are both basic and necessary if the group counseling process is to be therapeutic.

_____ 4. With its emphasis on personal responsibility and freedom, transactional analysis can be considered an existential approach to psychotherapy.

_____ 5. Relationships between the group leader and members need to be equal if the group's work is to be successful.

_____ 6. It is useful to teach group members how to explore their early decisions and the parental injunctions that are influencing them now.

_____ 7. It is the leader's function to challenge members to examine the decisions they made early in life and to determine whether these decisions are still appropriate.

_____ 8. Game playing, by its very definition, prevents the development of genuine intimacy.

_____ 9. People tend to accept uncritically the messages they received from their parents and from parental substitutes.

_____ 10. Contracts give direction to group sessions, increase the responsibility of members to participate actively in group work, and provide a basis for equal partnership between the members and the leader.

Summary of Basic Assumptions and Key Concepts of the Transactional Analysis Approach to Groups

1. TA is grounded on the assumption that we make current decisions based on our early experiences and messages we received in childhood. Decisions made then about how to behave may not be valid, useful, or empowering today.

2. The redecisional model of TA emphasizes that we react to stresses, receive messages about how we should be in the world, and make early decisions about ourselves and others that become manifest in our current patterns of thinking, feeling, and behaving. In TA groups the members relive the context in which they made these early decisions, and thus they are able to choose new decisions that are functional.

3. Awareness is an important first step in the process of changing our ways of thinking, feeling, and behaving. In the early stages of a group, techniques are aimed at increasing participants' awareness of their problems and their options for making substantive changes in their lives.

4. A basic premise of the TA approach is that people need to receive both physical and psychological "strokes" to develop a sense of trust in the world and a basis for loving themselves.

5. The primary goal of the therapist is to create and develop a meaningful relationship with members within which transformation can occur. The TA therapist pays attention to a working alliance that allows for goals to be mutually arrived at and agreed upon.

6. Decisions about oneself, one's world, and one's relationships to others are crystallized during the first 5 years of life. Such decisions are basic for the formulation of a life position, which develops into the roles of the lifescript.

7. To make new, appropriate decisions, group members are taught to recognize ego states, to understand how injunctions and messages they incorporated as children are affecting them now, and to identify lifescripts that are determining their actions. A basic assumption of TA is that we are in charge of what we do, how we think, and how we feel. People are viewed as being capable of going beyond their early programming and choices by making new choices in the present that will affect their future.

8. TA is largely a didactic and cognitive form of therapy, with the goal of liberating group members from the past and assisting them to redecide how they will live based on new awareness. Ultimately, group members come to realize that they can now initiate a new direction in life, changing what is not working while retaining what serves them well. In a group context members can experience their lifescripts unfolding before them through the interactions within the group. Group members represent family members from the past as well as people in the present. TA members have many opportunities to review and challenge their past decisions and to experiment with new decisions.

9. Members can best achieve their personal goals by being active in the group therapy process. To ensure that members actively and responsibly participate, they contract to work on specific issues, and these contracts direct the course of the group.

10. TA concepts and techniques are particularly appropriate for group work. It is the leader's role and function to create a climate in which people can discover for themselves how the games they are playing support chronic bad feelings and how they are clinging to these dysfunctional feelings to support their lifescripts and their early decisions.

Glossary of Key Terms for Transactional Analysis

- **Adult** An ego state that is the processor of information. It is the analytic, rational, and objective part of personality.
- **Autonomy** Awareness, spontaneity, and capacity for intimacy.
- **Basic psychological life position** A stance that people assume in early childhood regarding their own intrinsic worth and that of others.

- **Child** An ego state that consists of feelings, impulses, and spontaneous acts. This part of the personality can manifest itself in several ways, for example, the "Natural Child" or the "Adapted Child."
- **Contract** Specific and measurable statements of the objectives group participants intend to attain; contracts place the responsibility on members for clearly defining what, how, and when *they* want to change.
- **Controlling (Critical) Parent** An ego state that is critical, harsh, and fault-finding.
- **Counterinjunctions** The counterpart of injunctions that come from the Parent ego state; messages that convey "shoulds" and "oughts."
- **Decisions** A view that people incorporate about themselves based on the injunctions they accept or reject.
- **Ego state** One of the three distinct patterns of behavior and psychological functioning: Parent, Adult, and Child.
- **Games** A series of stereotyped and predictable patterns of behavior designed to prevent intimacy and to provide a negative payoff for at least one player.
- **Injunctions** Parental messages telling children what they have to do and be to get recognition. These messages, which are usually couched in some form of "Don't," may be verbal or nonverbal.
- **Lifescript** An unconscious plan for life made in childhood, reinforced by parents and by subsequent events, and culminating in a chosen alternative.
- **Nurturing Parent** An ego state that is supportive and caring.
- **Parent** An ego state that is an introject of parents and parent substitutes; combines the "shoulds" and "oughts" that individuals collect from significant people in their lives.
- **Psychological strokes** Verbal and nonverbal signs of acceptance and recognition, which are necessary for people to develop a sense of self-worth.
- **Racket** A habitual feeling (depression, guilt, anger, sadness) to which people chronically cling after a game.
- **Redecision** The process of reexperiencing early situations in which we made basic decisions about life, evaluating these decisions, and making new and more appropriate choices about life.
- **Redecision therapy** Aimed at helping people challenge themselves to discover ways in which they perceive themselves in victimlike roles and to take charge of their lives by deciding for themselves how they will change.
- **Script analysis** A process that helps members become aware of how they acquired their lifescript; that part of the therapeutic process by which the life patterns of clients are identified, allowing them to take steps toward changing their programming.
- **Strokes** A form of recognition. Strokes may be positive or negative, conditional or unconditional, physical or psychological.
- **Structural analysis** A tool by which clients become aware of the content and functioning of their ego states of Parent, Child, and Adult.
- **Transaction** An exchange of strokes between two or more people; the basic unit of human communication. Transactions may be complementary, crossed, or ulterior.
- **Transactional analysis (TA)** Both a theory of personality and an organized system of interactional therapy; an approach that emphasizes the cognitive and behavioral aspects of change.

Exercises and Activities for the Transactional Analysis Approach

Rationale

Not all of the following exercises deal with therapeutic procedures routinely used by all TA practitioners; however, they are designed to increase your awareness of matters such as these: In what ego state do you tend to function? What kind of strokes do you typically receive? Which of the parental messages that you picked up early in life do you still live by? How do your decisions made early in life still influence you? What games prevent intimacy? What is the basis for new decisions?

Many of these exercises are cognitively oriented and are geared to get you to think about your assumptions and your behavior. I encourage you to think of imaginative ways of developing your own exercises; for example, experiment with combining some of these cognitively oriented TA concepts with some of the emotionally focused techniques of Gestalt therapy. Use these exercises in your own small groups, and discuss specific aspects of this approach that you think you could use in the groups you lead.

Exercises

1. *The ego states: Parent, Adult, Child.* TA teaches people to recognize when they are operating in their Parent, Adult, and Child ego states. Each person in your group should choose an ego state and remain in it during a group exercise, thinking and speaking from the chosen state. The purpose of this exercise is to help you become aware of how you might function as a Parent without knowing it.

2. *Stroking.* TA stresses the need for strokes, both physical and psychological ones. In your group talk about the specific types of strokes you need to sustain you. What strokes do you seek? How do you get the strokes you want? Are you able to accept positive stroking, or do you have a need to discount it and set yourself up for negative stroking? You could also experiment with asking your group members for the strokes you want. Discuss in your group the idea of conditional strokes. Were you brought up to believe you would get strokes when you behaved in the expected manner? How does this relate to the strokes you get in your group?

3. *Injunctions.* Injunctions are messages we have been programmed to accept—that is, messages we have knowingly and unknowingly incorporated into our lifestyle. In this experiment each group member "becomes" his or her parent and gives injunctions. Each person should adopt the tone of voice he or she imagines the parent would have used. Get involved in the exercise, and really tell people the way you think they should be and should live. As a second part of this exercise, discuss a few of the following injunctions as they apply to you. What are some other messages you heard as a child? Add these to the list. Which of these messages still influence you?

    a. Don't be _____.
    b. You should always do what is expected.
    c. Don't be who you are.
    d. Don't succeed/fail.
    e. Don't trust others.
    f. Be perfect—never make a mistake.
    g. Be more than you are.
    h. Don't be impulsive.
    i. Don't be sexy.

STAGES OF DEVELOPMENT OF THE TRANSACTIONAL ANALYSIS GROUP

Dimension	Initial Stage	Working Stage	Final Stage
Key developmental tasks and goals	Group therapy begins with a contract, one that is acceptable to both member and leader. Group work is guided by the contract. An early basic task is to teach members the basics of TA, including how to recognize ego states, transactions, games, injunctions, rackets, and the significance of early decisions.	The basic developmental task is to recognize and work through impasses. Much work is done with reexperiencing early decisions and situations from childhood, with the aim of making new decisions that are more appropriate for the present. Members think about how they want to be different.	Focus is on actually making new decisions. Basic premise is that what was decided earlier can now be redecided. Members learn to thrive on positive strokes, and they recognize the power they possess. Contracts may be renegotiated, and new work may begin. Emphasis is on applying new learning in daily life.
Role and tasks of group leader	Leaders begin to teach members that they are responsible for how they think, feel, and act. Leaders provide structure for the group, teach the basic concepts of TA, and may use role playing and fantasy to have members relive certain scenes. Leaders help members identify and clarify goals and develop a contract that will specify the work to be done.	The group leader helps members recognize early decisions they made from a Child ego state. Then, from this same ego state, the members are encouraged to make new and more appropriate decisions. Leaders draw on a variety of techniques to help members work through impasses. Group becomes a rehearsal for living.	The leader mainly assists members in making new decisions and life-oriented contracts; members are encouraged to accept responsibility for changing their own lives. Leader challenges members to transfer their changes from the therapy group to daily life. Members are assisted to become their own therapists.
Role of group members	Members are expected to formulate a clear contract. They learn the ego state in which they are functioning, recognize the injunctions they've accepted, and see the importance of understanding and challenging early decisions. They learn the basics of TA and the key concepts they will need to know in participating in the group. Members begin to understand the games they play, along with understanding their lifescripts, basic life positions, and early decisions.	Members learn about the injunction/decision/racket complex. They identify lifescripts. Members work through early experiences both cognitively and affectively. They discover the context in which they accepted injunctions and made early decisions. They explore ways in which they have given their power away, and they experiment with actions geared toward empowerment. Members are expected to refine the contracts and update them.	Members decide how they will change. They may use the group to practice new behaviors. Feedback and support are given. Group members are encouraged to tell a new story in the group to replace their old story. Members devise other support systems outside the group. Members are expected to plan specific ways in which they will change their thinking, feeling, behavior, and body. Members are empowered by choosing new decisions that are more functional.

Techniques	Contracts are a basic tool. Imagery and fantasy techniques may be used. Role playing may be used to promote a here-and-now focus. The other techniques TA leaders tend to use are lifescript analysis and working with injunctions and decisions.	A wide range of cognitive and affective techniques is used, including structural analysis, transactional analysis, analysis of games, cognitive restructuring, empty-chair, lifescript questionnaire, and desensitization. Techniques in TA groups are designed to help members feel more intensely and to think and conceptualize.	Homework assignments may be used as a way of helping the members to fulfill their contracts. Gestalt techniques may be incorporated into the TA group, as may techniques drawn from behavioral methods, psychodrama, and other action-oriented approaches.
Questions to consider	Are you able to obtain a clear and specific contract from each of the members? How can you help members formulate a therapeutic contract? Are these contracts open to renegotiation? Are the members committed to working on them? How does the structure of the group reflect the nature of the members' contracts? What would you most want to teach the members about how a TA group functions? What is your role as leader in this group? What do you expect from the members? What kind of structuring do you most want to provide? To what degree have you explored your own injunctions and early decisions? How might this influence the way you lead your group?	What kind of information would you want to include in a lifescript questionnaire? How might you use this lifescript checklist in your TA group? What are some techniques for focusing on injunctions and early decisions? How can you become aware of members' games, life positions, and lifescripts by paying attention to their transactions with others in the sessions? How might you draw on techniques from Gestalt therapy, psychodrama, and behavior therapy in working with concepts in the TA framework? What are some ways in which you might help members work through early experiences that have an impact on their present behavior?	To what degree have the members recognized early decisions and the lifescript by which they have been living, and to what extent are they making new decisions? Are they acting on these redecisions in the group? Are they taking action outside of the sessions? What new contracts might you make with members as a group approaches the final stage? How can you teach members to find support outside of the group for maintaining the changes? What are some ways to reinforce redecisions by the client and by others in the group? What are some ways to prepare members for some new situations that they will face when they leave the group? How about preparing them for dealing with setbacks?

Reactions: Summarize your reactions to the transactional analysis perspective on group developmental stages. What do you like most? least? What aspects of this approach would you incorporate in your style of leadership?

j. Don't be aggressive.

k. Keep your feelings to yourself.

l. Think of others before yourself.

m. Never have negative thoughts.

Which of these injunctions might you have accepted uncritically? Which of them do you most want to modify? How can you modify them?

4. *Decisions and redecisions.* People tend to cling to early decisions and to look for evidence to support these decisions. However, TA assumes that what has been decided can be re-decided. In your group devote some time to identifying one of your early decisions. Then, determine what you are doing to keep this early decision in your life now. Finally, discuss what you might do to change an early decision so that it does not have an undue influence on you. For example, you may have decided early on to keep all of your negative feelings inside you; you may have been told both directly and indirectly that you were unacceptable when you expressed negative feelings or reactions. In this case you could discuss what you do now in situations where you experience negative reactions. Do you feel that you want to change your old decision?

5. *Exploring your rackets.* In TA a "racket" refers to the collection of bad feelings people use to justify their lifescripts and the feelings on which they base their decisions. Some possible rackets are:

a. an anger racket

b. a guilt racket

c. a hurt racket

d. a depression racket

For instance, if you develop a depression racket, you may actually seek out situations that will support your feelings of depression. You will continually do things to make yourself feel depressed, and thus you will feel this way enough of the time to be able to convince yourself that you are right to have these feelings. In your group spend time exploring how you may at times maintain old, chronic, bad feelings. What might be one of your major rackets? List some recent situations that you put yourself in or found yourself in that led to old, familiar feelings of depression, guilt, or the like.

6. *Games we play.* In this group exercise devote some time to listing some of the games that you played as a child to get what you wanted. For example, perhaps you played the Help-lessness Game. If you act helpless and pretend you cannot do something, others may treat you as helpless and do for you what you really don't want to do for yourself. Although you did get something from the game, you might consider whether the price you paid was worth what you got. In your group discuss some games you played as a child, then list what you got from each one. What games do you play now? Discuss what you get from these games. Evaluate the costs. What do you think you'd be like if you gave up these games?

7. *Life positions.* There are four basic life positions in TA:

I'm OK—You're OK.	*or*	I Count—You Count.
I'm OK—You're not OK.	*or*	I Count—You don't Count.
I'm not OK—You're OK.	*or*	I don't Count—You do Count.
I'm not OK—You're not OK.	*or*	I don't Count—You don't Count.

In small groups, take turns describing your life positions and explaining how they affect your life. To what degree do you genuinely like and appreciate yourself? Do you feel that you count as a person? What contributes to feeling that you matter or to feeling that your existence does not count? What are some of the situations that contribute to feelings of inadequacy that you may experience at times? How might you challenge these feelings? If we hope to change the life course that we are on, it helps to understand the components of this script, which to a large extent determine our patterns of thinking, feeling, and behaving.

8. *Changes in your life circumstances.* You may have felt basically inadequate as a child, yet now you may feel very adequate in many areas of your life. What factors do you think are responsible for this shift in the way you feel about yourself?

9. *A book of you.* Write your own table of contents for a book about your life, and then give your book a title. What title best captures the sense of your life now? What would you include in the chapters? Mention the key turning points and key events of your life in your table of contents so that others in your group will have a picture of who you are. Now, assume you want to revise your book. What revisions do you want to make, chapter by chapter? Do you want a new book title?

10. *"You are your parents" exercise.* This exercise can be done with a partner or in small groups. It will provide a format for looking at the influence your parents have on you and the quality of life you see your parents experiencing, and it will help you decide how you'd like to modify your own values and behavior. Close your eyes and see your parents at their present ages in a typical setting. Visualize the way they live. How is their marriage? How do they react to their children? What kind of life do they have? Now imagine yourself at their ages in the same setting. For a few minutes imagine that you value what they do and that your life is almost identical with theirs. In what ways would you modify the outcomes of this visualization exercise?

11. *Early decisions.* Assume that you are a group leader and that you determine that certain members have made the following decisions. Speculate about what factors may have contributed to each of these decisions:
    a. I'll always be a failure.
    b. I'm basically weak and helpless.
    c. I won't feel, and that way I won't experience pain.
    d. Regardless of what I accomplish, I'll never be good enough.

12. *Redecision work in groups.* Take the four statements above and assume that each of them represents a life orientation. How would you proceed in working with each of these approaches toward life? What new decisions would you like to see made? What would it take to change these decisions?

13. *Contracts.* TA groups work on a contract basis, which means that members clearly specify what they want to change as well as what they are willing to do to change. What do you think of the use of contracts in groups? If you were to become involved as a client in a TA group, what are some contracts you'd be willing to make? List one such contract, including a specific statement of some behavior you want to change and the steps you'd be willing to take to make this change.

14. *Personal critique.* What is your personal evaluation of the TA approach to group work? Consider questions such as the following in your critique:
    a. To what clients do you think TA is best suited?
    b. What contributions of TA do you think are most significant?
    c. What are the major limitations of TA? Explain.

d. What are the strengths and weaknesses of TA as applied to multicultural populations?

e. On what specific concepts from TA might you draw in working with ethnically diverse clients?

Questions for Reflection and Discussion

1. To what degree do you think children are "scripted" and then destined to live out their lives in accord with this script? Do you think children actually make decisions about the messages they receive, or do you think they accept the injunctions uncritically? How does your answer influence the manner in which you would work with a group?

2. Consider the possibility that you might be a leader of a TA group. How do you think your patterns of games, rackets, and early decisions would affect the way you worked with certain members in your group? Using what you know of yourself, are there any members with whom you might have particular difficulty working?

3. TA is generally a didactic model of group therapy. Would you be comfortable in the role of teaching, along with the structuring that would be expected if you were to function within this model? What aspects of this educational model might you incorporate into your style of group leadership, even if you did not adhere to TA theory?

4. TA is direct. As a leader you would be talking with participants about the games they play and the ways they cling to chronic bad feelings. To what degree do you think you would be able to be direct in working with members of your group to recognize their games and to help them design contracts for what they would change?

5. Compare and contrast TA with psychoanalytic therapy with respect to the group leader's role and functions. Which role seems more compatible with your leadership style and view of group counseling? Why?

6. A contract is a basic part of a TA group. How do you think you'd proceed with one or more group members who refused to negotiate a contract with you? What might you do with a member who argued that making a contract seemed rigid?

7. With its emphasis on personal responsibility and freedom, TA can be considered an existential approach to psychotherapy. Both existential therapy and TA emphasize the importance of clients assuming responsibility for their lives. How might you apply these principles if you were doing a group with involuntary members who denied responsibility for their problems and life situation?

8. In a TA group, both women and men can identify societal messages and stereotypes of what it means to be a female or a male. To what degree would you encourage members to question the messages regarding gender-role expectations that they may have received from their culture?

An Expert's Perspective on Transactional Analysis: by Mark E. Young

MARK E. YOUNG, PhD, is Professor of Counseling at University of Central Florida.

1. What attracted you to this particular theoretical orientation? How does this theory fit with the person you are?

I was attracted to transactional analysis (TA) because it focused not merely on personality and intrapsychic therapy but showed the relationship of personality to how we interact with others. It explained how one's background can shape the lifescript and how that script is played out unconsciously in the person's life. At the time I first learned about TA, I was working with a divorced client who was depressed and rather dependent. She was adopted at age 12 and had been in foster homes for years. When we moved her to group, at first she was accepted by the other members as being a fragile person that needed help. Soon they got tired of her complaining and unwillingness to change. I was able to see how her history manifested interpersonally as an "I'm not OK, You're OK" script. You could say that her ineffective way of getting attention and recognition was the result of a "Poor Me" game. The client eventually recognized how she was evoking rejection through her strategy of appearing helpless and hopeless. Her contract in the group was to "Ask for what I need." Thus, she didn't have to play a game of being fragile to get a hug, attention or talk about a problem.

This insight into how a person's unconscious intentions dramatically affect interpersonal behavior still fits for me. When a client is boring, aggressive, pitiful, or demanding in group, instead of thinking, "What's wrong with this person?" I think, "What is he or she trying to get from the group with this behavior?" A part of traditional TA that does not fit as well for me is teaching the client the jargon and mechanics of TA. Using words like "games," "rackets," and "cold pricklies" can be perceived as stigmatizing and tends to cheapen the important dynamics that they are describing.

2. What Key Concepts (1 to 3) of this theory are most applicable to the practice of group counseling?

Decisions and redecisions: Clients make decisions early in life about how they are going to interact with others and about the safety of relationships. They may be based on negative experiences or injunctions from parents. These include: "You can't trust anyone but your family," "Don't air your dirty laundry in public," "Most people will take advantage of you if you let them," or even, as one client said to me, "Love is chains." There comes a time when the group or the leader must confront a member's tendency to act in a particular pattern and challenge the client to "redecide" the story of his or her life. At such times, clients may recoil and say, "But that's just the way I am." The culture of the group should reinforce the notion that change is possible and that what we decided early on is a kind of a wall. Certainly it protects, but it also becomes a prison.

3. What Techniques (1 to 3) from this theory have the most practical value for group work practitioners?

Contracts: One of the principles of group therapy, championed by Claude Steiner, was the importance of a contract between the client and the group. The contract should be simple enough for an 8-year-old to understand, and it is designed by the leader in front of the group with each individual member. At first the client proposes that she would like to improve her relationship with her significant other. But this is rejected by the group and the leader as inappropriate. How could she work on that relationship in the group? How would the group know when she was not doing it? Through this refining process, the client's eventual goal evolved: "To become more open about my feelings, both positive and negative." The client agreed that withholding her emotions, thoughts, and opinions was a significant problem in her outside relationship and she could use the group as a laboratory for trying out new behavior.

The beauty of the contract is that every member knows what is expected of him or her. Without being confrontational, the leader can ask, "Tell me again, what is your contract?" Group members can identify client change when it occurs, sometimes before the leader or the client can notice it. The group can also tell the client when he or she is not practicing. Even more exciting is the fact that two members' contracts can coincide and work synergistically. If one member is working on expressing and the other is learning to listen, each can be fulfilling a different contract at the same time.

4. How does this theory have particular relevance for addressing diversity and social justice issues in group work?

I believe transactional analysis does have relevance for addressing diversity and has historically been concerned with social justice. Without going into a long history, it is important to note that Eric Berne was concerned with, and wrote about, culture and comparative psychiatry as early as 1939. In 1961, he wrote one of the first papers on cultural factors in group psychotherapy. More important, he was one of the first to break down the barriers between client and therapist and advocate an Adult to Adult contract, holding case conferences with the client present. After his death in 1970, a number of his adherents and chief collaborators began to discuss "radical psychiatry," which took Berne's ideas in a political direction consistent with the turbulent times. Their mantra was, "Therapy means change, not adjustment." This decreed that the therapist should always push for the individual to change himself or the system, not merely to adjust to societal demands. In many ways, this approach is consistent with Berne's ideas about equality, justice, and equitable treatment for clients. Even today the TA practitioner is concerned about a clear contract for change.

5. Raise a question from this theoretical framework that you consider especially important for group work practice.

How can I become a competent group leader according to TA? In essence there are three steps. First, formal education (especially in the neglected area of group dynamics); second, engaging in self-examination through becoming a client in a group; and third, self-correction, which means that the leader must examine the games he or she is playing in supervision and in therapy. For example, "Am I seeking approval from this very intelligent client rather than confronting her?"

Your Thoughts on Dr. Young's Perspective on Transactional Analysis Groups

1. What relevance do you see transactional analysis playing in dealing with social justice and multicultural issues?
2. What advantages do you see in using a contractual approach in group work? Are you interesting in using contracts in group you lead? Why or why not?
3. What are some possibilities of working with decisions and redecisions in groups?

Quiz on the Transactional Analysis Approach to Groups:
A Comprehension Check

Score ____%

Note: Please refer to Appendix I for the scoring key. Count 5 points for each error, and subtract the total from 100 to get your percentage score.

True/false items: Decide if the following statements are "more true" or "more false" as they apply to TA.

T F 1. TA tends to stress the experiential aspects of therapy and underplays the cognitive dimensions.

T F 2. A basic premise of TA is that once we make a decision in childhood we become scripted, which means that the decision is irreversible.

T F 3. Injunctions are given from the Child ego state of the parents.

T F 4. The TA group leader considers it essential to recognize and fully work through transference.

T F 5. TA shares with Gestalt therapy the basic assumption that awareness is an important first step in changing our ways of thinking, feeling, and behaving.

T F 6. Script analysis is aimed at helping members understand ways to change their early programming.

T F 7. The analysis of the lifescript of a group member is based on the drama of his or her original family.

T F 8. The TA therapist will expect the members to formulate a contract to guide the sessions.

T F 9. According to the Gouldings, people are scripted in a passive way.

T F 10. Berne's position is that people are to a large degree the victims of their injunctions.

Multiple-choice items: Select the *one best answer* among the alternatives given. Consider each question within the framework of TA.

_____11. Redecision therapy, as introduced by the Gouldings, is done primarily in the context of
a. individual therapy.
b. couples therapy.
c. family therapy.
d. group therapy.

_____12. Redecision therapy integrates TA concepts with techniques drawn from all the following approaches except
a. psychodrama.
b. family therapy.
c. fantasy and imagery.
d. Gestalt therapy.
e. person-centered therapy.

_____13. A contribution of TA to counseling with ethnically diverse clients is
a. its focus on dreams.
b. the structure it provides to help clients understand how their culture has influenced them.

c. the abundance of research on TA theory as it is applied to working with culturally diverse client populations.

d. the fact that TA always begins by exploring the client's cultural background.

_____14. The unpleasant feelings people experience after a game are called

a. injunctions.

b. parental messages.

c. script analyses.

d. rackets.

e. life positions.

_____15. Looking ahead, TA seems to be

a. getting more and more complex.

b. going back to its psychoanalytic roots.

c. moving toward becoming more and more cognitive.

d. focusing more on encouraging clients to emotionally reexperience crucial experiences when early decisions were made.

e. merging with Adlerian concepts.

_____16. Which of the following is not a key concept of TA?

a. strokes

b. rackets

c. lifestyle assessment

d. lifescripts

e. games

_____17. According to TA theory, strokes are

a. necessary only for highly dependent people.

b. necessary for healthy development.

c. needed for children but not for adults.

d. needed only in times of crisis.

_____18. Messages that are given from the Child ego state of the parents are known as

a. rackets.

b. lifescripts.

c. games.

d. injunctions.

e. counterinjunctions.

_____19. Messages that come from the Parent ego state of the parents are known as

a. rackets.

b. lifescripts.

c. games.

d. injunctions.

e. counterinjunctions.

_____20. Collections of bad feelings that people use to justify their lifescripts are known as

a. rackets.

b. counterinjunctions.

c. games.

d. injunctions.

e. basic decisions.

CHAPTER THIRTEEN

Cognitive Behavioral Approaches to Groups

Prechapter Self-Inventory for the Cognitive Behavioral Approach

Directions: Refer to page 77 for general directions. Indicate your position on these statements using the following code:

5 = I *strongly agree* with this statement.
4 = I *agree,* in most respects, with this statement.
3 = I am *undecided* in my opinion about this statement.
2 = I *disagree,* in most respects, with this statement.
1 = I *strongly disagree* with this statement.

_____ 1. Self-reinforcement is needed if participants hope to transfer the changes made in a group to everyday life.

_____ 2. Assessment is a necessary step in the initial phase of a group.

_____ 3. Evaluation of results is best done continually during all the phases of a group.

_____ 4. For change to occur, members must actively participate in group work, and they must be willing to practice outside of group sessions.

_____ 5. Specific goals increase the chances that members will do productive group work.

_____ 6. Members can change without having insight into their underlying dynamics.

_____ 7. Groups should aim at helping participants develop specific skills and self-directed methods of changing.

_____ 8. A good working relationship between the leader and members is a necessary, but not a sufficient, condition for change.

_____ 9. Mindfulness practices can be incorporated in a cognitive behavioral group.

_____ 10. Any group techniques or therapeutic procedures are best evaluated by both the group members and the leader to determine their effectiveness in meeting goals.

Summary of Basic Assumptions and Key Concepts of Cognitive Behavioral Group Therapy

1. The specific unique characteristics of cognitive behavior therapy include: (1) conducting an assessment, (2) precisely spelling out collaborative treatment goals, (3) formulating a specific treatment procedure appropriate to a particular problem, and (4) objectively evaluating the outcomes of therapy. Data-based assessment is a part of the treatment procedure, and there is a focus on transferring new skills learned in the group to everyday situations.

2. A basic assumption is that all problematic behaviors, cognitions, and emotions have been learned and that they can be modified by new learning. The behaviors clients express are considered to be the problem rather than merely symptoms of the problem.

3. Cognitive restructuring is based on the theory that our thoughts are causally linked to our behavior and emotions; the route to changing behavior and emotion is to change negative or self-defeating cognitions.

4. Group therapy is seen as a present-centered psychoeducational process whereby members are encouraged to try out more effective behaviors, cognitions, and emotions. The group leader does not focus on the member's past, or on unconscious material; rather, the focus is on changing dysfunctional thoughts and actions.

5. The structured nature of a cognitive behavioral groups appeals to many who facilitate psycho-educational groups, and this approach is becoming increasingly popular for many client groups and work settings. Cognitive behavioral group therapy is an efficient form of treatment for a wide range of specific problems for diverse client populations.

6. Cognitive behavioral practitioners use a time-limited, active, directive, transparent, collaborative, present-focused, didactic, evidence-based approach that relies on empirical validation of its concepts and techniques.

7. Members of a group are involved in a teaching and learning process and are taught how to develop a new perspective on ways of learning. The members must actively participate in the group work and be willing to experiment with new behavior by taking a role in bringing about changes in their thinking and behavior.

8. There are a wide variety of techniques, and cognitive behavioral group counselors have a great deal of flexibility in adapting techniques for the needs of group members. Practitioners from any orientation are able to profit from drawing on behavioral interventions and incorporating them in their group work.

9. The group leader is active and directive, functioning in some ways as a teacher. Some of the leader's functions include organizing the group, orienting and teaching members about group process, assessing problems and developing ways of resolving them, evaluating the progress of group sessions, planning procedures for change, modifying group attributes, and establishing transfer and maintenance programs for new behaviors. Cognitive behavioral leaders assess group problems as they arise. Data on group satisfaction, completion of assignments, participation, and attendance are typically collected and used as a basis for determining problems. Once the problems are identified and acknowledged by the members, they are dealt with by means of systematic procedures.

10. It is important for group leaders to help their clients assess the possible consequences of some of their newly acquired social skills within a particular cultural context. Group leaders need to be mindful of how cultural values can influence the behaviors of members, and they should help these members assess the advantages and disadvantages of making life changes.

11. A basic assumption is that a good working relationship between the leader and members is important in producing positive outcomes. With a sound working relationship, leaders can provide immediate social reinforcement for desired behaviors, model effective interpersonal skills, promote engagement in the therapy process, encourage clients to complete homework assignments, and build a sense of collaboration toward treatment goals.

12. The field of behavior therapy has significantly changed and continues to evolve. The theoretical foundations of behavior therapy have broadened, and the treatment strategies have become more diverse. As behavior therapy continues to expand, it increasingly overlaps with other theoretical approaches to therapy.

13. *Third-generation behavior therapies* (also called *third wave* approaches) emphasize mindfulness, acceptance, the therapeutic relationship, spirituality, values, meaning and purpose in one's life, meditation, being in the present moment, and emotional expression. These newer approaches are making an impact on behavior therapy, especially in treating a wide range of clinical problems.

14. Contemporary behavior therapy has much in common with cognitive behavior therapy in which the mechanism of change is both cognitive (modifying thoughts to change behaviors) and behavioral (altering external factors that lead to behavior change).

Glossary of Key Terms for Cognitive Behavior Therapy

- **Acceptance** A process involving receiving our present experience without judgment or preference, but with curiosity and kindness. Acceptance is an attitude of striving for full awareness of the present moment.

- **Acceptance and commitment therapy (ACT)** A program based on encouraging clients to accept, rather than attempt to control or change, unpleasant sensations.

- **Automatic thoughts** Personalized notions that are triggered by particular stimuli that lead to emotional responses.

- **Behavioral assessment** A set of procedures used to get information that will guide the development of a tailor-made treatment plan for each client and help measure the effectiveness of treatment.

- **Behavior rehearsal** Trying out new behaviors in a group session that are to be applied in everyday situations.

- **Behavior therapy** Refers to the application of diverse techniques and procedures that are rooted in a variety of learning theories.

- **Buddy system** A therapeutic alliance between members whereby they monitor and coach one another both inside and outside of the group.

- **Coaching** Providing members with general principles for carrying out specific forms of effective behaviors.

- **Cognitive behavior therapy** An approach that blends both cognitive and behavioral methods to bring about change.

- **Cognitive restructuring** Actively altering maladaptive thought patterns and replacing them with more realistic and constructive thoughts.

- **Cognitive therapy** An approach that perceives psychological problems as stemming from commonplace processes such as faulty thinking, making incorrect inferences on the basis of inadequate or incorrect information, and failing to distinguish between fantasy and reality.

- **Collaborative empiricism** A process through which the group leader assists members in forming hypotheses and testing their assumptions. Through a collaborative effort, group members learn to discriminate between their own thoughts and events that occur in reality.

- **Coping skills** A behavioral procedure for helping clients deal effectively with stressful situations by learning to modify their thinking patterns.

- **Dialectical behavior therapy (DBT)** A blend of cognitive behavioral and psychoanalytic techniques that generally involves a minimum of one year of treatment. This approach makes use of mindfulness and was developed to help clients regulate emotions and behavior associated with depression.
- **Feedback** Providing verbal reactions to behaviors of others in the group.
- **Mindfulness** Becoming increasingly observant and aware of external and internal stimuli in the present moment and adopting an open attitude toward accepting what is, rather than judging the current situation.
- **Mindfulness-based cognitive therapy (MBCT)** A comprehensive integration of the principles and skills of mindfulness applied to the treatment of depression.
- **Mindfulness-based stress reduction (MBSR)** A program developed mainly by Jon Kabat-Zinn that involves 8- to 10-week group sessions in which mindfulness techniques are applied to cope with stress and promote physical and psychological health.
- **Modeling** Learning through observation and imitation.
- **Multimethod group approach** The use of various coping strategies for dealing with specific problems, such as cognitive restructuring, problem solving, and behavioral rehearsal.
- **Problem solving** A cognitive behavioral technique that teaches individuals a method of dealing with their problems.
- **Reinforcement** A specified event that strengthens the tendency for a response to be repeated. In groups, social reinforcement is provided by the group leader and by other members.
- **Self-management** A collection of strategies based on the idea that change can be brought about by teaching people to use coping skills in problematic situations such as anxiety, depression, and pain.
- **Self-monitoring** The process of observing one's own behavior patterns as well as one's interactions in various social situations.
- **Social effectiveness training (or SET)** A multifaceted treatment program designed to reduce social anxiety, improve interpersonal skills, and increase the range of enjoyable social activities.
- **Social learning theory** A perspective, developed primarily by Albert Bandura, holding that behavior is best understood by taking into consideration the social conditions under which learning occurs.
- **Social skills training (or SST)** Behavioral techniques that are aimed at teaching members how to interact effectively with others.
- **Stress inoculation training** A form of cognitive behavior modification developed by Meichenbaum that involves educational, rehearsal, and application phases. Clients learn the role of thinking in creating stress and are given a set of skills to deal with future stressful situations.
- **Stress management training** An approach that teaches clients how to detect sources of stress and to learn methods of coping adequately with stress.
- **Therapeutic collaboration** A process whereby the therapist actively strives to engage the client's active participation in all phases of therapy.
- **Therapeutic homework** Aimed at putting into action what members explore during a group session; the attempt to integrate what takes place within the group with everyday life.
- **Third-generation behavior therapies** A term used interchangeably with "third wave approaches," these therapies include acceptance and mindfulness-based approaches.

Exercises and Activities for the Cognitive Behavioral Approach

Rationale

Cognitive behavioral group leaders use a variety of specific techniques. These evidence-based practices are used systematically to accomplish particular goals, and both the group members and the leader determine whether these methods are producing positive results. If members are not making progress, the therapeutic procedures can be modified. It is basic to the cognitive behavioral approach that therapeutic procedures and evaluation of these techniques proceed simultaneously.

Most of the cognitive behavioral techniques are designed to effect specific changes in thinking and bring about behavioral changes—that is, either to decrease or eliminate undesirable behaviors or to acquire or increase desired behaviors. The following exercises will show you ways to use learning principles in your work to change members' thoughts and behavior. You can apply many of the techniques presented in these exercises to your own life. As you experiment with these techniques in your small group or in class, determine which aspects of the cognitive behavioral approaches you would incorporate in your work as a group leader, regardless of the theoretical model you might be working with.

Exercises

1. *Setting up a cognitive behavioral group.* Assume that you are a cognitive behavioral group leader and are giving a talk at a gathering in a community where you hope to begin a group. What points would you emphasize to give these people a good picture of your group, your functions and role as a leader, and your expectations of them as participants? Assume that they respond enthusiastically and want to join your group. Where would you begin, and how would you proceed in setting up this group? What pregroup concerns would you have? What would you do during the initial meeting?

2. *Terminating and evaluating a group.* Assume that the above group meets for 20 weeks. It is now the 18th week. What specific issues would you be concerned with as a group leader? What evaluation procedures would you employ at the end of the group? What follow-up procedures would you use?

3. *Group leaders as skilled technicians.* Cognitive behavioral group leaders must be skilled technicians who also possess the human qualities that lead to the climate of trust and care necessary for the effective use of therapeutic techniques. From a cognitive behavioral perspective, what emphasis would you place on your relationships with the members of your groups? What specific skills do you see yourself as having that would be useful in a group? What are a few examples of skills that you would either like to acquire or refine as ways of enhancing your ability to function from a cognitive behavioral perspective? Discuss this in a group, and collectively generate a list of skills cognitive behavioral leaders need to possess.

4. *Relaxation exercises.* Many cognitive behavioral group therapists use self-relaxation techniques. Members are taught how to systematically relax every part of their body. They practice in the group and also daily at home. In your own group, one member can volunteer to lead a tension/relaxation procedure, going from head to foot. After the exercise discuss the possibilities for using relaxation procedures in any group. What is the value of

STAGES OF DEVELOPMENT OF THE COGNITIVE BEHAVIORAL THERAPY GROUP

Dimension	Initial Stage	Working Stage	Final Stage
Key developmental tasks and goals	Responsibilities and expectations of both the leaders and the members are outlined in a contract. Preparation of members is stressed. At the early stages the focus is on building cohesion, getting familiar with the structure of group therapy, and identifying problems to explore. Assessment is a vital aspect as is setting clear goals. A treatment plan, including procedures to be used to attain the stated goals, is developed and is constantly evaluated to test its effectiveness. Collaborative relationships are stressed from the beginning.	Treatment plan is implemented. A wide range of treatment procedures is used to solve specific problems, and the focus is on learning skills. Central part of this phase is work done outside of the group. The group is used as a place to learn and perfect skills and to gain support and feedback so that progress continues. Much of the learning in the group takes place through modeling and observation along with coaching. The emphasis is on identifying dysfunctional thoughts and behaviors and learning new skills as opposed to the exploration of feelings.	At this phase the transfer of learning from the group to everyday life is critical. Situations that simulate the real world are used so that this transfer is facilitated. Focus is on learning self-directed behavior and developing plans for maintaining and using new coping skills. It is assumed that the generalization of learning will not occur by chance, so sessions are structured in such a manner that transfer of learning will be maximized. Relapse prevention is emphasized at the ending stage.
Role and tasks of group leader	Leader's tasks are to conduct pregroup interviews and screen members, organize the group, prepare the members by telling them how the group will work, establish group trust and cohesion, assess the nature of the problems to be explored, and provide a structure for the group. Leaders are active, and they provide information. They assist members in formulating specific goals. Leaders model appropriate behavior and values. They offer reinforcement to members for acquiring newly developed skills and behaviors. They emphasize the importance of members taking action and planning for change.	Leaders develop an appropriate treatment plan based on the initial assessment, and they monitor those behaviors identified as problematic. They continually assess progress and teach them the members self-evaluation skills. Leaders reinforce desired behavior, and they assist members in learning methods of self-reinforcement. Leaders model, coach, and provide corrective feedback. They encourage members to form therapeutic alliances with one another. Leaders help members gradually increase their participation and involvement in setting new goals and making decisions.	Main function of leaders at this phase is to assist members in learning ways to transfer new skills to situations in daily life. They prepare members for dealing with setbacks and teach them skills needed to meet new situations effectively. Leaders arrange for follow-up interviews to assess the impact of the group and to determine the degree to which members have fulfilled their contracts. Leaders help members in preparing for generalization and maintenance of change. They overtrain members in the desired target behaviors. They devise ways of evaluating the effectiveness of a group and help members make a self-evaluation.

Role of group members	Members are involved in formulating the contract. They make a list of behaviors they want to change, or they clarify the problems they want to work on in the group. They determine baseline data for certain behaviors and begin to monitor and to observe their behavior in the group as well. The members are involved in the assessment process, which continues throughout the group. Members learn to identify their self-defeating cognitions.	Members report on the nature of their progress each week. Group time is used to define problem areas to work on in the group. Role playing of a cognitive behavioral nature is done to assist members in learning new skills. Members provide models for one another: they carry out specific behavioral assignments, keep records of their progress, assess their progress in light of the baseline data collected at the initial sessions, and report to the group each week.	Members decide what specific things they've learned in the group situation, and they practice new roles and behaviors, both in the group and in daily life. Feedback is provided so that skills and new behavior can be refined, and suggestions are made for maintaining these new behavioral changes. Members act as a support system for one another. They typically agree to carry out specific assignments at the end of a group and then report back at a follow-up meeting.
Techniques	Basic techniques include contracts, checklists, role playing, and assessment devices.	Many cognitive behavioral techniques are used, including reinforcement, modeling, desensitization, cognitive methods, cognitive restructuring, and homework.	Feedback is a main technique, as are role playing and developing self-reinforcement. Follow-up sessions are scheduled to assess outcomes.
Questions to consider	Central function of leader is to create trust needed for work on issues. In doing this, leader must strive to make the group attractive to members, create many functional roles that they can play in the group, and find ways to involve all members in the group interactions. How can you best carry out these tasks? How can you help the members develop specific and concrete goals? Are the goals that are established meaningful for the members? Have they been developed by the members and leader in a spirit of cooperation? What are specific things you expect of members?	In what ways will you assist members in assessment, monitoring, and evaluation throughout the working stage? How might you involve the members in developing a treatment plan for a group? What kind of structuring would you want to provide in a behavioral group? What specific behaviors would you most want to reinforce in members? In what ways might you involve other members in one person's work? How could you use members to provide assistance to one another between sessions? What ways could you think of to use a buddy system?	How can you change your role from that of a direct therapist to a consultant during the final stage? How can you encourage the members to assume an increasing share of the leadership tasks? What self-help skills and problem-solving strategies would you want to teach members as a group is approaching termination? What kinds of short-term and long-term follow-up sessions might you consider setting up before a group ends? Along with members, how can you evaluate the effectiveness of a given group?

Reactions: Summarize your reactions to the behavioral perspective on group developmental stages. What do you like *most? least?* What aspects of this approach would you incorporate in your style of leadership?

such procedures? Consider practicing these exercises to reduce stress. Give them at least a 3-week trial to determine some personal benefits.

5. *Social reinforcement.* Observe in your own class or group how social reinforcement works. For what are members reinforced? Pay attention to *nonverbal* responses, such as smiles, head nodding, and body posture, as well as verbal support and approval. Do you see ways you can systematically use social reinforcement in a group situation? What social reinforcers have the most impact on your behavior?

6. *Modeling.* Think about the importance you place on your role as a leader in modeling for members. Consider factors such as clear and direct speech, self-disclosure, respect, enthusiasm, sensitivity, respect for diversity, and caring confrontation. In your group discuss how you can model positive behavior. Also, observe the effect of a certain behavior on your group (for example, speaking enthusiastically). Do you notice that members tend to assume some of the traits of the leader? What are the implications of this influence? In addition to your own modeling as a group leader, participants can function as models, which will enhance observational learning on the part of other members. In what ways can you shape a group norm for this type of modeling? What behaviors would you like to see modeled in your groups?

7. *Behavior rehearsal in groups.* The aim of behavior rehearsal is to prepare members to perform desired behaviors outside the group, when modeling cues will not be available. Behavioral rehearsal is an integral part of modeling as members are typically asked to participate by performing a behavior immediately after it has been modeled for them. Feedback is a useful mechanism of change during behavior rehearsals. If you are in a small group, think of a particular behavior that you are willing to rehearse, and participate in a behavior rehearsal that you would want to carry out in your daily life. What possibilities do you see of using behavioral rehearsals in groups that you may be leading?

8. *Social skills training in groups: An introduction.* Assume that you are giving a talk to people who might be interested in joining the social skills training group you are forming. What would you tell them about your group? What are some examples of social skills that members might learn and practice? For whom is the group intended? How can it help them? What would they do in this group? What are some of the techniques you'd use during the group sessions? For this exercise, two group members can be the coleaders and explain the rationale for the group to the potential members; the others in the group can ask questions relating to what they will be expected to do in the group, how these activities will help them in daily life, and how they can apply what they learn.

9. *Stress management training in groups.* Review the section in the textbook on a group approach to stress management, especially Meichenbaum's stress inoculation program. Imagine that you are a participant in such a training group. What factors in your life contribute to your experience of stress? Identify some of your cognitions (beliefs or self-talk) that play a role in creating and maintaining stress. Consider keeping an open-ended diary in which you systematically record specific thoughts, feelings, and behaviors for at least 2 weeks. This process can be useful in teaching you to become aware of your own role in creating your stress. If you are in a group at this time, consider bringing into a session a specific concern about stress. After working on this concern in your group, develop a plan that will lead to practice in daily life situations. Assume that you want to begin a stress management group in your agency. What specific steps would you take in forming this group? What cognitive

behavioral techniques would you use? How would you explain the purpose of your group to prospective members?

10. *Mindfulness and acceptance-based approaches in groups.* Acceptance-based approaches that typically incorporate mindfulness skills training are becoming an increasingly important part of cognitive behavioral groups. Mindfulness practice involves training ourselves to focus our attention on our present experiencing without judging it. Some mindfulness skills include focusing on breathing, noting our present activity, identifying and labeling feelings, accepting all feelings, letting thoughts flow, assuming a nonjudgmental stance, and doing one thing at a time. What do you think about the relatively recent broadening of the cognitive behavioral approaches to include mindfulness and acceptance-based skills into therapeutic practice? What are some ways that you would like to incorporate mindfulness in your daily life? What are some specific ways that you might want to use mindfulness and acceptance-based strategies in your groups?

11. *Working on specific goals.* A real value of the behavioral approach is its specificity—its ability to translate broad goals into specific ones. State some broad goals you'd like to attain. Then, in your group, practice making these goals concrete. Make them specific to the degree that you actually *know* what it is that you want and can thus measure progress toward them. As a second part of this exercise, assume that members in one of your groups make the following kinds of broad and vague statements. Can you think of ways to make these goals clear and concrete?

a. "I'd like to be more spontaneous." Concrete goal is: _____

_____

_____

_____

_____

b. "I need to learn how to get in touch with my feelings." Concrete goal is: _____

_____

_____

_____

_____

c. "My goal is to become a more autonomous and actualized person." Concrete goal is: ____

_____

_____

_____

_____

d. "I have many fears that get in my way of living the way I want." Concrete goal is: _____

_____

_____

_____

_____

e. "I'd like to be able to relate better." Concrete goal is: _____

_____

_____

_____

_____

f. "I'd like to feel better." Concrete goal is: _____

_____

_____

_____

_____

g. "My goal is to understand myself better." Concrete goal is: _____

_____

_____

_____

_____

h. "I want to live better." Concrete goal is: _____

_____

_____

_____

_____

12. *Developing a treatment plan.* Building on the task that you accomplished in the previous activity, collaborate with other members of your group to develop a treatment plan that will address your specific goals. Assist other members in developing their treatment plans as well. Process the activity as a group afterward.

13. *Creating and carrying out homework.* Based on the goals you established in Exercise 11 and the treatment plan you developed in Exercise 12, brainstorm potential homework assignments that you could assign to yourself. Get input from your group. When you have come up with a list of options, identify the ones that you would most likely carry out. Consider how you would use homework as a tool in the groups that you lead. What would you do if certain members consistently fail to do their homework?

14. *Applying problem-solving strategies to everyday problems.* The seven stages in the problem-solving process are described in the text. Identify a problem in your life and use the seven-stage model to arrive at a solution. How effective is this approach to working through problems? Does this approach lend itself to solving particular types of problems or all problems?

15. *Groups designed for self-directed change.* Assume that you want to organize a group for people who are interested in self-directed change. For example, they may be interested in stopping smoking, taking weight off and keeping it off, or improving their self-discipline at work. How would you design a group of this nature?

16. *Applying a self-directed program to yourself.* In your group or class discuss the specific behavior you want to work on during the semester. Next, decide what you are willing to do

to change this behavior. Draw up a specific contract, and include details. (For instance, "I will lose 10 pounds by the end of the semester, regulate my eating habits, and ride a bicycle for 75 minutes a day for the rest of the semester.") Then practice your program, and report your progress to your group. Ask a fellow student to support you if you get discouraged or find that you have difficulty sticking to your program.

17. *Cognitive restructuring in groups.* Identify a few major cognitions that have a negative impact on the way people behave. Think of common self-defeating statements that you have heard. Can you think of some methods for helping group members challenge negative cognitions and also develop a new and more effective set of beliefs and thoughts? Can you think of possible homework assignments to supplement the work done in the group sessions? What steps might you suggest to members in learning new ways of thinking?

18. *Self-reinforcement methods.* Cognitive behavioral group work teaches members how to reinforce themselves so that they are not dependent on external rewards to maintain newly acquired skills. In your class or group, experiment with ways you can *reinforce yourself* after successes. Brainstorm this topic in your group. Self-reinforcement may involve learning ways to praise yourself *and* at the same time remind yourself of certain realities that you tend to forget. An example is writing notes to yourself and putting them on the mirror. These notes could say "I am worthwhile," "I am enough," "I have a right to my own feelings," "I'll like myself better if I treat myself with regard," or "I can take time for myself."

19. *Guidelines for applying cognitive behavioral methods with children and adolescents.* A number of cognitive and behavioral concepts and strategies are useful in group work in the schools. Here are some suggestions for working within a behavioral framework with a variety of groups in a school setting:

_____ Cognitive behavioral groups fit well with the restrictions often imposed on group counseling in schools. Create formats that capitalize on the educational components, especially imparting information and teaching a range of coping skills.

_____ As a group leader, you can model many of the specific behaviors you hope members will acquire.

_____ Strive to create a collaborative spirit between you and the members of the group. Students will become more motivated to actively participate in the group if they have an opportunity to contribute to the goals and the procedures to attain them.

_____ Make use of homework methods to maximize learning. Involve group members in creating their own homework. Make sure the homework fits their goals.

_____ Assist members in formulating concrete personal goals, and teach members how to assess the degree to which they are accomplishing their goals. At each session, ask members to reflect on what they have done in the group to make it productive for them.

_____ Employ a variety of cognitive behavioral strategies to teach young people how they might more effectively cope with problems.

_____ Even if the group is structured around a particular theme or topic, it is still important to pay attention to the process issues that are occurring within the group. Allow time to talk about matters such as trust, interpersonal relationships within the group, and the cohesion level in the group.

_____ Use cognitive behavior rehearsal methods to summarize key learning and help members translate what they are learning in the group sessions to various facets of daily life.

_____ Teach members how to give and receive feedback. Specific feedback can be most useful in groups with children and adolescents. Oftentimes the feedback in these groups will be of a global nature. Apply a behavioral format in giving feedback.

Form small groups within your class and choose a specific type of group that you want to design (either for children or adolescents). In your small group, decide on the specific focus and purpose of your group and outline the structure of the group. How long will your group last? How might you best apply these guidelines to the group you are designing? This activity is aimed at helping you think about ways you can concretely apply behavioral methods to working with a group in the school setting.

20. *Personal evaluation and critique of cognitive behavioral groups.* Discuss in your class or group what you consider to be the major strengths and weaknesses of the cognitive behavioral approaches to groups. Consider questions such as these:

a. How can any group leader (regardless of theoretical orientation) draw on cognitive behavioral concepts and procedures?

b. How would it be for you to use cognitive behavioral techniques as a group leader?

c. If you were leading a group composed of members with culturally diverse backgrounds, what cognitive behavioral techniques do you think might be particularly effective?

d. What do you see as the major strengths and limitations of cognitive behavioral group approaches in working with multicultural populations?

e. From a cognitive behavioral perspective, what kind of teaching would you want to do if you were beginning a group with culturally diverse clients?

Questions for Reflection and Discussion

1. What are some of the distinguishing features of a cognitive behavioral group that separate it from many of the other models covered in this book? To what extent do you think you could incorporate some cognitive behavioral concepts and techniques into relationship-oriented and experiential therapies?

2. What role does assessment play in a cognitive behavioral group? Should assessment be viewed as an ongoing process?

3. What cognitive behavioral techniques would you most want to include in your groups? How might you broaden the base of your style of leadership by including cognitive and behavioral methods?

4. What are some practical advantages of pregroup interviews and follow-up individual interviews and group sessions? In what ways might you build these into the design of a group?

5. Select a particular kind of group you would be interested in organizing. Thinking from a cognitive behavioral perspective, what are some of the factors you would consider from the time you announced the group to the final session? How would you design this group at each of its stages? Share your proposal with others in your class.

6. What are your thoughts about the "new wave" of the cognitive behavioral field that includes the mindfulness-based and acceptance approaches? What are the main advantages of combining the various mindfulness-based approaches with the more traditional behavioral approaches? What mindfulness-based techniques would you like to learn more about?

7. What are your reactions to the focuses of cognitive behavior therapy—its emphasis on cognition and behavior rather than feelings and insight, interest in current problems rather than exploration of the past, and reliance on empirical validation as a basis for clinical practice?

8. Identify as many elements as you can from the cognitive behavioral perspective that will be operative in any group. For example, discuss the role of modeling, social reinforcement, teaching, and feedback in a group. How can systematically paying attention to some of these factors enhance a group?

9. What are the major shortcomings and limitations of the cognitive behavioral model, as applied to group work?

10. What do you consider to be the most important contributions of the cognitive behavioral approaches?

An Expert's Perspective on Cognitive Behavioral Therapy Groups: by Sherry Cormier

SHERRY CORMIER, PhD, is Professor Emerita of Counseling, Rehabilitation Counseling, and Counseling Psychology at West Virginia University.

1. What attracted you to this particular theoretical orientation? How does this theory fit with the person you are?

What I like about cognitive behavioral therapy (CBT) is that it is an approach for the whole person. In using this theory, the therapist works with feelings, thoughts, and actions, which makes it a comprehensive approach. Initially, I became interested in this approach because of its emphasis on helping students learn practical skills to use in individual and group counseling. This approach fits with me because I am someone who believes in possibilities for people. To me, this approach seems to foster greater possibilities for change.

2. What Key Concepts (1 to 3) of this theory are most applicable to the practice of group counseling?

Theories of learning: One key concept useful for group counseling is that this approach is based on theories of learning. People learn, unlearn, and relearn behaviors that are maladaptive or adaptive. There is so much room for learning and growth in a group setting. The power of the group is huge to help participants work on new skills and behaviors as well as to get feedback about existing skills and behaviors that are ineffective.

Here is an example: Robin was someone who was used to being sarcastic and caustic in her interactions with others. She joined a social skills group because she was lonely and didn't have any real friends. In the group, Robin was able to hear that her communication style pushed people away. The group helped Robin learn to communicate with more "warm fuzzies" that drew people to her. In real life, Robin was able to generalize the skills she learned in this CBT group to make and keep new friends after unlearning and relearning a different style of communicating with people.

3. What Techniques (1 to 3) from this theory have the most practical value for group work practitioners?

Skills training: Many groups are formed to help clients learn new skills, such as social or relationship skills, communication and assertion skills, test taking, and studying skills.

Self-management: A big part of the CBT approach is helping people learn things in groups that translate to their life outside of the group. One way this goal is accomplished through a CBT group is to use techniques that focus on self-directed behavior. These techniques include such things as personal goal setting, contracting for self-change, self-monitoring, self-reward, and stimulus control. All of these techniques are designed to help the group members become more self-directed in a variety of situations outside of the group.

Mindfulness: This is a way to direct and increase our attention to the present moment. Groups are often more effective when they focus on the here-and-now as opposed to the past or the future. Mindfulness is a way to accomplish this in a group setting. Continued practice of mindfulness both within and outside of a group setting fosters tranquility and equanimity, two qualities that are helpful in today's fast-paced stressful world.

4. How does this theory have particular relevance for addressing diversity and social justice issues in group work?

Cognitive behavioral therapy has a number of advantages for working with groups with diverse members. This approach is generally compatible with the cultural values of a wide range of clients. Many clients who feel disempowered because of social justice issues such as discrimination and oppression like a CBT approach because the emphasis on practical change is empowering to them. At the same time, CBT not only focuses on changing an individual person but also changing facets of societal and cultural systems that are contributors to problems and issues.

5. Raise a question from this theoretical framework that you consider especially important for group work practice.

What kinds of clinical problems is a CBT group best suited for? One of the features of the CBT approach is its focus on evidence; that is, the exploration and accumulation of scientific data to assess the effectiveness of CBT treatment with a given clinical disorder. The evidence base for CBT groups suggests that these groups are very effective for clients with depression and moderately effective for clients with anxiety and phobias. There is also accumulating evidence to support the use of mindfulness-based CBT groups. A few more unusual applications of CBT groups involve the combination of CBT and play therapy in a group setting for sexually abused children as well as a CBT group approach with adults with hoarding issues. Finally, CBT groups have been used effectively with veterans with posttraumatic stress disorder issues.

Your Thoughts on Dr. Cormier's Cognitive Behavioral Therapy Perspective on Groups

1. What do you understand by the concept of mindfulness? What applications can you see in terms of applying mindfulness principles and practices in groups you will lead?
2. Dr. Cormier claims that there is a great deal of room in CBT groups for teaching life skills. What are some examples you can think of that illustrate the teaching and practicing of life skills?
3. CBT uses methods that have the support of research evidence. What value do you place on evidence-based practice as it applies to group counseling?

Quiz on the Cognitive Behavioral Approach to Groups: A Comprehension Check   Score _____ %

Note: Please refer to Appendix I for the scoring key. Count 5 points for each error, and subtract the total from 100 to get your percentage score.

True/false items: Decide if the following statements are "more true" or "more false" as they apply to cognitive behavioral group therapy.

T   F   1. An assumption of the cognitive behavioral orientation is that the behaviors clients express *are* the problem and not merely symptoms of the problem.

T   F   2. CBT groups emphasize creating an agenda at the beginning of each session to prioritize members' goals and attend to ways that time will be spent. This agenda is created solely by the leader of a group.

T   F   3. Cognitive behavioral group therapy is generally long term.

T   F   4. In cognitive behavior therapy, assessment and treatment proceed simultaneously.

T   F   5. The cognitive behavioral leader typically assumes an inactive style of leadership to allow members to direct the group process.

T   F   6. There is no single model that, strictly speaking, can be called a "cognitive behavioral group."

T   F   7. One of the group leader's functions is to collect data to determine the effectiveness of treatment, both for the individual members and for the group as a whole.

T   F   8. Mindfulness-based cognitive therapy is a comprehensive integration of the principles and skills of mindfulness applied to the treatment of depression.

T   F   9. One of the drawbacks of the mindfulness and acceptance approaches that are a part of cognitive behavioral therapy is that none of them have been empirically validated.

T   F   10. Mindfulness-based stress reduction programs aim to teach people how to live more fully in the present rather than ruminating about the past or being overly concerned about the future.

Multiple-choice items: Select the *one best answer* among the alternatives given. Consider each question within the framework of cognitive behavioral group therapy.

_____11. Which of the following mindfulness-based programs involves teaching participants sitting meditation, mindful yoga, and a body scan meditation that helps a client to observe all sensations in his or her body?
   a. dialectical behavior therapy
   b. acceptance and commitment therapy
   c. mindfulness-based cognitive therapy
   d. mindfulness-based stress reduction

_____12. A limitation of cognitive behavior therapy is its
   a. lack of research to evaluate the effectiveness of techniques.
   b. de-emphasis of the role of feelings in the therapeutic process.
   c. lack of clear concepts on which to base practice.
   d. lack of attention to a good client–therapist relationship.
   e. overemphasis on early childhood experiences.

_____13. Contemporary cognitive behavior therapy places emphasis on
   a. the interplay between the individual and the environment.
   b. helping clients acquire insight into the causes of their problems.
   c. a phenomenological approach to understanding the person.
   d. encouraging clients to reexperience unfinished business with significant others by role-playing with them in the present.
   e. working through the transference relationship with the therapist.

_____14. Dialectical behavior therapy is used to treat persons with
   a. borderline personality disorder.
   b. anxiety disorders.
   c. depression.
   d. eating disorders.
   e. all of the above.

_____15. Through a collaborative effort and process of evaluation, group members learn to discriminate between their own thoughts and events that occur in reality. They learn the influence that cognition has on their feelings and behaviors and even on environmental events, particularly the distortions that they have acquired. This is best described as
   a. countertransference.
   b. collaborative empiricism.
   c. cognitive rehearsal.
   d. cognitive structuring.
   e. collaborative structuring.

_____16. Which of the following statements is _not_ true regarding acceptance and commitment therapy?
   a. In this approach, acceptance is equivalent to tolerance.
   b. It is designed to help clients learn that attempts at suppressing negative or unwanted thoughts or painful feelings does not work.
   c. The goal of this approach is to allow for increased psychological flexibility.
   d. This approach emphasizes action, and it makes use of concrete homework and behavioral exercises as a way to create larger patterns of effective action that will help clients live by their values.
   e. There are more than 100 acceptance and commitment therapy skills to choose from, which are individualized for each client.

_____17. Factors that enhance the application of cognitive behavioral therapy to diverse populations include
a. its ability to be individualized to each person.
b. its emphasis on the external environment.
c. its psychoeducational emphasis.
d. the active nature of the approach.
e. all of the above.

_____18. Which of the following is *not* a characteristic of cognitive behavioral approaches?
a. Reliance on the principles and procedures of the scientific method
b. Specifying treatment goals in concrete and objective terms
c. Focusing on the client's current problems and the factors influencing them
d. An emphasis on observing overt behavior
e. Application of the same procedures to every client with a particular dysfunctional behavior

_____19. Dialectical behavior therapy (DBT) is a blend of cognitive behavioral therapy and
a. psychoanalytic concepts and techniques.
b. the mindfulness training of Eastern psychological and spiritual practices.
c. traditional behavior therapy.
d. Adlerian therapy.
e. both (a) and (b).

_____20. In behavioral groups, _____ is a major intervention provided by the group leader and by other members.
a. social reinforcement
b. the empty chair technique
c. free association
d. social restructuring
e. the social microcosm

CHAPTER FOURTEEN

Rational Emotive Behavior
Therapy in Groups

Prechapter Self-Inventory for Rational Emotive
Behavior Therapy (REBT)

Directions: Refer to page 77 for general directions. Indicate your position on these statements using the following code:

5 = I *strongly agree* with this statement.
4 = I *agree,* in most respects, with this statement.
3 = I am *undecided* in my opinion about this statement.
2 = I *disagree,* in most respects, with this statement.
1 = I *strongly disagree* with this statement.

_____ 1. Group members can learn how they disturb themselves by applying the A-B-C theory to their problems.

_____ 2. For groups to be effective, leaders need to convince members to practice new behaviors both inside and outside the group.

_____ 3. Because REBT tends to be a forceful approach, the group leader must exert caution in interpreting certain beliefs as being irrational.

_____ 4. The most efficient way to bring about lasting emotional and behavioral change is for group members to change their way of thinking.

_____ 5. Once irrational beliefs have been discovered, they can be counteracted in a variety of ways and replaced with a rational set of beliefs.

_____ 6. A large part of the leader's task is to be a teacher, especially in teaching members how to detect and dispute irrational beliefs.

_____ 7. Homework assignments are a basic part of group counseling.

_____ 8. Effective group therapy includes cognitive, emotional, and behavioral elements.

_____ 9. A major function of the group leader is to enable members to recognize their "shoulds," "oughts," and "musts."

_____ 10. The REBT group leader tends to consider the relationship between the group leader and the members as being important to the group process, but mainly as a means to an end of getting results.

Summary of Basic Assumptions and Key Concepts
of Rational Emotive Behavior Therapy for Groups

1. People's belief systems result in emotional disturbances. Situations alone do not determine emotional disturbances; rather, it is people's evaluations of these situations that are crucial.

People have a tendency to fall victim to irrational beliefs, and although these beliefs were originally incorporated from external sources, people internalize and maintain them by self-indoctrination.

2. REBT stresses the importance of the therapist giving and showing unconditional acceptance of members. It emphasizes the group therapist's skill in challenging, confronting, and convincing the members to practice activities that will lead to positive change. REBT employs a wide variety of cognitive, behavioral, and emotive techniques, and it is therefore a truly integrative approach to group counseling. REBT practitioners are flexible and creative in their use of methods, making sure to tailor the techniques to the unique needs of the members of a group.

3. The leader helps group members identify and challenge the irrational beliefs they originally unquestioningly accepted, demonstrates how they are continuing to indoctrinate themselves with these beliefs, and teaches them how to modify their thinking by developing rational alternative beliefs.

4. In an REBT group the members acquire skills in generalizing what they are learning in the group to present and future problems. Ultimately, group leaders teach members how to become their own therapists.

5. Cognitive methods used in REBT groups include teaching the A-B-Cs of REBT, active disputation of faulty beliefs, teaching coping self-statements, psychoeducational methods, and cognitive homework.

6. Emotive techniques (such as role playing, rational-emotive imagery, and shame-attacking exercises) tend to be vivid and evocative in nature, yet the main purpose is to dispute clients' irrational beliefs. It is assumed that the best way to change feelings is by changing self-defeating thoughts. Group leaders teach members that once they have achieved intellectual insight they can use a variety of methods in changing their thoughts, behavior, and feelings.

7. Behavioral methods in groups are designed to motivate members to take actions that will result in thinking and feeling differently. REBT stresses that meaningful cognitive change is unlikely unless clients are willing to behave differently. Some of the techniques include behavioral homework assignments, cognitive and behavioral role playing, reinforcement, skill training, and feedback.

8. REBT emphasizes that our newly acquired insights must be put into action. REBT practitioners employ a directive role in encouraging members to commit themselves to practicing in everyday situations what they are learning in the group sessions. They view what goes on during the group as important, but they realize that the hard work between sessions and after therapy is terminated is even more crucial. The use of the homework method is a route to translating insights into concrete action programs.

9. REBT lends itself to short-term group-oriented procedures, and group members are often able to make significant changes with brief therapy.

10. REBT group leaders assume the role of psychological educator, and they encourage members to commit to practicing what they learn in the group sessions in daily life. Leaders strive to promote clear thinking, engage members in problem-solving experiments, and minimize emotional distress.

11. REBT is particularly applicable to group therapy and is frequently the treatment of choice. The group leader can help others to learn and apply the principles and procedures of

REBT in group sessions. Group work affords many opportunities to agree on homework assignments, to practice assertiveness skills, to take risks by practicing different behaviors, to explore self-defeating thinking, to learn from the experiences of others, to interact therapeutically and socially with each other in after-group sessions, and to have their behavior observed by the group therapist and the other members.

12. REBT has certain advantages in working with multicultural populations. If members are not challenged too quickly, they can be invited to examine the premises on which they behave. A sensitive practitioner can encourage members to begin to question how they may have uncritically accepted as truth all of the messages from their culture. Without encouraging them to abandon respect for their cultural heritage, the therapist can invite them to examine their beliefs and understand their consequences.

Glossary of Key Terms for Rational Emotive Behavior Therapy

- **A-B-C theory** The theory that people's problems do not stem from activating events but rather from their beliefs about such events. Thus, the best route to changing emotions is to change one's beliefs about situations.
- **Cognitive homework** Cognitive assignments that clients complete between sessions, which consist of ways of applying the A-B-C theory to many of the problems in daily life.
- **Cognitive restructuring** A central technique of cognitive therapy, which teaches people how to make themselves less disturbed.
- **Cognitive therapy** An approach and set of procedures that attempts to change feelings and behavior by modifying faulty thinking and believing.
- **Distortion of reality** Erroneous thinking that disrupts one's life; can be contradicted by the client's objective appraisal of the situation.
- **Humor** To combat the exaggerated thinking that leads people into trouble, REBT employs a good deal of humor. It teaches group members to laugh—not at themselves, but at their self-defeating beliefs.
- **Internal dialogue** People's self-talk, or inner speech; the debate that often goes on "inside their head."
- **Irrational belief** An unreasonable conviction that leads to emotional and behavioral problems.
- **Musturbation** A term coined by Albert Ellis to refer to behavior that is absolutist and rigid; self-constructed, self-repeated, and self-learned "musts," "oughts," and "shoulds" that can result in emotional disturbance.
- **Psychoeducational methods** The use of audiotapes, videotapes, and books as adjuncts to group counseling.
- **Rationality** The quality of thinking, feeling, and acting in ways that will help us attain our goals. Irrationality consists of thinking, feeling, and acting in ways that are self-defeating and that thwart our goals.
- **Rational emotive behavior therapy (REBT)** A cognitive behavioral model of therapy that stresses the reciprocal interactions among cognition, emotion, and behavior.
- **Rational-emotive imagery** A form of intense mental practice for learning new emotional and physical habits. Clients imagine some of the worst things they can think of and then train themselves to develop appropriate emotions in place of disruptive ones.

- **Rational emotive therapy (RET)** Ellis changed the name of his model to RET in the early 1960s.
- **Rational therapy** The original name for Albert Ellis's approach, which was developed in the mid-1950s.
- **Self-acceptance** Learning to accept oneself unconditionally in spite of imperfections.
- **Self-instructional therapy** An approach to therapy based on the assumption that what people say to themselves directly influences the things they do. Training consists of learning new self-talk aimed at coping with problems.
- **Self-rating** People have a strong tendency not only to rate their acts and behaviors as "good" or "bad," "worthy" or "unworthy," but also to rate themselves as total beings on the basis of their performances. This stems from rigid demands.
- **Shame-attacking exercises** A strategy encouraging people to act in ways that make them feel uncomfortable due to their fear of looking foolish and feeling embarrassed. The aim of the exercise is to teach people that they can function effectively even if they might be perceived as doing foolish acts.

Exercises and Activities for the Rational Emotive Behavior Therapy Approach to Groups

Rationale

The rationale underlying most of these exercises and REBT techniques is that most of us make irrational assumptions about ourselves and the world that lead to emotional and behavioral disturbances. The essence of REBT is that rational thinking can lead to more effective living. To combat stubborn and persistent irrational beliefs, it is necessary to work and practice diligently and to replace faulty thinking with logical thinking.

The following activities and exercises are designed to help you experience the process of challenging your own thinking and to become aware of the consequent feelings of your belief system. As you work through these exercises on your own, with another person, and with a small group, think about ways in which you, as a group leader, could incorporate them in group practice.

Exercises

1. *Learning to recognize and challenge your internal dialogue as a group counselor.* Leaders often incorporate a wide range of dysfunctional beliefs that impair their capacity to function as effectively as they might in their groups. In a number of his writings (cited in Chapter 14 of the textbook), Ellis has identified several irrational ideas that we often internalize and that inevitably lead to self-defeat. Here are a few typical irrational beliefs that can be applied to group counselors:
   a. "I *must* have love and approval from *all* of the members in my group. My worth as a counselor and as a person is dependent on the affirmation of each client."
   b. "As a group facilitator, I *must* always perform competently and perfectly. There is *absolutely* no room for any mistakes, for this implies failure, and any failure is catastrophic."
   c. "Because I strongly desire that group members treat me considerately and fairly, they *absolutely must* do so! If they don't, I will certainly feel miserable and be unable to function effectively."

STAGES OF DEVELOPMENT OF THE RATIONAL EMOTIVE BEHAVIOR THERAPY GROUP

Dimension	Initial Stage	Working Stage	Final Stage
Key developmental tasks and goals	Key task is to teach members the A-B-C theory of how they create and can "uncreate" their own disturbances, how they can detect their irrational beliefs, and how they can critically examine these faulty beliefs. Members need to learn that situations themselves do not cause emotional problems; rather, their beliefs about these situations cause the problems. Thus, changing beliefs (not situations) is the road to improvement.	Group focuses on identifying and examining members' "musts," "shoulds," and "oughts." Members learn that if life is not the way they want it to be, this may be unfortunate but not catastrophic. In place of self-defeating assumptions, members incorporate beliefs that are grounded in reality. Members learn a variety of ways to continue challenging their *musturbatory philosophy.*	Ultimate aim is that participants internalize a rational philosophy of life, just as they internalized a set of irrational beliefs. This phase is one of reinforcement of new learning to replace old patterns. Emphasis is on teaching people better methods of self-management. It is important for members to commit themselves to continue to work and practice new behavior in real life.
Role and tasks of group leader	Group leader shows members how they have caused their own misery by teaching them the connection between their emotional and behavioral disturbances and their beliefs. Leader teaches members how to dispute irrational beliefs and ways to substitute rational beliefs.	Leader confronts members with the beliefs they originally accepted without question and with which they continue to indoctrinate themselves. Leader strives to modify members' thinking by challenging their underlying basic assumptions about reality.	Therapist continues to act as teacher by showing members methods of self-control, giving them homework assignments that involve active practice in real life, and correcting any lasting faulty patterns. Leader encourages use of self-help methods for continuing change.
Role of group members	Members need to be willing to discipline themselves and work hard, both during the sessions and between sessions. They are active, both in and out of the group, for they learn by practicing and doing. Members gain awareness of specific ways in which they perpetuate the dysfunctional thinking that creates their problems. They learn how they disturb themselves and how to become undisturbed.	Members learn how to analyze, dispute, and debate by using scientific methods to question their belief systems. Members ask, "What evidence supports my views?" Members learn a new, rational set of beliefs. They learn how to dispute dysfunctional and self-defeating self-talk. Members carry out activity-oriented homework assignments as a way of challenging their beliefs.	Group members integrate what they have learned and continue to make plans for how they can practice overcoming self-defeating thinking and emoting outside of the group. They continue giving themselves cognitive, emotive, and behavioral assignments in daily life. They acquire a more rational and effective philosophy of life that allows them to face new challenges with confidence.

Techniques	Educational methods: use of tapes, books, and lectures; suggestions; information giving; interpretation; group feedback and support; other directive, confrontational, didactic, philosophic, and action-oriented methods. Therapist employs a wide range of cognitive, emotive, and behavioral techniques to fit the needs of the client.	Rapid-fire and forceful techniques that emphasize cognitive factors are used. These include persuasion, homework assignments, desensitization, role playing, modeling and imitation, behavior rehearsal, operant control of thinking and emoting, group feedback and support, cognitive restructuring, and assertiveness training.	There is continued use of emotive/evocative and cognitive behavioral techniques that people can use on their own after therapy terminates. Members can continue working with and practicing new ways of thinking and behaving as they encounter new problems. Members are encouraged to use self-help resources such as reading.
Questions to consider	What would you want to teach members about the ways they create their own disturbances? What are some common faulty beliefs that you might expect members to bring to a group? In what ways do you think a member's belief system is connected to how the person behaves and feels? How can you challenge members and help them recognize their irrational thinking without adding to their defensiveness? What kind of relationship would you want to create with the members before you attempted to use forceful and directive procedures? What behavioral techniques would you employ in an REBT group at the early stage? How can you best prepare culturally diverse clients for an REBT group?	To what degree have you recognized and challenged your own "musts," "shoulds," and "oughts"? To what extent have you looked at your own self-defeating assumptions and behavior? Do you agree that the role of leader is to challenge members with beliefs they have accepted without thinking and questioning? What are some specific methods you might teach the members for analyzing, disputing, and debating unexamined assumptions? What are some examples of REBT homework that you are likely to use during the working stage? Can you keep from imposing your values on members? Do you challenge them to think for themselves?	If you employ directive strategies and encourage members to take a specific course of action, are you clear about your own motives? Are you willing to state your motivations to your clients? Do you share with them your values that pertain to choices they might make? How can you teach members ways to maintain constructive thinking once they leave a group? How can you help members maintain gains they have made in challenging self-defeating attitudes? Might you want to integrate any other therapeutic techniques from other approaches during the final stages? If so, what? What are some ways you could evaluate the effectiveness of your group as it moves toward termination?

Reactions: Summarize your reactions to the rational emotive behavior therapy approach to group developmental stages. What do you like *most*? *least*? What aspects of this approach would you incorporate in your style of leadership?

d. "If I don't get what I want from each member, it's terrible, and I *can't stand it*. The group *must* act exactly the way I want when I want it."

e. "It's easier to avoid facing life's difficulties and responsibilities than to undertake more rewarding forms of self-discipline. I should be able to run my group without too much effort and *must not* have to change my way or style to get the group to work better."

2. *Dysfunctional self-statements*. Many group counselors have a strong tendency to make and keep themselves emotionally disturbed by internalizing self-defeating beliefs such as the ones listed above. I asked the students in one of my group counseling classes to list their own irrational beliefs, the underlying assumptions they often make, and a sample of their internal dialogue when they are coleading groups. These self-statements included the following:

a. "I should always know what to say, and it's essential that I have the right answers."

b. "I should be able to fix all the problems posed by members of my group."

c. "I must not be weak, and I shouldn't ask for help."

d. "If I'm not thoroughly prepared, I'm not likely to be totally competent, as I must be."

e. "I must have the right technique for each situation, or else everything might fall flat, and the consequences would be a disaster."

f. "I mustn't lose control. I should always be perfectly in control of every situation in a group."

g. "I must be a perfect role model, which means being an outstanding group leader at all times."

h. "I fear that I may look foolish, and this should never happen!"

i. "I expect myself to be successful with all of my group members all of the time."

j. "I feel I need the approval of virtually all the people in my group."

k. "If a group session doesn't go well, I typically feel responsible and guilty."

l. "If a group member stops coming to the sessions, I blame myself because that should never happen."

m. "I must always be available to any member who might need me."

n. "If a participant in my group is in pain, I should take it away."

o. "I should know everything."

p. "It would be terrible if I made a mistake in the groups I lead, for that would mean I'm a failure."

Review the self-statements listed here and circle the letter preceding each self-statement that you imagine you could (or do) make. Reflect on the nature of some of the beliefs you hold about who and what you think you *should be* in order to be an effective group counselor. List three of your beliefs that are not helpful to you in your development as a group leader:

1. _____

_____

_____

_____

2. _____

_____

_____

_____

_____

3. _____

_____

_____

_____

Your internal dialogue. Now consider the nature of your internal dialogue regarding your functioning as a group leader. You might think about what goes on in your head just before you begin a group session. What messages do you give yourself about what you should be and must do if your group is to be successful?

3. *Challenging your internal dialogue.* How can you deal effectively with your self-defeating internal dialogue? There are no answers that will silence your internal dialogue permanently. However, by becoming aware of what you are telling yourself and by challenging your dysfunctional beliefs, you take a step in the right direction. It could be an important step to speak out in a group that you are leading, especially when you become aware of negative thinking. Doing so can be excellent modeling for the members, for it can teach the members ways to combat their own self-defeating beliefs.

a. After you've identified a few self-defeating self-statements that you most often make, practice methods of disputing these statements. Also, attempt to replace the irrational belief with a rational and effective belief. For example, if you say, "I must be approved of or accepted by all of the members of my group," a disputation might include: "Where is it written that my own approval depends on getting approval from others? If a client disapproves of me, can't I still feel like a worthwhile person and group leader?" An example of a rational and effective belief is: "While it's true that I don't enjoy disapproval, I'm able to tolerate it. I don't have to be accepted by everyone to feel accepted by myself." Use the "REBT Self-Help Form" at the end of this exercise section as a concrete way to record and work on your beliefs.

b. Give yourself specific homework assignments to critically evaluate some of the beliefs that interfere with your effectiveness.

c. Identifying and disputing ineffective beliefs, as well as substituting effective beliefs, could be a lively and productive group activity. Spend some time in your class or group discussing how some of your beliefs actually interfere with your effectiveness as a group leader and what you are doing to change what you are telling yourself.

d. Write constructive sentences that you might suggest to a group member who repeated self-defeating sentences such as the following:

a. "I've always been stupid, and I suppose I'll always be that way."

b. _____

_____

_____

a. "I need to please everyone, because rejection is just terrible."

b. _____

_____

_____

a. "Because my parents never really loved me, I guess nobody else could ever love me."

b. _____

_____

_____

a. "Basically, I'm a worthless person."

b. _____

_____

_____

4. *Creating assignments for group members*. Think of some in-group assignments or home-work exercises for members who demonstrate problems such as the following, and write them down. Bring these assignments to your class or group and share ideas with one another.

a. A woman says very little during the group sessions because she's afraid she'll sound stupid and that other members will laugh at her. One possible assignment is: _____

_____

_____

_____

b. A woman believes men are always judging her in a critical fashion. She avoids men, both in the group and outside of it, because she doesn't want to feel negatively judged. One possible assignment is: _____

_____

_____

_____

c. A member of a group you're leading tells you that he feels and believes that he *must* gain universal approval. When someone is displeased with him, he feels devastated. Because of this he tries hard to figure out what every person in the group wants from him, and then he goes out of his way to meet these expectations. He says he is sick of being the "super nice guy" and desperately wants to change. One possible assignment is: _____

_____

_____

_____

d. A member describes his drive to be perfect and says that he carefully avoids situations and activities that make it difficult for him to feel that he's performed perfectly. He wants to relax and not be obsessed with the thought that he must be perfect in anything he attempts. One possible assignment is: _____

_____

5. *Role playing with a cognitive focus.* Think of a situation that causes you difficulty—one that you'd be willing to share in your group or class—and role-play it. For example, you may feel upset because you can't get your father's approval. Have a person play *your role* first, and you role-play your demanding father who refuses to give approval no matter what is accomplished. After about 5 minutes or so, reverse roles: be yourself while someone else plays your father as you portrayed him. Continue this for about another 5 minutes. Afterward, do a *cognitive evaluation* of this interchange in your group. Here are some questions you might include in your evaluation:

   a. How did you appear to others as you played yourself talking with your father?
   b. Do you need his approval to survive?
   c. What will become of you if he never gives you his approval?
   d. What might you have to do to get his approval?
   e. How do you imagine you'd feel if you did what might be required to gain his acceptance?
   f. Can you gain self-acceptance, even if acceptance is not forthcoming from him?
   g. In what ways do you treat others like your father?

6. *REBT groups in specific settings.* Imagine that you want to conduct an REBT group in the agency, school, or institution in which you work (or may someday work). Convince your supervisor, principal, or agency director of the advantages of practicing REBT in a group over practicing it on an individual basis. What are some unique advantages of REBT in groups in the particular setting where you expect to work? What can you say to your supervisor to increase the chances that you will be given the support to design a group? This can be a productive exercise in your group or class. Another student can play the role of the school principal or the director of the agency.

7. *REBT with children and adolescents.* Explore some specific ways school counselors could apply REBT concepts and techniques to group work with both children and adolescents. In your group devise a specific kind of psychoeducational group or a group with an educational focus. Here are a few guidelines and questions to consider when creating a group to address the special needs of students:

   _____ Consider your group as an approach to reeducate students. What areas would be a useful focus for reeducation?

   _____ Identify some specific self-defeating beliefs of both elementary school children and high school adolescents that you would target in your group. What are some beliefs about self and others that many children and adolescents cling to that lead to emotional and behavioral problems?

   _____ What kind of cognitive techniques might be appropriate with both children and adolescents?

   _____ What kind of action plans could you think of that would assist young people in practicing new cognitive and behavioral skills outside of the group?

   _____ Apply selected cognitive, emotive, and behavioral techniques that were discussed in this chapter to your group. How might you be able to increase the cooperation of the students so they are more likely to actively participate in these interventions?

8. *REBT with culturally diverse populations.* In your class or group discuss what you consider to be some of the major advantages and disadvantages of employing REBT techniques in working with culturally diverse groups. Consider these questions as you critique REBT in working with diverse client populations:

   a. Specifically, what cultural variables would you want to take into account in applying REBT techniques and concepts?

   b. Who is the judge of what constitutes a "faulty belief"? Does culture play a role in determining whether a belief is helpful or unhelpful?

   c. Clients from many cultures will be drawn to the teaching aspects of REBT and the active and directive role of the group leader. How comfortable might you be in structuring a group around educational lines and assuming the role of teacher and coach? How would you combine providing members with cognitive information and facilitating personal exploration?

   d. How might you demonstrate respect for the cultural values and beliefs of the culturally diverse members in your group, yet at the same time challenge them to evaluate the degree to which some of their values are helping or hindering them in their lives?

9. *REBT Self-Help Form.* For at least a week, pay attention to various situations you encounter, especially areas of self-talk or beliefs that influence your behavior. Use the REBT Self-Help Form to record at least one event that contributes to an emotional upset or some self-defeating behavior. Identify any beliefs that you think are not constructive that you hold about a particular event; dispute each faulty belief; and replace it with a rational belief. Bring the completed form to your class or group the following week and use it to talk about how your beliefs influence both your behavior and the way you feel about certain events.

10. *Applying exercises to yourself.* After identifying some of your own irrational beliefs, brainstorm ideas in your group about how you might apply cognitive, behavioral, and emotive techniques that you would be willing to carry out in daily life. Assist other classmates in developing specific REBT exercises to challenge their irrational fears. As each of you envisions carrying out these exercises in your own life, discuss the pros and cons of using these methods. Practice how you might introduce the use of similar exercises as a group leader through role playing.

Questions for Reflection and Discussion

1. In your own experiences as a group member or a group leader, what are some of the common self-defeating beliefs you have most frequently heard? What opportunities does a group offer to critically evaluate such ideas? What would be helpful to you in challenging some of your self-limiting beliefs?

2. REBT strongly encourages clients to examine illogical assumptions about life. Do you believe people will make changes on an emotional and behavioral level if the focus is primarily on cognitive aspects?

3. As a psychoeducational model, REBT stresses teaching, learning, practicing new skills, logical thinking, carrying out homework assignments, and reading. As a group leader, to what degree are you comfortable with this focus? What aspects of REBT would you want to include in your approach to groups, regardless of your theoretical orientation?

REBT Self-Help Form

A (Activating Event)

- Briefly summarize the situation you are disturbed about (what would a camera see?)
- An A can be *internal or external, real or imagined.*
- An A can be an event in the *past, present, or future.*

C (Consequences)

Major unhealthy negative emotions:

Major self-defeating behaviors:

Unhealthy negative emotions include:
- Anxiety
- Shame/Embarrassment
- Depression
- Rage
- Hurt
- Low Frustration Tolerance
- Jealousy
- Guilt

IBs (Irrational Beliefs)

To identify IBs, look for:
- Dogmatic demands (musts, absolutes, shoulds)
- Awfulizing (It's awful, terrible, horrible)
- Low frustration tolerance (I can't stand it)
- Self/other rating (I'm/he/she is bad, worthless)

D (Disputing IBs)

To dispute, ask yourself:
- Where is holding this belief getting me? Is it *helpful or self-defeating?*
- Where is the evidence to support the existence of my irrational belief? Is it *consistent with reality?*
- Is my belief *logical?* Does it follow from my preferences?
- Is it really *awful* (as bad as it could be?)
- Can I really not *stand* it?

RBs (Rational Beliefs)

To think more rationally, strive for:
- Non-dogmatic preferences (wishes, wants, desires)
- Evaluating badness (it's bad, unfortunate)
- High frustration tolerance (I don't like it, but I can stand it)
- Not globally rating self or others (I—and others—are fallible human beings)

E (New Effect)

New healthy negative emotions:

New constructive behaviors:

Healthy negative emotions include:
- Disappointment
- Concern
- Annoyance
- Sadness
- Regret
- Frustration

Source: © Windy Dryden & Jane Walker 1992. Revised by Albert Ellis Institute, 1996. Reprinted by permission.

4. Compare and contrast REBT with Gestalt therapy. What are some of the major differences? Do you see any room to integrate the differing dimensions of these two therapies? If so, what factors might you combine in a group you were leading?

5. REBT calls for an active/directive group leader. Compare this role with that of the person-centered group leader who gives as little direction as possible to the members. Which leader role are you more comfortable with, and how do you think these contrasting leadership styles will change a group? Do you see any way to combine some aspects of REBT with the person-centered approach?

6. Albert Ellis invented the PYA (Push Your Ass) technique, which deliberately forces group members to confront fears that get in their way of behaving the way they want to. The idea is that by learning to face and cope with fearful situations, we will conquer our fears. How would the PYA technique work for you personally? As a group leader, would you be inclined to suggest this technique for members who are held back by their fears?

7. What criteria would you employ to determine whether a group member's ideas were rational and functional? How would you determine whether certain assumptions were self-defeating or constructive?

8. To what degree do you think the group leader's values become a central part of REBT group therapy? How do you think the values held by the leader and by the members influence the group process?

9. Some might criticize REBT group therapy on the ground that a participant is subjected to undue group pressure, from both the leader and the other members. This pressure could take the form of persuasion, giving advice, and expecting members to do certain outside assignments. What are your reactions to this criticism? If you were to incorporate REBT methods, what safeguards might you devise so that members would not be subjected to pressure to change their way of thinking?

10. Like any other action-oriented approach, REBT insists that newly acquired insights be put into action, largely through homework assignments. What do you think of a model that is based on action outside of the sessions? In what ways might you assist members in creating and carrying out behavioral assignments? What ideas do you have that would lead to collaborative efforts in designing meaningful homework assignments?

An Expert's Perspective on Rational Emotive Behavior Therapy Groups: by Debbie Joffe Ellis

DEBBIE JOFFE ELLIS, MDAM (Medical Doctor of Alternative Medicine), is a licensed psychologist and mental health counselor who travels around the world presenting workshops on REBT.

1. What attracted you to this particular theoretical orientation? How does this theory fit with the person you are?

I was attracted to the holistic nature of rational emotive behavior therapy. REBT reminds us that our thoughts, emotions, and behaviors are interconnected, and it strongly emphasizes the importance and benefit of identifying one's core philosophy about life and being willing to change self-defeating, unrealistic, or negative thoughts. I also loved the vigor and precision REBT utilizes in its process of encouraging us to change our irrational unhealthy thoughts into healthy rational ones.

More than other approaches, REBT emphasizes the importance of unconditional acceptance, which is compatible with my philosophy of life and approach when providing therapy. I love the compassion and kindness these attitudes beget, and I was drawn to the authentic nature of REBT's creator, Albert Ellis (who became my beloved husband a couple of decades after I first studied REBT). He was a most compelling and convincing model of this approach.

The REBT approach fits the person I am. I appreciate doing things thoroughly and well. REBT offers elegant solutions that can lead to empowering and lasting changes for people who want to experience greater joy in their lives. I like the flexibility REBT encourages with its embrace of a variety of techniques and homework activities. I value its use of humor when appropriate, and I am warmed and inspired when sharing the humanistic attitude and respect REBT offers each individual.

2. What Key Concepts (1 to 3) of this theory are most applicable to the practice of group counseling?

Psychoeducation (cognitive): Teaching REBT principles in a group setting is a powerful activity. Hearing the self-defeating views of other group members helps members more easily identify any similar attitudes that they may hold. Members are encouraged to help dispute such unhelpful views—those they hold and those they hear from other members. All work together under the group leader's guidance to assign each member homework, and this too can expand and reinforce healthy thinking in each individual. All are encouraged to be affirming of themselves and others when progress is made and to practice empathy and offer practical suggestions in discussion when any obstacles, difficulties, or blocks are reported by any of the members.

Unconditional acceptance (emotive): All members of the group receive reinforcement of the principles of REBT and become more adept at working on compassionately increasing them in their lives. The group leader will immediately point out any words a member may say that indicate the member feels worthless (absence of unconditional self-acceptance), that the member is damning other people (absence of unconditional other acceptance), or overgeneralizations from the member that all of life is awful when only certain specific events may be bad in the member's life (absence of unconditional life acceptance). Group members are encouraged to point out any self-defeating beliefs spoken by members, and members are encouraged to replace them with positive statements.

Modeling (behavioral): The group leader does his or her best to model unconditional other acceptance by never criticizing the worth or personhood of any member, and only constructively and caringly pointing out any flaws in his or her behaviors and/or attitudes.

3. What Techniques (1 to 3) from this theory have the most practical value for group work practitioners?

Role playing: A group member acts out the issue of another member who takes on the role of the rational person and disputes his or her own unhelpful attitudes.

Shame-attacking exercises: Members push themselves, within the group setting, to practice uncomfortable behaviors they want to be more comfortable doing. This is particularly helpful for individuals seeking to rid themselves of "needing" approval from others.

A-B-C approach: The group works together in applying the A-B-C approach to presented issues of individual group members: (A) clearly describe the Activating event; (C) describe the emotional and behavioral Consequences; (B) identify as many irrational Beliefs as possible that followed from "A"; (D) Dispute every irrational belief identified; (E) come up with Effective new philosophies or beliefs with regard to the activating event. The leader then assigns relevant homework activities.

4. How does this theory have particular relevance for addressing diversity and social justice issues in group work?

A main contributor to conflict is the irrational demand that others be like us, or that they behave in the ways we think they "should." REBT is at its core a most civil, humanistic, and ethical approach. One of its important aspects is its encouragement to each and every one of us to practice high frustration tolerance (HFT) along with unconditional acceptance. The group leader models and encourages healthy attitudes of tolerance and acceptance.

Group members may have the opportunity through their group experience to accept the diversity in others present and to share their own attitudes about various differences in others. They may then choose to work on changing any attitudes they discover that are intolerant, prejudicial, and unjust with the help and encouragement of members of the group and the group leader.

5. Raise a question from this theoretical framework that you consider especially important for group work practice.

How can the group leader remain effective and accepting in the face of disruptive behavior? The most effective REBT group leader will demonstrate and express firmness and clarity as appropriate, along with empathy, compassion, and unconditional acceptance. REBT clearly distinguishes the difference between the worth and acceptability of every human being, and the worth and acceptability (or lack of) of their behavior.

REBT encourages us to take action to change poor behaviors and events when we can (and to accept those we can't change). For a group leader to allow disruptive behavior to continue in a group would be disrespecting the individuals within it, including the one who may be acting inappropriately. An effective REBT group leader would remind attendees that our behaviors have consequences and calmly express clear boundaries and limits for participation. The worth of the person would not be at issue in any sense, the issue would be the inappropriate behavior of the person, and the group leader would use the experience of the disruption and inappropriate behavior as a learning opportunity for all present. REBT leaders tolerate difference, diversity, fallibility, and relapses and encourage ongoing efforts to increase unconditional acceptance, but leaders do not put off any appropriate assertive verbal confrontation for the good of all present.

Your Thoughts on Dr. Joffe Ellis's Rational Emotive Behavior Therapy Perspective on Groups

1. What aspects of REBT group work do you find most interesting? What concepts or techniques from REBT might you like to apply in your practice of group counseling?
2. What do you understand by the A-B-C approach to group therapy?
3. REBT is a psychoeducational approach. What value do you place on psychoeducation in groups you intend to lead? What can REBT offer to group members when it comes to learning how thinking influences feelings and behaviors?

Quiz on Rational Emotive Behavior Therapy: A Comprehension Check

Score _____%

Note: Please refer to Appendix I for the scoring key. Count 5 points for each error, and subtract the total from 100 to get your percentage score.

True/false items: Decide if the following statements are "more true" or "more false" as they apply to rational emotive behavior therapy.

T F 1. For Ellis, there are some distinct advantages for practicing REBT in a group context rather than in individual counseling.

T F 2. Generally, traumatic situations, in and of themselves, cause people to be emotionally disturbed.

T F 3. Group members need to be taught how to think logically and give themselves new internal dialogues if they hope to change.

T F 4. In negotiating shame-attacking exercises, leaders should not discourage members from doing anything that is illegal, immoral, or that will unduly alarm other people; it is better to not place any limits on members when they are mustering up the courage to engage in such an activity.

T F 5. REBT is basically an educational model.

T F 6. Ellis originally developed REBT to try to make psychotherapy shorter and more efficient than most other systems of therapy.

T F 7. REBT considers the nature of the therapeutic relationship between the group therapist and the members to be central to the outcomes of a group.

T F 8. Group members are taught to use logical analysis as a way of understanding their faulty premises.

T F 9. REBT group leaders tend to be highly active and directive.

T F 10. Ellis believes people become emotionally disturbed because stressful situations lead to a breakdown of their coping mechanisms.

Multiple-choice items: Select the *one best answer* among the alternatives given. Consider each question within the framework of rational emotive behavior therapy.

_____11. Cognitive therapy is based on the assumption that
    a. our feelings determine our thoughts.
    b. our feelings determine our actions.
    c. cognitions are the major determinants of how we feel and act.
    d. the best way to change thinking is to reexperience past emotional traumas in the here-and-now.
    e. insight is essential for any type of change to occur.

_____12. In REBT, the therapy techniques are designed to
    a. assist clients in substituting rational beliefs for irrational beliefs.
    b. help clients experience their feelings more intensely.
    c. help clients rate themselves as human beings as a route to self-acceptance.
    d. enable clients to deal with their existential loneliness.
    e. teach clients how to think only positive thoughts.

_____13. According to REBT, people develop psychological disturbances because of
    a. a traumatic event.
    b. failure to receive love from significant others.
    c. their beliefs about and reactions to certain events.
    d. unfinished business from their past.
    e. inadequate bonding with their mother during infancy.

_____14. All of the following are _cognitive_ methods of REBT except for
    a. shame-attacking exercises.
    b. disputing irrational beliefs.
    c. coping self-statements.
    d. teaching the A-B-Cs.
    e. psychoeducational methods.

_____15. All of the following are _emotive_ methods used in REBT groups except for
    a. unconditional acceptance.
    b. rational emotive imagery.
    c. the use of humor.
    d. shame-attacking exercises.
    e. the analysis of one's lifescript.

_____16. In REBT groups, the members would be most concerned about
    a. understanding the childhood origins of their emotional disturbances.
    b. understanding the problems of other members.
    c. merely freeing themselves of their symptoms.
    d. minimizing ways in which they create their own disturbances.
    e. reexperiencing the traumatic situations under which they made critical decisions about themselves and their place in the world.

_____17. REBT can best be considered as
    a. an educational method.
    b. a didactic process.
    c. the process of challenging ideas and thinking.
    d. a teaching/learning process.
    e. all of the above.

_____18. In REBT groups, role playing
    a. is rarely done as it needlessly stirs up emotion.
    b. is limited strictly to cognitive aspects.
    c. is designed to evoke intense feelings.
    d. involves a cognitive/emotive evaluation of both feelings and beliefs.
    e. involves a member acting out all the various roles of a present conflict.

_____19. Which of the following would have the least applicability to an REBT group?
    a. interpretation of early memories
    b. unconditional acceptance
    c. role playing
    d. feedback
    e. reinforcement and penalties

_____20. When REBT group practitioners ask members to imagine some of the worst things they can think of and then to train themselves to develop appropriate emotions in place of disruptive ones, this is an example of
    a. systematic desensitization.
    b. teaching the A-B-Cs.
    c. rational-emotive imagery.
    d. future projection.
    e. cognitive dissonance.

CHAPTER FIFTEEN

Choice Theory/Reality Therapy in Groups

Prechapter Self-Inventory for Choice Theory/Reality Therapy

Directions: Refer to page 77 for general directions. Indicate your position on these statements using the following code:

5 = I *strongly agree* with this statement.
4 = I *agree,* in most respects, with this statement.
3 = I am *undecided* in my opinion about this statement.
2 = I *disagree,* in most respects, with this statement.
1 = I *strongly disagree* with this statement.

_____ 1. The group counselor's main task is to encourage the group members to evaluate their present behavior and to make more effective choices.

_____ 2. By changing how we are acting, we inevitably change what we think and feel.

_____ 3. We perceive the world in the context of our own needs, not as it really is.

_____ 4. Self-evaluation is the cornerstone of reality therapy; asking members to evaluate each component of their total behavior is a major task in reality therapy.

_____ 5. The only person whose behavior we can control is our own; the way we can control events in our environment is through what we choose to do.

_____ 6. Group work should mainly aim to change actions rather than feelings or attitudes.

_____ 7. Generally, it is not the group leader's role to evaluate the behavior of group members; rather, the leader should assist members in evaluating their own behavior.

_____ 8. The goal of reality therapy is to help people fulfill their needs, to make more effective choices, and to gain better control of their lives—without infringing on others' rights.

_____ 9. Unless clients are willing to accept responsibility for their behavior, they will not be able to change it.

_____10. Group members are able to change when they accept that what they are doing, thinking, and feeling is not simply happening to them but that they are making choices.

Summary of Basic Assumptions and Key Concepts of the Choice Theory/Reality Therapy Approach to Groups

1. Choice theory/reality therapy is grounded on the premise that human behavior is purposeful and originates within the individual rather than from external forces. All behavior is motivated by the striving to fulfill five basic psychological needs: survival or self-preservation, love and

belonging, power or inner control, freedom or independence, and fun or enjoyment. This approach focuses on solving problems and on taking charge of one's life. By evaluating what we are doing and what we want, we are able to achieve opportunities for choice.

2. We perceive the world against the background of our needs and wants rather than as objective reality. We create our own inner world. We are not locked into any one mode of behavior, although we must behave in some way. Behavior is the attempt to control our perceptions of the external world to fit our internal and personal world (or what we want).

3. Choice theory teaches that the only person whose behavior we can control is our own. How we feel is not controlled by others or by events. Choice theory explains how and why we make the choices that determine the course of our lives. With its emphasis on connection and interpersonal relationships, choice theory is well suited for group counseling.

4. Choice theory is based on the assumption that all we can do from birth to death is behave. Everything we do can be understood within the context of *total behavior,* which is made up of four inseparable components: acting, thinking, feeling, and physiology. All total behavior is chosen, yet we have much more direct control over the acting and thinking components than over the feeling and physiological components.

5. Reality therapy (the WDEP system) is the methodology for implementing the key concepts of choice theory. Reality therapy is active, directive, structured, psychoeducational, and focuses on *doing* and on *action plans*. Attitudes, feelings, insight, transference, one's past, and unconscious motivations are not emphasized. This approach deals with helping clients solving problems and cope with the demands of reality by making more effective choices. People can improve the quality of their lives through honestly examining their wants, needs, and perceptions.

6. Group leaders strive to establish an empathic and trusting counseling relationship, which is the foundation for the effective use of reality therapy. Once this therapeutic alliance has been established, leaders teach members the basics of choice theory and its applications to their lives.

7. The reality therapy group leader assists members through a process of skillful questioning and exploration aimed at getting them to assess what they want. Leaders tend to focus on the strengths and resources of members rather than on their failures. This is done by encouraging members to look at their unused potential and to use it to fulfill their needs and gain more effective control of their lives.

8. Group leaders tend to focus on what members can do in the present to change their behavior. Members are guided in the process of self-evaluation, and they are also taught how to make a plan for action, to commit themselves to doing what it will take to change, and to follow through with their action plan. Accountability is a vital part of reality therapy. Group leaders do not encourage members to spend much time exploring the past but consistently assist members in dealing with what they are doing currently. Group therapists focus especially on the client's relationships, no matter what the presenting problem is, for it is assumed that the problem relationship is generally part of our present lives.

9. Grounded in choice theory, the WDEP system assists people in satisfying their basic needs. These strategies are designed to promote change: W = wants; D = direction and doing; E = self-evaluation; and P = planning. The WDEP framework involves a collaborative approach in which the group leader and members join together in determining goals and plans of action.

10. The practice of reality therapy involves two major components: (1) the counseling environment and (2) specific procedures that lead to changes in behavior. This is referred to as the cycle of counseling. A great deal of emphasis is placed on creating a supportive environment that allows clients to change. Through a process of skillful questioning, leaders help members recognize, define, and refine how they wish to meet their needs. The procedures that lead to change are based on the assumption that we are motivated to change (1) when we are convinced that our present behavior is not getting us what we want and (2) when we believe we can choose other behaviors that will get us closer to what we want. Members explore what they want, what they have, and what they are not getting. Leaders function by holding a mirror before the members and asking, "What do you see for yourself now and in the future?"

See the chart on pages 215–216 for details of basic concepts of choice theory and reality therapy.

Glossary of Key Terms for Choice Theory/Reality Therapy

- **Autonomy** The state that exists when individuals accept responsibility for what they do and take control of their lives.
- **Commitment** The act of sticking to a realistic plan aimed at change.
- **Choice theory** The view that humans are internally motivated; based on an internal control psychology that explains how and why we make the choices that determine the course of our lives.
- **Counseling environment** The practice of reality therapy that involves a leader's personal involvement with the members and those leader attitudes and behaviors that promote change.
- **Cycle of counseling** Specific ways of creating a positive climate in which counseling can occur. The proper therapeutic environment provides the foundation for the implementation of counseling strategies.
- **Essential human needs** The innate forces that motivate all behavior that consist of survival, belonging, power, freedom, and fun.
- **Involvement (or therapeutic alliance)** Therapist's attempt to be part of the client's quality world, namely, the world of wants.
- **Paining behaviors** Choosing misery by developing symptoms (such as "headaching," "depressing," and "anxietying") because these seem to be the best behaviors available at the time.
- **Picture album** The perceptions and images we have of how we can fulfill our basic psychological needs.
- **Quality school** Applying concepts of choice theory to the classroom and to groups in the schools.
- **Quality world** Another phrase for "picture album." Our view of what we have in our present world and what we would like to have. These are intense wants, not whims.
- **Reality therapy** An approach based on the key concepts of choice theory that was founded by William Glasser.
- **Responsibility** The act of satisfying one's needs in ways that do not interfere with others' fulfilling their needs.

CYCLE OF COUNSELING, COACHING, MANAGING, SUPERVISING, & PARENTING

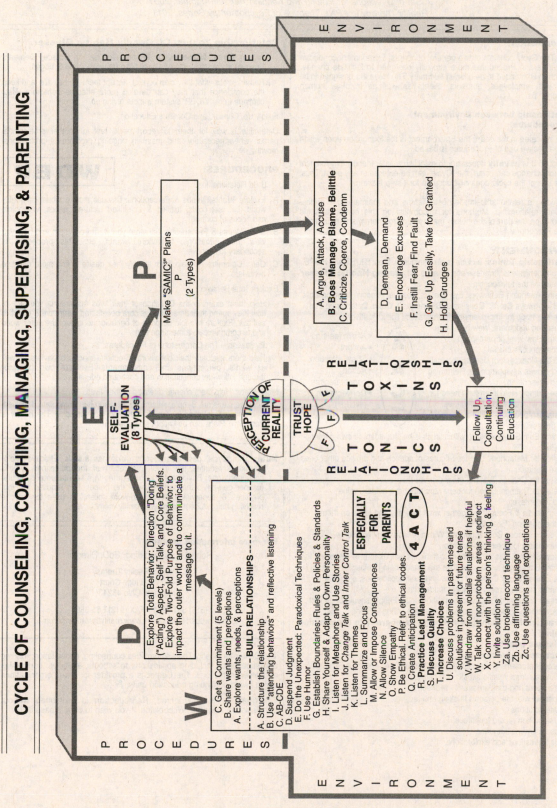

ENVIRONMENT

PROCEDURES

E

P

Make "SAMIC³" Plans
P
(2 Types)

A. Argue, Attack, Accuse
B. Boss Manage, Blame, Belittle
C. Criticize, Coerce, Condemn

D. Demean, Demand
E. Encourage Excuses
F. Instill Fear, Find Fault
G. Give Up Easily, Take for Granted
H. Hold Grudges

SELF-EVALUATION (8 Types)

PERCEPTION OF CURRENT REALITY

TRUST
HOPE

RELATIONSHIP TOXINS

RELATIONSHIP TONICS

Follow Up,
Consultation,
Continuing
Education

D

Explore Total Behavior: Direction "Doing"
("Acting") Aspect, Self-Talk, and Core Beliefs.
Explore Two-Fold Purpose of Behavior: to
impact the outer world and to communicate a
message to it.

W

C. Get a Commitment (5 levels)
B. Share wants and perceptions
A. Explore wants, needs, & perceptions
-----------**BUILD RELATIONSHIPS**----------
A. Structure the relationship
B. Use "attending behaviors" and reflective listening
C. AB-CDE
D. Suspend Judgment
E. Do the Unexpected: Paradoxical Techniques
F. Use Humor
G. Establish Boundaries: Rules & Policies & Standards
H. Share Yourself & Adapt to Own Personality
I. Listen for Metaphors and Use Stories
J. Listen for *Change Talk* and *Inner Control Talk*
K. Listen for Themes
L. Summarize and Focus
M. Allow or Impose Consequences
N. Allow Silence
O. Show Empathy
P. Be Ethical. Refer to ethical codes.
Q. Create Anticipation
R. **Practice Lead Management**
S. **Discuss Quality**
T. **Increase Choices**
U. Discuss problems in past tense and
   solutions in present or future tense
V. Withdraw from volatile situations if helpful
W. Talk about non-problem areas - redirect
X. Connect with the person's thinking & feeling
Y. Invite solutions
Za. Use broken record technique
Zb. Use affirming language
Zc. Use questions and explorations

ESPECIALLY FOR PARENTS

4 A C T

PROCEDURES

ENVIRONMENT

Developed by **Robert E. Wubbolding, EdD**
from the works of William Glasser, MD, the founder of choice theory/reality therapy

Copyright 1986 Robert E. Wubbolding, EdD
19th Revision 2015

SUMMARY DESCRIPTION OF THE
"CYCLE OF COUNSELING, COACHING, MANAGING, SUPERVISING, & PARENTING"

The Cycle is explained in detail in books by Robert E. Wubbolding: Reality Therapy for the 21st Century, 2000
A Set of Directions for Putting and Keeping Yourself Together, 2001
Reality Therapy In APA's *Theories of Psychotherapy* Series, 2011

Introduction:

The Cycle consists of two general concepts: Environment conducive to change and Procedures more explicitly designed to facilitate change. This chart is intended to be a **brief** summary. The ideas are designed to be used with employees, students, clients as well as in other human relationships.

Relationship between Environment & Procedures:

1. As indicated in the chart, the Environment is the foundation upon which the effective use of Procedures is based.

2. Though it is **usually** necessary to establish a safe, friendly Environment before change can occur, the "Cycle" can be entered at any point. Thus, the use of the cycle does **not** occur in lock step fashion.

3. Building a relationship implies establishing and maintaining a professional relationship. Methods for accomplishing this comprise some efforts on the part of the helper that are Environmental and others that are Procedural.

ENVIRONMENT:

Relationship Tonics: a close relationship is built on TRUST and HOPE through friendliness, firmness and fairness. **Cf. Caring Habits: Glasser**
A. Structure the relationship.
B. Using Attending Behaviors: Eye contact, posture, effective listening skills.
C. AB = "Always Be . . ." **C**onsistent, **C**ourteous & **C**alm, **D**etermined that there is hope for improvement, **E**nthusiastic (Think Positively).
D. Suspend Judgment: View behaviors from a low level of perception, i.e., acceptance is crucial.
E. Do the Unexpected: Use paradoxical techniques as appropriate; Reframing and Prescribing.
F. Use Humor: Help them fulfill need for fun within reasonable boundaries.
G. Establish boundaries: the relationship is professional.

4 ACT
• Affirm feelings
• Accept
• Show affection
• Action consequences
• Conversation (WDEP)
• Time together

H. Share Self: Self-disclosure within limits is helpful; adapt to own personal style.
I. Listen for Metaphors: Use their figures of speech and provide other ones. Use stories.
J. Listen for *Change Talk* and *Inner Control Talk*.
K. Listen to Themes: Listen for behaviors that have helped, value judgements, etc.
L. Summarize & Focus: Tie together what they say and focus on them rather than on "Real World."
M. Allow or Impose Consequences: Within reason, they should be responsible for their own behavior.
N. Allow Silence: This allows them to think, as well as to take responsibility.
O. Show Empathy: Perceive as does the person being helped.
P. Be Ethical: Study Codes of Ethics and their applications, e.g., how to handle suicide threats or violent tendencies.
Q. Create anticipation and communication hope. People should be taught that something good will happen if they are willing to work.
R. **Practice lead management, e.g., democracy in determining rules**.
S. **Discuss quality.**
T. **Increases choices.**
U. Discuss problems in the past tense, solutions in present or future tense.
V. Withdraw from volatile situations if helpful.
W. Talk about non-problem areas - redirect.
X. Connect with the person's thinking and feeling.
Y. Invite solutions.
Za. Use broken record technique.
Zb. Use affirming language.
Zc. Use questions and explorations.

Relationship Toxins: Cf. Deadly Habits: Glasser

Argue, **Boss Manage,** or Blame, Criticize or Coerce, Demean, Encourage Excuses, Instill Fear, or Give up easily, Hold Grudges.

Rather, stress what they **can** control, accept them as they are, and keep the confidence that they can develop more effective behaviors. Also, continue to us "WDEP" system without giving up.

Follow Up, Consult, and Continue Education:

Determine a way for them to report back, talk to another professional person when necessary, and maintain ongoing program of professional growth.

PROCEDURES:

WDEP

Build Relationships:

A. Explore **W**ants, Needs & Perceptions: Discuss picture album or quality world, i.e., set goals, fulfilled & unfulfilled pictures, needs, viewpoints and "locus of control."
B. Share Wants & Perceptions: Tell what you want from them and how you view their situations, behaviors, wants, etc. This procedure is secondary to A above.
C. Get a Commitment: Help them solidify their desire to find more effective behaviors.

Explore Total Behavior:

Help them examine the **D**irection of their lives, as well as specifics of how they spend their time. Discuss core beliefs and ineffective & effective self talk. Explore two-fold purpose of behavior: to impact the outer world and to communicate a message to it.

Evaluation – The Cornerstone of Procedures:

Help them evaluate their behavioral direction, specific behaviors as well as wants, perceptions and commitments. Evaluate own behavior through follow-up, consultation and continued education.

Make **P**lans: Help them change direction of their lives.

Effective plans are **S**imple, **A**ttainable, **M**easurable, **I**mmediate, **I**nvolved, **C**onsistent, **C**ontrolled by the planner, and **C**ommitted to. The helper is **P**ersistent. Plans can be linear or paradoxical.

Note: The "Cycle" describes specific guidelines & skills. Effective implementation requires the artful integration of the guidelines & skills contained under Environment & Procedures in a spontaneous & natural manner geared to the personality of the helper. This requires training, practices & supervision. Also, the word "client" is used for anyone receiving help: student, employee, family member, etc.

For more information contact:

Robert E. Wubbolding, EdD, Director

Center for Reality Therapy
5490 Windridge Court
Cincinnati, Ohio 45243

(513) 561-1911 • FAX (513) 561-3568
E-mail: wubsrt@fuse.net • www.realitytherapywub.com

The Center for Reality Therapy provides counseling, consultation, training and supervision including applications to schools, agencies, companies and other institutions. The Center is a provider for many organizations which award continuing education units.

- **Self-evaluation** Clients' assessment of current behavior to determine whether it is working and meeting their needs.
- **Total behavior** The integrated components of doing, thinking, feeling, and physiology. Choice theory assumes that all elements of behavior are interrelated.
- **WDEP system** Key procedures applied to the practice of reality therapy groups. The strategies help clients identify their wants, determine the direction their behavior is taking them, make a self-evaluation, and design plans for change.

Exercises and Activities for Choice Theory/Reality Therapy in Groups

Rationale

Reality therapy is a practical approach with many uses and applications for a variety of types of groups. As you review the basic concepts and principles of choice theory, think about ways to translate them into your practice with different kinds of groups. Also, reflect on how you could apply choice theory to help you get what you want and to gain more effective control of your own life. Some of the following exercises, activities, and questions can be used on your own, and others can be used in small groups. After you have worked with this material and answered the questions, you will be in a better position to know which of these ideas you might want to employ in the groups you lead or will lead.

Exercises

1. *Are you meeting your needs?* Choice theory holds that total behavior is purposeful, that it originates from within the individual rather than from external sources, and that psychological needs are powerful motivating forces. Choice theory also contends that we develop pictures in our head (an inner picture album) of specific wants. Our inner pictures make up our ideal world, or the way we want life to be. We are motivated to mold the external world to match our ever-changing inner world. Discuss the ways in which your needs are being met, as well as how you see them influencing your daily behavior. Arrange the following five needs in the order of priority to you. As you review these needs, attempt to identify what you consider to be your key strengths.
   a. **Survival (or self-preservation).** To what degree are you maintaining vitality and good health rather than merely surviving?
   b. **Love and belonging.** What do you do to meet your needs for involvement with others? In what ways do you feel a sense of belonging? Are you able to both give and receive love?
   c. **Power (or inner control).** When do you feel a sense of power? To what degree do you experience a sense of inner control? In what areas of your life do you feel most competent? When do you feel recognized?
   d. **Freedom (or independence).** To what degree do you feel that you are in charge of your life and are moving in the direction that you want?
   e. **Fun (or enjoyment).** What activities do you do for enjoyment? Do you have as much fun as you would like? What specific changes might you want to make in this area of your life?

STAGES OF DEVELOPMENT OF THE CHOICE THEORY/REALITY THERAPY GROUP

Dimension	Initial Stage	Working Stage	Final Stage
Key developmental tasks and goals	First task is to create member-to-member relationships and a sense of involvement in the group. Leader-to-member relationships based on trust are essential. Major goal of initial stage is to get members to look at the degree to which current behavior is meeting their needs and to determine the direction of their behavior.	Focus is on present behavior rather than feelings. Past is important only insofar as it influences present behavior. The central goal is to create a climate wherein members will learn to understand how their irresponsibility and poor choices have led to their personal problems; in this way members can make better choices.	Specific plans for achieving desirable behavior patterns must be established. Although plans are crucial for behavioral change to occur, a noncritical therapeutic milieu must be created to give members the strength to carry out their plans. It is important that the plan be "owned" by the member.
Role and tasks of group leader	Group leader has the task of fostering involvement among the members by being active with every member. Leader may question, ask others to make comments, and encourage interaction in the group. Modeling is crucial. Leader nudges members to look at what they are getting from their behavior.	Leader encourages members to evaluate their own behavior, asks members whether their behavior is meeting their needs, and firmly rejects excuses and rationalizations. Leader teaches members how to apply the basics of choice theory to their lives. Counselor avoids labeling people with diagnostic categories.	Leader assists members in formulating realistic plans for change and creates a noncritical therapeutic climate that helps them believe change is possible. Leader does not give up even if members fail to carry out their plans; he or she insists on finding a short-range plan that will lead to success.
Role of group members	Members concentrate on current behavior and problem areas. Focus may be on how each member attempts to gain love and feelings of self-worth and success. Members are expected to face their problems and to make plans to solve them. Making these plans for change begins early in the group. Members explore their "picture album" and whether what they are doing is getting them what they want. They define what they expect and want from the leader and other members. Members examine the direction of their lives.	Members evaluate their own behavior. They must understand what they are doing *now* as well as what they are getting from this behavior. After they decide if they have what they want, members must decide for themselves if they are willing to change their patterns of behavior. The focus is on choosing better behaviors to satisfy their needs. The work is aimed at teaching members how they can gain better control of their lives. The cornerstone of the approach is to assist members in self-evaluation.	Realistic plans to change behavior are made and carried out. If members do not carry out their plans, they are expected to state when they will complete them. They are to accept responsibility for what they do and to make commitments. Plans help members change the direction of their lives. Effective plans are simple, attainable, measurable, immediate, consistent, and controlled by the planner. Action plans assist members in achieving their long-range goals.

Techniques	In keeping with the goal of establishing involvement, leader will encourage members to talk about any subjects of interest to them. An attempt is made to find out what members want from the group. Leader invites members to explore their wants, perceptions, and needs.	Confrontation; insistence on importance of evaluating behavior and making decisions; avoidance of punishment. Leader uses techniques of skillful questioning. Other techniques are use of humor, use of paradox, and designing action plans.	Contracts; behavioral strategies such as role playing, behavior rehearsal, homework assignments, and so on; encouragement and support. Plans are refined and members commit to a plan to bring about changes once the group is over. Plans must be meaningful for members.
Questions to consider	Once you have established a relationship with members, focus on current behavior. In doing so, questions you may want to ask are: • What are you doing now? • What did you do this week? • What did you want to do differently this past week? • What stopped you from doing what you wanted to do? • What will you do tomorrow? If members seem reluctant to accept responsibility for their own problems, what might you do? How will you help members discuss their relationships? How would you help members establish clear and realistic goals? Would you focus exclusively on behavioral goals? Would you work with feelings and thoughts as well?	A central task is to get members to look at what they are doing to decide whether their course of action is working. How can you challenge members in a nonjudgmental way to make an evaluation of their behavior? How can you avoid imposing your values on members? How can you challenge members to make an honest evaluation if they seem resistant? What if the members cling to what you consider self-defeating ways of behaving? What do you see as your role in planning with members, checking with them about how well the plan is working, and making revisions in plans as needed? How can you use the group process in helping members make and follow through with their commitments? How will you get members to be more involved with people outside the group?	How might you avoid giving up on certain members, even if they fail to meet their commitments? What might you do with members who do not seem willing to carry out short-range plans? What are some ways to use the group sessions to help members practice new behaviors that they will try out in daily situations? What methods might you employ to encourage members to practice outside the group what they are learning in the session? What are some ways to help members express and explore their fears of failing? How can you reinforce success and small gains? Can you think of ways to encourage members to take action even though they feel defeated? What follow-up procedures might you use to assess the extent to which members make and maintain positive changes after a group?

Reactions: Summarize your reactions to the choice theory/reality therapy perspective on group developmental stages. What do you like *most*? *least*? What aspects of this approach would you incorporate in your style of leadership?

2. *Choosing your total behavior.* Choice theory is based on the assumption that we choose our total behavior, which is composed of the interrelated elements of doing, thinking, feeling, and physiology. In our attempt to gain more effective control, we behave in the world to get the picture we want at that time. Every total behavior is our best attempt to get what we want. Considering this set of basic assumptions, discuss the following questions as they apply to you in your group.
   a. What experiences have you had that either support or discredit the notion that you have the ability to change what you are doing and some ability to change what you are thinking? Do you find it is easier to change what you are doing and thinking rather than what you are feeling? Why or why not?
   b. To what extent do you find that when you begin to *act* differently you also change what you are thinking and feeling? Can you provide any personal examples?
   c. Reality therapists claim that it is inaccurate to speak of being depressed, having a headache, or being anxious. It is more accurate to say that we are "depressing," "headaching," or "anxietying." In your group provide examples of states over which you think you have some control. To what degree do you think that some of your behaviors (or actions, thoughts, feelings, physiology) are beyond your control?
3. *Effective and ineffective control.* How does what you say about yourself affect the way people view and treat you? Answer these questions about how you perceive yourself.
   a. What are some of your self-fulfilling prophecies?
   b. If your parents were to describe you in terms of the degree of your success, what might they say about you? What do you imagine your best friend would say? If you are in a group now, how do you think other members might perceive you?
   c. Is there a difference between the way you see yourself now and the way you'd like to be? If so, what changes would you like to make? What are some of the ways that you restrict your possibilities by adhering to fixed notions that make it difficult for change to occur? Do you tell yourself that you can't be other than you are—that you can't change?
   d. What would you say about your current ability to control your life?
4. *Involvement.* Reality therapy stresses the importance of involvement (or a spirit of caring) as the foundation for the group process. Ask yourself these questions:
   a. If you are in a group now, to what degree do you experience a sense of involvement with the leader and the other members.
   b. In what ways do you think a group leader might demonstrate his or her involvement with the participants? How would you involve yourself with the members in your groups?
5. *Applying WDEP to the cycle of counseling.* (Refer to the chart on the cycle in Chapter 15.) The cycle of counseling involves both the counseling environment and procedures; see if you can answer these basic questions.
   a. W = Explore your wants, needs, and perceptions. What is it that you want? If you had what you wanted now, how would your life be different?
   b. D = Explore the direction in which your total behavior is moving you. What are you currently doing, and is it working for you?
   c. E = It is essential to make a self-evaluation of your current behavior. What changes are you willing to make in your life?
   d. P = Make plans designed to change the direction of your life. It is essential that there be a commitment to the plan. What are you willing to commit to changing?

6. *Self-evaluation.* A central procedure in reality therapy consists of asking members to assess what they are doing to determine whether they are getting what they want and whether their behavior is working for them. Spend some time thinking about how making an evaluation of your behavior could benefit you.

   a. As you review your behavior on a given day, what would you most want to change about yourself? Are there any specific actions or thoughts that you would like to change because they are not working for you? To what degree do you think you are getting what you want? What are you willing to do to make the changes you want? Are you committed to taking action to change?

   b. What are some values that are important to you? What difficulties do you think you may have in allowing the members in your groups to make their own evaluations?

7. *Developing an action plan for change.* Think about what you would do in each of these situations.

   a. Think about a particular behavior that you want to change and are willing to change. If you are in a group at this time, work out a specific plan that will lead to change. Discuss the details of the plan with those in your group. One of the best ways to understand the process of formulating personal plans is for you to develop such a plan yourself.

   b. What commitments would you, as a leader, expect from those who participate in your groups? What methods would you use to assist them in formulating specific action plans? How do you imagine you'd handle participants who continually made plans but then returned to group without having followed through on most of them? How would you reframe this failure to a success?

   c. How would you, as a group member, deal with other members who talked about wanting to change but refused to make any concrete plans to put into action outside the group?

   d. As a practitioner of reality therapy, how would you make your group members accountable for implementing their plans of action? How could you include the other group members in the process of holding a particular member accountable for his or her plan? What might others do to cross the line between being helpful in holding a member accountable and being intrusive?

8. *Role-playing activity with involuntary group members.* In your class or group discuss some reality therapy strategies you might use if you were leading or coleading an involuntary group. After this discussion, each member can assume the identity of an involuntary client and then role-play this person in your group. Two students can function as coleaders and demonstrate ways of working with such a client. Attempt to keep within the reality therapy perspective. Allow enough time before the end of the session for processing. What was it like to lead this group by staying within the parameters of this approach? What was the experience like for those who role-played an involuntary client?

9. *Role-playing activity with a specific value issue.* Think about a specific concern of a group member that might pose difficulties for you as a group leader. Identify a particular value conflict a member is experiencing that you think would be challenging for you. Here are some issues members are likely to present:

   a. The client is an adolescent girl who is being pressured by her boyfriend to engage in sexual relations.

   b. The client is having difficulty accepting the religion with which he was brought up, yet he hesitates to leave the religion because of his fears and guilt feelings.

c. The client discloses that he is having an affair and is not certain whether he wants to remain married and keep the affair going or leave his wife for the other woman.

d. The client is a member of a cultural group that values loyalty to one's family. This woman is contemplating leaving her husband because of her deep dissatisfaction with what she refers to as a "dead-end relationship." What mainly stops her are the "internal voices" that remind her that she would bring shame to her entire family if she were to divorce.

10. *Reality therapy with diverse client populations.* Consider the strengths of reality therapy as they pertain to working with culturally diverse client populations. Apply the WDEP system to group work from a diversity perspective. In your groups also consider other factors that could be strengths of reality therapy with multicultural populations such as your active role as a leader who teaches and provides structure, the emphasis on making plans for change, the emphasis on belonging, and the value of self-evaluation. Can you think of any potential disadvantages or cautions in applying reality therapy with diverse client populations? How would you implement the WDEP system with clients who tend to communicate more indirectly that you do?

11. *Using reality therapy in school-based groups.* As a group, develop a brief proposal for using reality therapy as the basic format for a counseling group with either elementary school children or high school adolescents. In designing your group, consider these guidelines:

_____ The group will deal primarily with present concerns of the members.

_____ The group leader teaches the members how to evaluate the direction their behavior is taking them to determine what changes, if any, they are willing to make.

_____ The group leader strives to get involved in an active and personal way with the members.

_____ The interventions are mainly directed at what members are doing and thinking.

_____ Group members spend time exploring the degree to which their basic needs of survival, love and belonging, power, freedom, and fun are being met.

_____ The group leader raises helpful questions at the beginning of a group.

_____ The emphasis is on the quality worlds of the members.

_____ The group would involve considerable teaching and developing homework to carry outside of the group.

_____ Considerable emphasis is given to assisting each member in developing a concrete and realistic plan of action to bring about change.

12. *Role-playing activity for a particular age group.* You can do this activity in your group or in a small group within the larger class. Pick an age category who will be in your group. For example, you might have a group for children who are coping with divorce, a group for adolescents who want to explore social and personal problems, a group for veterans of war who are experiencing adjustment problems, a group of homeless people in a shelter, or a group for elderly clients who are in a day-care facility. Each person role-plays a particular individual in the chosen group. Identify a concern for which you think you have empathy and with which you could get involved through role playing. Two students can volunteer to be the coleaders. Apply what you know of choice theory and the interventions made in reality therapy to leading this group. After the session, discuss the possible advantages and disadvantages of working with this type of group with this approach. How would you apply the WDEP system differently at the various stages of group development?

Questions for Reflection and Discussion

1. Choice theory is based on the premise that we can control what we do and think. If we change what we are doing and thinking, it is highly likely that we will also change how we are feeling. Do you agree with this assumption? What are the implications of this viewpoint in working with clients who suffer from depression? How does this assumption fit for you personally? Discuss the possible ease and difficulty in changing actions.

2. Choice theory assumes that everything we do, think, and feel is generated by what happens inside of us. Thus, the proper focus for therapy is not to discuss the external world but to deal with the internal world of the client. What are the implications of this perspective for your group practice? How would this view influence your interventions in a group?

3. In many respects reality therapy is at the opposite end of the therapeutic spectrum from psychoanalytic therapy. What contrasts do you see between these two models? Do you see any similarities?

4. What are some of the unique advantages of practicing reality therapy in groups as opposed to individual counseling? How can others in the group help a member make a behavioral evaluation, form a realistic plan, and commit to an action program?

5. Compare and contrast choice theory/reality therapy with the experiential therapies (person-centered therapy, Gestalt therapy, psychodrama, and the existential therapies). To what extent do you think choice theory/reality therapy incorporates or fails to incorporate elements of these approaches? How would you blend choice theory/reality therapy with the experiential therapies in your groups?

6. Some of the more cognitively oriented therapies (TA, rational emotive behavior therapy, and other cognitive behavioral therapies) emphasize the role of one's thoughts, values, beliefs, and attitudes as crucial determinants of behavior. Reality therapy focuses mainly on actions. How would you blend choice theory/reality therapy's emphasis on acting with the emphasis of the cognitive therapies on thinking? What kinds of interventions could you devise that would make use of both cognitive and behavioral dimensions? How might you incorporate interventions aimed mainly at an exploration of feelings with this cognitive behavioral emphasis?

7. What are your reactions to those who criticize reality therapy on the ground that it is simplistic? To what extent do you agree with the reality therapist's contention that the procedures are simple to discuss but that putting them into practice requires considerable therapeutic skill and creativity?

8. Reality therapy requires members to make an honest and accurate assessment of their current behavior to determine whether it is working for them. In considering some of the groups that you want to organize, how might you assist members in making this self-evaluation? What problems might you anticipate with respect to actually getting members to make such a self-evaluation?

9. What are a few key concepts of choice theory that have the greatest applicability in working with cultural diversity within your groups? What reality therapy techniques might you most draw from as a way to work within the framework of the diverse cultural backgrounds of the members of your groups?

10. What are some specific concepts of choice theory that have relevance for group work with children and adolescents? How might you modify some of the techniques of reality therapy in working with children and adolescents in groups? What particular value do you see in using a reality therapy framework in devising groups in the school setting?
11. What two or three reality therapy techniques are especially useful to you and why?

An Expert's Perspective on Choice Theory/Reality Therapy in Groups: by Robert E. Wubbolding

ROBERT E. WUBBOLDING, EdD, is Professor Emeritus of Counseling at Xavier University, Cincinnati, Ohio, and director of the Center for Reality Therapy in Cincinnati.

1. **What attracted you to this particular theoretical orientation? How does this theory fit with the person you are?**

   I have always believed in personal responsibility and that human beings have free will. Reality therapy places human choice as a cornerstone in both theory and practice. The system allows for empathy and compassion for people who make mistakes, who choose harmful or self-destructive behaviors, and who are rejected by other people. I believe it is applicable to all cultures. I, myself, have taught it on every continent except Antarctica.

2. **What Key Concepts (1 to 3) of this theory are most applicable to the practice of group counseling?**

   Here-and-now concerns: In my view, most people join groups because of issues or problems that they see as "here-and-now" concerns. A counselor utilizing reality therapy does not ignore the past but acknowledges that it has an impact on current choices, actions, thoughts, and feelings. As William Faulkner, the American novelist said, "The past is not dead. In fact, it is not even past." However, choice theory/reality therapy emphasizes human motivation as current in that people make choices based on current unfulfilled hopes, dreams, desires and wants.

   "As if" principle: I believe that not all behaviors are 100% chosen, but that they are generated from within a person and are best treated with the principle summarized by two words: *as if*. Group counselors using reality therapy focus on actions, cognition, and feelings as generated from within the person. They deal with these components *as if* group members have at least some control over them. This perception of group members is very empowering to clients, especially those who believe that they have no choice and are completely victimized by other people or systems.

3. **What Techniques (1 to 3) from this theory have the most practical value for group work practitioners?**

   Define what you want to gain: Reality therapy and skilled reality therapists incorporate dozens, if not hundreds, of techniques for facilitating groups. In general, helping clients define what they want to gain or work on is a helpful and multifaceted technique with voluntary groups.

Self-evaluation of current behavior: Members of any type of group, voluntary or involuntary, are asked about their current behavior: how they have been spending their time recently, what thoughts go through their minds about being here in the group and about themselves, how they feel about entering the group and about group membership. The counselor's skill in self-evaluation interventions helps clients link with each other. Questions such as, "When Susan said she had done _____, do you think that was helpful to her and to other people, Charley?"

New vocabulary for conflict: When the group reaches the conflict stage, the skilled counselor helps members formulate a new kind of vocabulary that is more courteous, less harsh, and noncritical. The reality therapist can intervene by helping group members reformulate "That is the stupidest thing I ever heard" to "I couldn't disagree more with what you just said." Helping group members communicate in a more need-satisfying way with the use of nonexplosive and courteous statements facilitates group growth and the satisfaction of the need for belonging.

4. **How does this theory have particular relevance for addressing diversity and social justice issues in group work?**
The fact that human beings choose their behavior, or at least generate it from within, transcends cultural differences. I contend unabashedly that this principle has universal applicability. I demonstrate this fact in workshop training sessions around the world. Individuals coerced into groups, such as court ordered clients, clients in correctional programs, and in addiction programs often perceive the world as being against them. It is their perception, *not the counselor's* that is primary. Whether the counselor believes oppression or social justice is an issue is mostly irrelevant in group counseling. Of course, the counselor can work to alleviate unfairness and discrimination outside counseling sessions and can serve as a community educator.

A group unwillingly present for counseling often perceives that they are "put upon" and treated unfairly by people in power. They have an external sense of control. A counselor can begin by asking them to talk about how they have been treated badly. The counselor need not agree or disagree with them. As they describe their plights, they begin to feel inclusion in the group. As this feeling increases, the reality therapist listens for language that indicates that they have made choices, that they have at least some control in their lives. A skilled counselor can elicit hints of personal responsibility for future decisions and then proceed to help clients make more effective choices. The counselor can translate and reframe their frustrations into wants or desires to be free of coercion. After these wants are out in the open, the counselor then assists clients to evaluate their behavior, to validate their efforts to cope and to make realistically doable plans.

5. **Raise a question from this theoretical framework that you consider especially important for group work practice.**
Does reality therapy apply to severe emotional and mental problems? Reality therapy began in a mental hospital and a correctional institution, both of which were populated by people with severe mental and behavioral diagnoses. Whether reality therapists counsel individuals or groups, they listen empathically to clients' stories but focus on the healthy,

sane part of the person. They acknowledge the disorder and diagnose it, yet when counseling they talk to the healthy portion of the human being. For instance, when a reality therapist conducts a group with antisocial clients, the focus is on behaviors that are not antisocial. In a mental hospital, the reality therapist facilitates the patients' discussion of their current relationships, what they're doing when they are acting normally, how they have fun without acting in ways that the rest of society would disapprove of. When the effective behaviors become the focus of counseling, the group members develop a sense of inclusion and eventually the feeling of cohesion based on healthy behaviors rather than on their diagnoses.

I do not believe that the reality therapist needs to be an expert diagnostician. To be an effective reality therapist does not require experiences similar or identical with those of their clients. When I worked at a halfway house for women ex-offenders, they often asked in the group counseling, "How can you help me if you don't take drugs and if you've never been in prison?" In the beginning of my work, I became defensive when answering this question. Before long I realized that the best response is what I learned in a telephone conversation with Dr. Glasser. "The fact that I have not been in prison is the very reason I can help you. I am an expert at staying out of prison. I am an expert at living without drugs. You know more about drugs and prison than I do. I know how to stay out of prison and live a life free of drugs and secure a permanent job. That is why I can help you."

Your Thoughts on Dr. Wubbolding's Choice Theory/Reality Therapy Perspective on Group Work

1. What do you understand by Dr. Wubbolding's WDEP approach to practicing group counseling? What aspects of this model would you want to use as a group counselor?
2. Dr. Wubbolding emphasizes the importance of group members' making a self-evaluation of their current behaviors? What difference do you see between a group leader evaluating a member behavior versus a group member making his or her own evaluation?
3. Planning for change is critical in a reality therapy group. What ideas do you have for assisting members in making specific action plans that can help them accomplish their goals?

Quiz on Choice Theory/Reality Therapy: A Comprehension Check   Score _____%

Note: Please refer to Appendix I for the scoring key. Count 5 points for each error, and subtract the total from 100 to get your percentage score.

True/false items: Decide if the following statements are "more true" or "more false" as they apply to choice theory/reality therapy.

T   F   1. Reality therapy emphasizes an inner self-evaluation.
T   F   2. Reality therapy is basically an active, directive, didactic model.
T   F   3. In many ways Glasser's approach is grounded on phenomenological and existential premises.

T F 4. The essence of choice theory is that we are determined by events during our early childhood.

T F 5. Reality therapists would probably encourage their clients to get into contact with their buried feelings before they would expect them to change their behavior.

T F 6. One of the main functions of the group leader is to make an evaluation of each member's current behavior.

T F 7. Reality therapy emphasizes discussion of feelings and attitudes, for the assumption is that behavior will not change unless attitudes change first.

T F 8. Reality therapy has been used effectively in addiction treatment and recovery programs for more than 30 years.

T F 9. Reality group therapists tend to avoid asking group members questions, for doing so often leads to defensiveness.

T F 10. Group members are expected to make plans for change and also to commit to these plans.

Multiple-choice items: Select the *one best answer* among the alternatives given. Consider each question within the framework of choice theory/reality therapy.

_____11. Reality therapy rests on the central idea that
a. we need insight into the cause of our problems if we hope to change.
b. we choose our behavior and are responsible for what we do, think, and feel.
c. environmental factors largely control what we are doing.
d. the way to change dysfunctional behavior is to reexperience a situation in which we originally became psychologically stuck.
e. our family of origin sets our patterns for interacting with others.

_____12. With which one of the following conclusions would Glasser disagree?
a. We are most likely to change if we are threatened by punishment.
b. We do not have to be the victim of our past.
c. We have more control over our life than we believe.
d. We strive to change the world outside of us to match our internal pictures of what we want.
e. We strive to gain more effective control of our life to fulfill our needs.

_____13. The core of reality therapy consists of
a. teaching clients how to acquire rational beliefs instead of irrational ones.
b. helping clients understand their unconscious dynamics.
c. giving clients opportunities to express unresolved feelings.
d. teaching clients to take effective control of their own life.
e. identifying clients' cognitive distortions by means of a Socratic dialogue.

_____14. Glasser identifies four psychological needs (plus survival) as the forces that drive us. Which of the following is *not* one of those needs?
a. transcendence
b. belonging
c. power
d. freedom
e. fun

_____15. All of the following are basic concepts of choice theory/reality therapy except
     a. total behavior.
     b. musturbatory beliefs.
     c. quality worlds.
     d. self-evaluation.
     e. planning and action.

_____16. All of the following procedures are commonly used by reality therapy except
     a. exploring wants, needs, and perceptions.
     b. exploring parental messages and early decision.
     c. focusing on current behavior.
     d. planning and commitment.
     e. engaging in self-evaluation.

_____17. Which of the following is *not* emphasized in choice theory/reality therapy?
     a. Focus on what one is doing
     b. A time-limited focus
     c. Exploration of how basic needs are being met
     d. A focus on understanding the origin of a client's problem

_____18. Another term for one's "quality world" is
     a. a basic psychological life position.
     b. a personal lifescript.
     c. fictional finalism.
     d. an inner picture album.

_____19. What is Glasser's thinking about depression?
     a. We depress or anger ourselves, rather than being depressed.
     b. Depression is due to unresolved childhood issues.
     c. The more effective way to treat depression is with the use of drugs and medication.
     d. Depression is best understood as anger turned inward.

_____20. Choice theory tends to focus on
     a. feeling and physiology.
     b. doing and thinking.
     c. coming to a fuller understanding of the past.
     d. the underlying causes for feelings of depression or anxiousness.
     e. how the family system controls our decisions.

CHAPTER SIXTEEN

Solution-Focused Brief Therapy and Motivational Interviewing in Groups

Prechapter Self-Inventory for Solution-Focused Brief Therapy

Directions: Refer to page 77 for general directions. Indicate your position on these statements using the following code:

5 = I *strongly agree* with this statement.
4 = I *agree,* in most respects, with this statement.
3 = I am *undecided* in my opinion about this statement.
2 = I *disagree,* in most respects, with this statement.
1 = I *strongly disagree* with this statement.

_____ 1. It is the therapist's role to create opportunities for the members to view themselves as being resourceful.

_____ 2. The leader has the task of moving the group from a problem focus to a solution focus, or to keep the group members on a solution track instead of a problem track.

_____ 3. If members concentrate on telling problem-saturated stories, they tend to keep themselves from moving in a positive direction.

_____ 4. A key goal is to create a group context in which the members are able to learn more about their personal abilities and then learn to solve their concerns on their own.

_____ 5. A task for group leaders is to engage in conversations with their clients about what is going well, about future possibilities, and explore what will likely lead to a sense of accomplishment.

_____ 6. People tend to respond better to a present and future approach to counseling than they do to a past orientation that dwells on why they have certain problems that they cannot solve.

_____ 7. Because success tends to build on itself, small changes are crucial in the process of change.

_____ 8. Asking group members to consider that a miracle takes place opens up a range of future possibilities.

_____ 9. The group counselor supplies the optimism, but the group members generate what is possible and contribute the movement that actualizes it.

_____ 10. Gathering information about a problem is not necessary for change to occur.

Prechapter Self-Inventory for Motivational Interviewing

Directions: Refer to page 77 for general directions. Indicate your position on these statements using the following code:

5 = I *strongly agree* with this statement.
4 = I *agree,* in most respects, with this statement.
3 = I am *undecided* in my opinion about this statement.
2 = I *disagree,* in most respects, with this statement.
1 = I *strongly disagree* with this statement.

_____ 1. Leaders need to reflectively listen to members to understand their subjective world.

_____ 2. Group leaders have the task of understanding members' perspectives without judgment or criticism.

_____ 3. Although members may see advantages to making life changes, they also may have many reservations and fears about changing.

_____ 4. Reluctance to change is a normal and expected part of the therapeutic process.

_____ 5. When the power relationship between leader and members is equalized, group members become empowered.

_____ 6. Although the group leader guides members in making a commitment to change, the leader does not decide where members should go.

_____ 7. It is good for group leaders to focus on what is working well for participants rather than dwelling on members' problems.

_____ 8. It can be helpful for members to acknowledge the discrepancies between their values and their behavior.

_____ 9. The therapeutic relationship is of critical importance in contributing to successful outcomes in a group.

_____10. Group therapy practice can be based on a person-centered philosophy, yet at the same time employ active and directive therapeutic strategies.

Summary of Basic Assumptions and Key Concepts of Solution-Focused Brief Therapy (SFBT)

1. SFBT is centered primarily on solutions rather than an exploration of problems. There is very little interest in identifying and exploring the causes of a problem, and little time is spent taking a family history or looking at past influences. The focus of therapy is almost exclusively on the present and future.

2. There are advantages to a positive focus on solutions and on the future. By concentrating on successes, beneficial changes are likely to occur. There are also advantages to keeping therapy simple and brief.

3. Participants in a counseling group have the capability of behaving effectively, even though this effectiveness may be temporarily blocked by negative cognitions. Problem-focused thinking prevents people from recognizing effective ways they have dealt with problems. There is a movement from problem-talk to solution-talk.

4. No problem happens all of the time. There are always exceptions to a problem situation, and these exceptions are important to discuss. By talking about these exceptions, members

can get control over what had seemed to be an insurmountable problem. The climate of these exceptions allows for the possibility of creating solutions.

5. Group members can be trusted in their intention to solve their problems. There are no universal solutions to specific problems that can be applied to all people. Each individual is unique and so, too, is each solution. Members can make progress by beginning with small changes, which pave the way for larger changes. Members' problems are solved one step at a time.

6. Some of the major tenets of SFBT are: (a) If it ain't broke, don't fix it; (b) If it works, do more of it; and (c) If it's not working, do something different.

7. Little attention is paid to pathology or to giving clients a diagnostic label. People are not viewed as being locked into a set of behaviors based on a history or a psychological diagnosis. Interventions in a group are based on the assumption that people are competent, and that given a climate where they can experience their competency, they are able to solve their own problems.

8. The solution-focused model emphasizes the role of group members establishing their own goals and preferences. This is done when a climate of mutual respect, dialogue, inquiry, and affirmation are a part of the group process.

9. The future is a hopeful place, and people are the architects of their own destiny. Group leaders strive to establish collaborative relationships with members, which they do by showing members how they can use the strengths and resources they already possess to construct solutions.

10. Solution-focused brief therapists adopt a "not knowing" position, or a nonexpert stance, as a way to put clients in the position of being the experts about their own lives. The therapist-as-expert is replaced by the client-as-expert. Therapists do not assume that they know more about the lives of clients than clients do.

Summary of Basic Assumptions and Key Concepts of Motivational Interviewing (MI)

1. The MI approach involves embracing a belief system or set of assumptions about human nature and the process of human change. Although motivational interviewing was initially designed as a brief intervention for problem drinking, it has been effectively applied to a wide range of problems including substance abuse, compulsive gambling, eating disorders, anxiety disorders, depression, suicidality, chronic disease management, and health-related practices.

2. Group counselors can integrate the principles of motivational interviewing with a number of approaches, especially person-centered therapy, cognitive behavior therapy, choice theory/reality therapy, and solution-focused brief therapy.

3. Motivational interviewing emphasizes the relational context of therapy, known as the "MI spirit," which is primarily aimed at reducing ambivalence about change and increasing intrinsic motivation. When this MI spirit is applied to group counseling, the group leader establishes collaborative partnerships with members and draws on the ideas and resources of the group members rather than relying on the group leader as expert. All choices ultimately rest with the members rather than with the leader. MI is a collaborative conversational style for strengthening an individual's own motivation to change.

STAGES OF DEVELOPMENT OF THE SOLUTION-FOCUSED BRIEF THERAPY GROUP

Dimension	Initial Stage	Working Stage	Final Stage
Key developmental tasks and goals	First task is to set the mood for focusing on solutions from the beginning. Group members are given an opportunity to describe their problems briefly. The leader helps members to keep the problem external in conversations, which tends to be a relief to members because it gives them an opportunity to see themselves as less problem-saturated.	Rather than engage in detailed accounts of their problems, members have the task of shifting from a fixed problem state to a world with new possibilities that lead to creative solutions. People tend to respond better to a present and future orientation than they do to a past orientation that dwells on why they have certain problems that they cannot solve.	Specific plans for achieving personal goals need to be established. Members devote time in the group to talk about what they learned that they could transfer to their everyday living.
Role and tasks of group leader	The group leader works with members in developing well-formed goals as soon as possible. Questions that might be posed are: "What will be different in your life when your problems are solved?" "What will be going on in the future that will tell you and the rest of us in the group that things are better for you?"	Leaders give primary attention to creating collaborative relationships with members because of their belief that doing so opens up a range of possibilities for present and future change. One way of creating an effective therapeutic partnership is for the facilitator to show the members how they can use the strengths and resources they already have to construct solutions.	The group leader assists group members in monitoring their progress and eventually determining when they have accomplished their personal goals. Prior to ending a group experience, leaders assist members in identifying things they can do to continue the changes they have already made into the future.
Role of group members	The leader asks members about those times when their problems were not present or when the problems were less pressing. The members explore these exceptions and talk about what they did to make these events happen. The members engage in identifying exceptions with each other. This improves the group process and promotes a solution focus rather than problem focus. Members discuss what they need to do before they see their problem as being solved and what will be their next step.	Members look for what is working in their lives, rather than talking about what cannot be changed. By zeroing in on those aspects that are working, members are able to apply this knowledge to effectively address their concerns in the shortest time possible. Members may address any changes that they have made since the time they decided to join the group. The members share specific times when the problem did not exist. Doing this reminds members that their problems are not all powerful and have not existed forever.	Members design an action plan aimed at change. As a result of the group experience, the members have identified many of their competencies that they can bring to bear in attaining their plans for change. The group leader asks members a variety of questions to get members thinking of ways they can draw on their resources.

| Techniques | Some questions asked by SFBT group leaders during the initial stage might include:

• If a miracle happened and the problem you have was solved overnight, how would you know it was solved, and what would be different?

• I'd like for you to talk about the times before a problem started to interfere with your lives. What were you doing at these times to keep the problem at bay?

• At some time in the future when the problems that brought you to this group are less pressing than now, what will you be doing? | Leaders ask members to observe their behavior and to note any changes in feelings, moods, actions, or communication. By use of the scaling technique, members rate on a scale of zero to one the degree to which they show improvement on specific dimensions. Scaling questions enable clients to pay closer attention to what they are doing and how they can take steps that will lead to the changes they desire. Members are also asked what needs to be done before they see their problem as being solved and also what will be their next step.

The assumption is that talking about problems will produce more problems, while talking about change will produce change. Leaders concentrate on small, realistic, achievable changes that may lead to additional positive outcomes. Because success tends to build upon itself, modest goals are viewed as the beginning of change. | Clients are encouraged to experiment with patterns that have a better chance of working. Leaders typically allow time in each group session for sharing feedback with one another. This kind of summary feedback assists members in carrying their learning outside of the group sessions into daily living. Members are invited to give one another feedback and identify the changes they have observed in each other over the course of the entire group. |
| Questions to consider | If members seem reluctant to talk about the times when their problems did not exist, and instead insisted on talking about their problems, what might you do?

How will you help members identify their strengths and search for possibilities?

How would you help members establish clear goals at the first session? Would you focus primarily on what members are doing? How much might you attend to feelings that members might bring up?

If members wanted to talk about the past, would you allow this? How might you re-direct the focus to present and future behavior? | Members are encouraged to engage in change—or solution-talk rather than problem-talk. The miracle question is a goal setting technique that is useful when a member has no clue of what a miracle might look like. Leaders might ask other group members to brainstorm with the disillusioned member about what they think his or her miracle might look like. This sparks creative conversations and can create cohesion in the group. How can you get members to focus on possibilities and solutions, especially if they come to the group with the expectation of talking about their problems and finding answers to what troubles them? | What are some ways to use the group sessions to help members practice new behaviors that they will try out in daily situations? What methods might you employ to encourage members to practice outside the group what they are learning in the session?

What are some ways to help members express and explore their fears of failing? How can you reinforce success and small gains? Can you think of ways to encourage members to take action even though they feel defeated?

What follow-up procedures might you use to assess the extent to which members make and maintain positive changes after a group? |

Reactions: Summarize your reactions to the solution-focused brief therapy perspective on group developmental stages. What do you like most? Least? What aspects of this approach would you incorporate in your style of leadership?

4. MI emphasizes being purposeful and getting to the point—the direction, purpose, and point is to guide group members toward positive change. MI is *directive* in the sense that leaders steer the conversation in the direction of considering change without persuading members to change. MI group leaders encourage members to determine whether they want to make certain changes, and if so, what kinds of changes will occur and when they will occur. MI stresses client self-responsibility and promotes working cooperatively with the client to generate alternative solutions to behavioral problems.

5. MI works on the premise that people who seek therapy are often ambivalent about change and that motivation may ebb and flow during the course of therapy. Group counselors have the task of understanding and working with ambivalence about change rather than working against clients' struggles. Leaders attempt to understand both sides of a member's ambivalence from his or her perspective. They do not fight with a member; rather, they roll with the resistance. The goal of exploring members' ambivalence is to minimize the ambivalence and to build intrinsic motivation. Group leaders encourage members to explore their ambivalence and strive to build intrinsic motivation.

6. During a later phase of MI work, members show signs of readiness to change, which is manifested by a decreased resistance to change, increased talk about change, expressing a desire to change, experimenting with possible change actions between sessions, and envisioning a future picture of having made desired changes. Leaders pay particular attention to members' arguments for changing compared to their arguments for not changing.

7. MI is based on a person-centered philosophy and includes using open-ended questions, employing reflective listening, affirming and supporting the client, summarizing and linking at the end of sessions, and eliciting and reinforcing *change-talk*.

8. Similarities between solution-focused brief therapy and motivational interviewing include a nonpathological, health-promoting emphasis; acceptance of reluctance to change as normal; de-emphasizing diagnosis and labeling of clients; using client strengths and resources; and working within a framework of brief intervention. Many of the methods used in SFBT apply equally well to MI.

9. MI is a phenomenological approach whereby the counselor attempts to see life from the client's perspective; goals are developed from that vantage point. In MI group members are not persuaded to adopt advice by the counselor; rather, they are invited to consider a menu of alternative interventions or options.

10. Motivational interviewing can be a stand-alone treatment, but it also lends itself to various forms of psychotherapy integration. MI can be integrated with cognitive behavioral and other therapies. MI can be a significant factor in assisting clients in making a commitment to the therapy process, thus improving client involvement, adherence, and retention in cognitive behavioral and other action-oriented therapies.

Glossary of Key Terms for Solution-Focused Brief Therapy and Motivational Interviewing

- **Ambivalence** Ambivalence refers to having simultaneous and conflicting thoughts or feelings about making a change. MI is designed to evoke, explore, and resolve ambivalence.
- **A not knowing position** This implies that group counselors allow themselves to enter the conversation with curiosity and with an intense interest in discovery, rather than have a preconceived idea about the client.

- **Change-talk** MI practitioners emphasize the value of change-talk. Once members show signs of wanting or needing to change, the therapist guides individuals in taking steps necessary to bring about the changes they want.
- **Cooperation** MI avoids a confrontational style and promotes an invitational style in which cooperation is a major element for successful counseling. From the perspectives of both MI and SFBT, cooperation allows clients to experience support from the therapist, which facilitates openness toward future possibilities and new directions.
- **Exception questions** This is a solution-focused technique of directing clients' attention to times when the problems did not occur as a way to help clients build on successful problem-solving skills.
- **Formula first session task (FFST)** This is a form of homework a group leader might give members to complete between their first and second sessions. The FFST technique puts the emphasis on future solutions rather than past problems.
- **Miracle question** A solution-focused technique of asking clients to imagine how life would be different if they were to wake up tomorrow and no longer have a particular problem. The way this might be presented is: "If a miracle happened and the problem you have was solved overnight, how would you know it was solved, and what would be the signs that something was different?"
- **MI spirit** The relational context of therapy, in which the group leader assumes the role of establishing collaborative partnerships with members, drawing on the ideas and resources of the members, and preserving their autonomy.
- **Motivational interviewing (MI)** This is a humanistic, client-centered, directive counseling approach; MI is deliberately directive and has the specific goals of reducing ambivalence about change and increasing intrinsic motivation.
- **Positive psychology** Solution-focused counseling has parallels to this approach, which pays attention to what is right and what is working for people rather than dwelling on deficits, weaknesses, and problems.
- **Pretherapy change** Any changes made before the initial session; therapists often ask: "What changes have you notice that have happened since you decided to come to this first group session?"
- **Reframing resistance** In MI resistance is viewed as an interactional phenomenon, the result of client and counselor not seeing eye-to-eye.
- **Scaling questions** A technique of asking clients to rate a behavior or feeling on a scale of zero to 10 to determine changes.
- **Solution-focused brief therapy (SFBT)** An approach to therapy that emphasizes helping clients find solutions rather than talking about problems. This is a future-focused, goal-oriented therapeutic approach.
- **Solution-focused counseling** This approach is grounded on the optimistic assumption that people are resourceful and competent and have the ability to construct solutions that can change the direction of their lives; also referred to as solution-focused brief therapy.
- **Temporal sensitivity** Both SFBT and MI are time-sensitive counseling approaches, with their respective ties to brief interventions in addiction counseling and to brief therapy.

Exercises and Activities for Solution-Focused Brief Therapy and Motivational Interviewing

Rationale

Techniques in the solution-focused approach and motivational interviewing are geared to assisting clients in discovering their internal resources and competencies. A number of solution-focused brief therapy techniques are frequently used, including pretherapy change, exception questions, the miracle question, scaling questions, formula first session tasks, homework, and summary feedback. See how some of these methods fit for you, both personally and as a group leader.

The following activities and exercises are designed to help you experience the process of applying some concepts and techniques of solution-focused brief therapy and motivational interviewing, both as a member and as a leader. As you work through these exercises on your own, with another person, and with a small group, think about ways in which you, as a group leader, could incorporate them in your group practice.

Exercises

1. *Pretherapy change.* Solution-focused brief therapists often ask clients at the first session, "What have you done since you called for an appointment that has made a difference in your problem?" Asking about pretherapy change tends to encourage clients to rely less on the therapist and more on their own resources to reach their goals.
    a. Think of yourself as a member of a group. How might you address this pretherapy change question? What value would you find in this kind of question?
    b. Now, think of yourself as a facilitator of a solution-focused group. What uses might you make of asking members what they had already done since they first decided to join the group? What are some other ways leaders can encourage members to begin to identify the strengths they already have?

2. *Exception questions.* These questions direct clients to those times in their lives when their problems did not exist. Exploring exceptions offers group members opportunities for evoking resources, engaging strengths, and creating possible solutions. Examples of questions looking for exceptions include, "When was the last time that things were better?" "Talk about times when things were going well for you? What were you doing then?" "What are some things that you have done that helps with your problem?" "How will you know when you are handling your problem well?"
    a. Put yourself in the place of a group member. Identify one problem that you would want to explore in a group. Can you think of any time in your life when you did not have the problem? What was different then? What might you do to use your resources more fully to create solutions? Explore ways that such questions could suggest multiple answers and encourage members to think of what they could do to create a different future. Do you find any personal value in thinking about this kind of question?
    b. Thinking of yourself as a group leader, what advantages can you see in asking members to come up with exceptions to their problems? Can you think of ways you might be able to focus members on exceptions to their problems in your groups during the initial sessions?

3. *The miracle question.* Members can be asked: "If you were to wake up tomorrow and you no longer had your problem, how would your life be different?" Allowing group members to describe themselves without their problem involves a future focus that encourages group members to consider a different kind of life than one dominated by a particular problem. This question focuses clients on searching for solutions. Members can also be asked questions such as "How will you know when things are better?" "What will be some of the things you will notice when life is better?"

   a. From the vantage point of you being a group member, how would you answer this question: "If a miracle were to happen and the problem you have was solved overnight, how would you know that your problem had been solved and what would be different?" What process did you go through in imagining that a particular problem of yours would be gone?

   b. As a group leader, what are some ways that you could introduce the miracle question? When would you want to do this in a group? What would you most be hoping to accomplish? Explore ways that you could use the miracle question as a strategy to help members formulate specific goals they could pursue in a group?

4. *Scaling questions.* This technique asks clients to observe changes in feelings, moods, thoughts, and behaviors. On a scale of zero to 10, clients are asked to rate some change in their experiences. Scaling questions enable clients to see progress being made in specific steps and degrees.

   a. Think of as many uses as you can of the scaling technique. How might you use this in your personal life? When might you want to introduce a scaling question to members of your group?

   b. What are some specific values you can think of in asking members to rate changes in their experiences, both in and out of the group?

5. *Homework.* A basic part of a solution-focused group involves often asking clients to observe events that they would like to see occur more frequently in the future. They can also practice some form of new behavior outside of the group and then report on changes or improvements at the next session.

   a. As a group member, what kind of homework is most meaningful to you? What motivates you to complete homework? Do you operate best when homework is assigned to you or when you devise your own homework?

   b. Think of yourself as leading a group. How would you introduce homework to members in your sessions? Would you be inclined to suggest homework to individual members? Would you ask members to suggest homework to each other? Would you expect members to design their own tasks to complete both in the sessions and outside the group? What are your thoughts about accountability for homework assignments? How might doing tasks outside of the group assist members in accomplishing their goals?

6. *Summary feedback.* Both group leaders and members may provide summary feedback in the form of genuine affirmations or pointing out particular strengths that certain members have demonstrated. Solution-focused practitioners typically allow time in each group meeting for sharing feedback with one another.

   a. What kind of feedback have you found helpful in the groups in which you were a member? What increases your chances of considering feedback from other members or the leader in a nondefensive manner?

b. As a leader, how might you structure a session so that useful feedback can be shared? Do you see possible ways to combine feedback with suggesting tasks for members to complete as homework? What value do you see in arranging for feedback for each group session?

7. *Being a group member.* What do you imagine it would be like for you to be a member of a solution-focused group? What about being in a group structured by motivational interviewing principles? What issues do you think you'd want to pursue in these groups? What kind of member do you think you'd be in such groups?

8. *Working with ambivalence.* Ambivalence refers to having simultaneous and conflicting thoughts or feelings about making a change. In motivational interviewing a member's reluctance to change is viewed as a normal and expected part of the therapeutic process. Although members may see advantages to making life changes, they also may have many concerns and fears about changing. In a small group, identify some aspect of your life where you may experience ambivalence. Are there any behaviors that you want to change, yet at the same time are hesitant about changing? What would be most helpful to you in resolving your conflicting feelings about changing a behavior?

9. *Role of group leader.* Review the section in the textbook on the role of the solution-focused group leader. Solution-focused group counselors adopt a "not knowing" attitude to put group members into the position of being the experts about their own lives. In this approach, the therapist-as-expert is replaced by the client-as-expert. What would it be like for you to work within the framework of this model? Could you function within this model if it were your primary orientation? Why or why not?

10. *Personal evaluation and critique.* In your group or class discuss the concepts of the solution-focused and motivational interviewing approaches to group work that you find most valuable. Consider some of these questions in your discussion:

    a. What key themes or concepts would you take from each of these approaches and apply to groups you lead?

    b. What are the limitations of these approaches? What disadvantages do you see in limiting yourself strictly to a solution-focused orientation or to a motivational interviewing framework?

    c. Do you think solution-focused brief therapy has something to offer every client in a group? For what people do you think it is the most appropriate? What clients might have difficulty with this perspective?

    d. Do you think motivational interviewing has something for all the members of a group? For what kinds of groups do you think MI is most suited?

    e. What do you see as both the strengths and limitations of the solution-focused approach and the motivational interviewing perspective in working with groups composed of culturally diverse populations? What are some ways that you could apply the notion that people are creative, resourceful, and competent with certain cultural backgrounds of members?

    f. How are you able to relate in a personal way to the solution-focused approach and to the motivational interviewing approach? What ways can you understand yourself better by reflecting on the exceptions to your problems and the times when your problems did not get the best of you? How is your self-understanding related to your ability to encourage group members to explore their own resources for creating solutions in their personal lives?

g. With what age populations and client populations might SFBT and motivational interviewing best fit? Can you think of ways to apply SFBT and motivational interviewing ideas and methods in group work with children and adolescents? What value do you see in using a solution-focused framework or a motivational interviewing perspective in designing groups in a school setting?

11. *Using SFBT or MI in school-based groups.* As a group, develop a brief proposal for using solution-focused brief therapy or motivational interviewing as the basic format for a counseling group with either elementary school children or high school adolescents. In designing your group, consider these guidelines:

_____ The group will deal primarily with present and future concerns of the members.

_____ The group leader teaches the members how to think in terms of exceptions to their problems.

_____ The group leader strives to get involved in an active and personal way with the members and also attempts to create collaborative relationships with members.

_____ Group members spend time exploring exceptions to problems they bring to the group.

_____ The group leader raises helpful questions at the beginning of a group to assist members in thinking about what they did that was different.

_____ Members are given summary feedback and some homework tasks at the end of each session.

12. *Integrating solution-focused therapy with the practice of motivational interviewing.* In small groups discuss some ways that you could integrate some of the basic ideas of solution-focused therapy with motivational interviewing. Consider the possibilities of blending concepts and techniques such as these that are common to both approaches:

_____ Emphasis on the present concerns of group members

_____ A time-limited framework that stresses results

_____ A collaborative and respectful therapeutic relationship

_____ Emphasis on members making choices about the personal goals they wish to pursue

_____ A recognition of client strengths and preferences

_____ Creating an optimistic attitude that change is possible

_____ Emphasis on the internal frame of reference of clients

13. *MI and the transtheoretical model of the stages of change.* The transtheoretical model of Prochaska and Norcross (described in the textbook) suggests that different stages of change are associated with different levels of readiness to change. People are assumed to progress through a series of five identifiable stages in the counseling process: precontemplation, contemplation, preparation, action, and maintenance. Identify changes that you would like to make in your life and discuss what stage you are currently at in terms of your readiness to change. How will you, as well as your significant others, know when you are at a more advanced stage? If you are in the maintenance stage, identify the strategies you have adopted to support and maintain your changes. What words of encouragement can you offer others to support the changes they want to make?

14. *MI perspective on resistance.* Discuss in class or in small groups how MI views the concept of resistance. How does this perspective compare to the way other major therapeutic approaches view resistance? Which approach offers you the most useful way to conceptualize

resistance? Which offers you the least useful perspective? As a client, how would you prefer your resistance to be viewed and worked with?

15. *Reframing resistance.* After discussing the concept of resistance based on the questions listed above, role-play working with resistance in small groups. As a group leader, experiment with ways you can assist a member in increasing his or her intrinsic motivation and desire to engage in the therapeutic process. Ask for feedback from your group members about how effective your strategies were. Did you successfully demonstrate the MI spirit? After a while, switch roles and be a member who feels ambivalent about engaging in the group. Reflect on how well your group leader captures the MI spirit and helps you to be more receptive to participation in the group and to change.

Questions for Reflection and Discussion

1. Solution-focused brief therapy eschews the past in favor of both the present and the future. What implications does this time perspective have for you as a group leader? What are your thoughts about getting group members to work toward present and future solutions?

2. Solution-focused brief therapists strive to get their clients away from talking about their problems, and instead, talking about solutions. What do you think of this orientation toward solutions? How would you deal with members who insisted that they wanted to talk about the problems that brought them to your group? How natural might it be for you to focus on constructing solutions with group members rather than resolving problems?

3. What are your thoughts about the value of keeping therapy brief? How do you think SFBT and motivational interviewing contribute to limiting the time frame of a group? With what kinds of groups do you think a brief orientation is most called for? Can you think of groups that you might lead for which a brief approach would not be appropriate?

4. Both SFBT and motivational interviewing are strength-based approaches that assume that individuals have inner resources. What thoughts do you have about the value of asking group members to talk about their resources, talents, and strengths, and to adopt a positive focus on what they are doing that is working in their lives? If you build your group on the notion of helping members recognize their strengths and resources, what implications does this have for the way you would work with members of your groups?

5. Solution-focused practitioners often ask clients the *miracle question*. What value do you see in asking group members to imagine their problems would vanish one night when they were asleep? How does the miracle question enable members to think of ways of creating solutions? What are some specific ways you might make therapeutic use of how members respond to this question? What ways can you think of to use the miracle question to promote interpersonal interaction within the group?

6. Practitioners with a solution-focused and motivational interviewing perspective are concerned with establishing collaborative relationships with the members of their groups. With both of these approaches, group leaders replace the therapist-as-expert with the client-as-expert philosophy. To what degree is this a stance that you are ready to assume? If you were to assume the stance that clients are the experts in their own lives, how would this influence your way of facilitating a group?

7. Compare and contrast both solution-focused brief therapy and motivational interviewing with the experiential therapies (person-centered therapy, Gestalt therapy, psychodrama,

and the existential therapies). To what extent do you think SFBT and MI incorporate or fail to incorporate elements of these approaches? How would you blend the principles of SFBT and MI with the experiential therapies in your groups?

8. What are a few concepts or techniques of SFBT and MI that you think have the greatest applicability in working with cultural diversity in your groups? What specific techniques might you be most inclined to draw from as a way to work within the framework of the diverse cultural backgrounds of the members of your groups?

9. Group leaders who think in terms of both SFBT and MI assist members in becoming their own advocates for change and the primary agents of change in their lives. There are many possibilities for combining solution-focused therapy and motivational interviewing with a variety of groups. What are some ways you can think of to combine these two approaches in applying them to your work with groups?

10. MI enjoys an extensive and impressive record of well-conducted and compelling research. Conduct a literature search on MI and bring research articles to class for discussion. To what client and student populations has MI been successfully applied? What populations might benefit from MI that have not been researched? Compared to using therapeutic approaches that are less empirically validated, how might incorporating MI into your clinical practice convince agency directors and school principals of the value of your approach? In general, how can the research literature enhance your practice as a clinician?

An Expert's Perspective on Solution-Focused Brief Therapy in Groups: by John J. Murphy

JOHN J. MURPHY, PhD, is a Licensed Psychologist and Professor of Psychology and Counseling, University of Central Arkansas.

1. What attracted you to this particular theoretical orientation? How does this theory fit with the person you are?

My attraction to SFBT was purely pragmatic. I was working as a school psychologist in an urban district with large caseloads and high levels of poverty. SFBT not only met the demand for efficiency but helped to energize students and families by acknowledging and building on their strengths, successes, and resources. These conversations were very different from the problem-based interactions they typically had with helping professionals, which made them more effective in engaging their attention and energy. On a personal level, my mother was an optimistic, open-minded person who modeled her own home-spun version of solution-focused thinking and practice. I was taught to see the good in people and to treat them with dignity and respect—two core values of SFBT. In addition, I signed up for this business to lift people up, which is one of the reasons I personally resonate with SFBT and other approaches that privilege people's input and resources.

2. What Key Concepts (1 to 3) of this theory are most applicable to the practice of group counseling?

Focus on exceptions: Focusing on what clients are already doing (exceptions) and what they already have (strengths and resources) can be applied by any practitioner to any group, problem, or goal. As conceptually simple as this concept is, it is not something that comes naturally to people who are struggling with a problem or to practitioners who, like most of us, were trained to assess and correct problems rather than build on people's strengths and resources. By asking about strengths and resources, practitioners are inviting group members to stop and think about what is "right" with them, which is a refreshing and empowering experience for clients who are more aware of their problems than their possibilities. This paradigm shift in the way we view clients and the way they view themselves is no small matter given that many clients enter counseling discouraged and demoralized by their struggles with the problem.

3. **What Techniques (1 to 3) from this theory have the most practical value for group work practitioners?**
   Building on exceptions: The core SFBT technique of building on exceptions has great practical value for group practitioners. Clients often become more hopeful when they realize that the problem is not constant and that they have some degree of relief and influence in their lives.

   "What is better?" question: Another practical solution-focused technique that any group leader can use is to begin group sessions by asking clients to respond to the question, "What is better?" A colleague who leads substance abuse recovery groups told me that this question has a powerful and positive impact on the effectiveness of group discussions and meetings. When asked in a respectful way that is not intended to minimize the reality and frustration of problems, it encourages people to look at *all* aspects of their personal identities and stories—the failures and the successes, the pain and the possibilities, the weaknesses and the strengths.

4. **How does this theory have particular relevance for addressing diversity and social justice issues in group work?**
   SFBT theory urges practitioners to partner with group members in developing customized goals and interventions that boost members' ownership and involvement in the group and in their own care. The collaborative, client-driven nature of SFBT is directly responsive to the fact that many minority clients report experiences of disempowerment and marginalization in their interactions with helping professionals. SFBT practitioners ensure that group members' perceptions and feedback are given top priority, that group discussions revolve around members' goals, and that the group interventions and solutions emerge largely from members' unique perspectives, strengths, successes, and other resources—all of which support culturally responsive services by "putting clients first" and keeping them there throughout the group counseling process.

5. **Raise a question from this theoretical framework that you consider especially important for group work practice.**
   SFBT gives clients a significant voice in their own care and treatment, but how do you justify giving a voice to people who are too young or too disturbed to know what is in their best interest? This is a question of cultural respect and social justice. I've worked with many clients, from children through older adults, who were considered incapable of contributing to their own solutions and care—but ended up doing just that when given

the opportunity. Children, along with adults diagnosed with mental illnesses, have had a profound absence of participation in the therapeutic process. Most children and adolescents enter services as mandated clients subjected to the whims, well-intended as they are, of adults who make decisions and judgments on their behalf. Under these oppressive circumstances, it is incumbent on practitioners to provide ample space and opportunity for group members' input and contributions. This position does not deny that certain developmental and psychological challenges can make it very difficult for some clients to participate in meaningful ways. Even then, however, we should bear in mind that clients are the owners of their lives and, as such, should be afforded the respect and dignity to participate in counseling to the extent desirable and possible for them.

Your Thoughts on Dr. John Murphy's SFBT Perspective on Group Work

1. Dr. Murphy states that the concept of focusing on what clients are already doing (exceptions) and what they already have (strengths and resources) can be applied by any practitioner to any group, problem, or goal. To what degree do you agree with this perspective?

2. What do you think of the way Dr. Murphy answered this question that he raised: SFBT gives clients a significant voice in their own care and treatment, but how do you justify giving a voice to people who are too young or too disturbed to know what is in their best interest?

3. As a way to begin a group session, a practical solution-focused technique that a group leader can use is to ask group members to respond to the question, "What is better?" Can you think of some advantages in using this question to focus group members?

Solution-Focused Brief Therapy: A Comprehension Check   Score ____%

Note: Please refer to Appendix I for the scoring key. Count 5 points for each error, and subtract the total from 100 to get your percentage score.

True/false items: Decide if the following statements are "more true" or "more false" as they apply to solution-focused brief therapy.

T F   1. Solution-focused brief therapy is both future-oriented and goal-oriented.

T F   2. In SFBT the therapist-as-expert is replaced by the client-as-expert.

T F   3. A main therapeutic task is to help clients imagine how they would like things to be different and what it will take to bring about these changes.

T F   4. This approach is based on the assumption that talking about problems will be the path to resolving them.

T F   5. Behavioral tasks and homework are a basic part of this therapy approach.

T F   6. Solution-focused brief therapists generally avoid asking questions, since doing so is viewed as being confrontational.

T F   7. An assumption of this approach is that the future is both created and negotiable.

T F   8. This approach is based on giving clients an accurate diagnosis so a treatment plan can be designed based on solutions.

T   F   9. Members of a solution-focused brief therapy group are expected to gain insight if they hope to solve their problems.

T   F   10. Solution-focused brief therapy does not work very well with children and adolescents in school settings.

Multiple-choice items: Select the *one best answer* among the alternatives given. Consider each question within the framework of solution-focused brief therapy.

_____11. Solution-focused counseling is appropriate for school settings for a number of reasons. Which of the following is *not* one of these reasons?

    a. The approach encourages the acceptance and accommodation of diverse opinions and beliefs, which is appropriate for many school counselors who work in schools with diverse student groups.

    b. Solution-focused counseling is perceived as effective and practical because it emphasizes "what works" rather than "why" something is a problem.

    c. The model underscores the importance of small changes and co-constructed goals.

    d. Counselors are able to provide effective counseling to more students in less time.

    e. Because it has a strong research base, school counselors find it easier to get reimbursed for their services by insurance companies.

_____12. With which one of the following conclusions would a solution-focused brief therapist disagree?

    a. People are resilient, resourceful, and competent.

    b. We do not have to be the victim of our past.

    c. Clients choose the goals they wish to accomplish, which reduces resistance.

    d. It is best to focus on what is not working in a client's life so that the therapist can provide suggestions on more effective ways of behaving.

    e. Clients can build solutions to their problems without any assessment of the nature of their problems.

_____13. The core of solution-focused brief therapy consists of

    a. teaching clients how to acquire rational beliefs instead of irrational ones.

    b. helping clients understand their unconscious dynamics that block their ability to function effectively in daily life.

    c. giving clients opportunities to express unresolved past conflicts.

    d. assisting clients in discovering a range of solutions and enabling them to do more of what is working for them.

    e. identifying clients' cognitive distortions and teaching clients methods of cognitive disputation.

_____14. The main person who is considered the founder of SFBT is

    a. Bill O'Hanlon.

    b. Steve de Shazer.

    c. John Murphy.

    d. Linda Metcalf.

    e. John Peller.

_____15. All of the following are basic concepts of solution-focused brief therapy except for

    a. looking for what is not working.

    b. a positive orientation.

    c. focusing on solutions, not problems.

_____ d. a not-knowing position of the group leader.

e. creating a therapeutic partnership.

_____16. All of the following are generally steps involved in a solution-focused brief group except for

    a. the group leader setting the tone for the group.

    b. the facilitator working with members in developing well-defined goals as soon as possible.

    c. members completing a very detailed form that identifies some of their past problems that they think are getting in the way of living effectively.

    d. searching for exceptions to the problem.

    e. the group facilitator assisting the members with task development.

_____17. Which of the following is _not_ emphasized in solution-focused brief therapy?

    a. a focus on the future

    b. a time-limited focus

    c. a focus more on solutions than on problems

    d. a focus on understanding the origin of a client's problem

    e. identifying small changes

_____18. Which of the following is _not_ a solution-focused brief therapy technique?

    a. exception questions

    b. miracle questions

    c. scaling questions

    d. exploring with clients how they view the origin of a problem

    e. considering solutions and possibilities

_____19. Solution-focused brief therapists believe

    a. life is change, and change is inevitable.

    b. their function is to prescribe ways that clients can solve problems.

    c. the present is more important than the future.

    d. understanding the past is essential in working out current problems.

    e. it takes a long time for clients to begin to make substantial changes.

_____20. All of the following are characteristics of SFBT that makes it an appropriate approach in working with diverse client populations except for the

    a. the emphasis on the experience of clients, rather than working from the counselor's framework.

    b. not-knowing position frequently assumed by solution-focused practitioners.

    c. discussion of solutions rather than problems.

    d. focus on strengths rather than weaknesses.

    e. brief and structured nature of the therapy.

Motivational Interviewing: A Comprehension Check   Score _____%

Note: Please refer to Appendix I for the scoring key. Count 5 points for each error, and subtract the total from 100 to get your percentage score.

True/false items: Decide if the following statements are "more true" or "more false" as they apply to motivational interviewing.

T   F   1.   MI is a humanistic, client-centered, directive counseling approach.

T   F   2.   MI was initially designed as a brief intervention for chronic disease management.

T   F   3.   MI primarily involves using many techniques to persuade group members to change.

T   F   4.   Since its inception, clinical and research applications of MI have grown at a remarkable pace, and this trend is reflected in more than 800 publications and 200 random clinical trials on MI.

T   F   5.   Like solution-focused therapy, MI emphasizes the relational context of therapy.

T · F   6.   MI does *not* give much credence to diagnostic labels because of the dehumanizing aspect of attaching a label to a client.

T   F   7.   MI is considered synonymous with the transtheoretical model of the stages of change.

T   F   8.   MI works on the premise that people who seek therapy are often ambivalent about change and that motivation may ebb and flow during the course of therapy.

T   F   9.   From a motivational interviewing perspective, resistance is viewed as an intrapsychic phenomenon.

T   F   10.   Motivational interviewing can be a stand-alone treatment, but it also lends itself to various forms of psychotherapy integration.

Multiple-choice items: Select the *one best answer* among the alternatives given. Consider each question within the framework of motivational interviewing.

_____11.   MI was developed by _____ in the early 1980s.
     a. Miller and Rollnick
     b. White and Epston
     c. Haley and Madanes
     d. de Shazer and Weiner-Davis
     e. Erickson and Erickson

_____12.   MI emphasizes the relational context of therapy, which is known as
     a. the social microcosm.
     b. the MI spirit.
     c. the collaborative spirit.
     d. the relational spirit.
     e. contextual connectedness.

_____13.   MI works by _____ motivation for change and adherence to treatment.
     a. forcing
     b. confronting clients to acquire
     c. activating clients' own
     d. reinforcing
     e. promoting catharsis to support

_____14.   Which of the following statements best describes MI?
     a. MI is a theory and school of psychotherapy.
     b. MI is a set of prescribed techniques.
     c. MI is a way of being with people and a style of helping.
     d. MI is best considered as a specialized form of cognitive behavior therapy.

_____15. MI has been effectively applied to which of the following problems?
 a. suicidality
 b. eating disorders
 c. anxiety disorders
 d. depression
 e. all of the above

_____16. Which of these statements best captures what is known about the clinical and research applications of MI?
 a. Over the past 30 years, clinical and research applications of motivational interviewing have grown at a remarkable pace.
 b. Since its inception in 1965, MI has produced very little empirical evidence despite much anecdotal support from clinicians.
 c. Despite MI's broad applicability, research on MI has focused exclusively on the clinical population of substance abusers.
 d. The vast majority of research on MI has been qualitative.
 e. MI was initially used in a career counseling context; not surprisingly, much of the research on MI is published in journals of vocational psychology.

_____17. MI is said to be rooted in the philosophy of _____, but with a "twist."
 a. self-psychology
 b. psychoanalysis
 c. Adlerian psychotherapy
 d. client-centered therapy
 e. family systems theory

_____18. MI is designed to evoke and explore
 a. ambivalence.
 b. creativity and spontaneity.
 c. resentment.
 d. inferiority feelings.
 e. happiness and joy.

_____19. In MI reluctance to change is viewed as
 a. defiance against the therapist.
 b. a normal and expected part of the therapeutic process.
 c. extreme rigidity and a sign of personality pathology.
 d. laziness.
 e. an aggressive impulse that has been repressed.

_____20. Which of the following skills or interventions is _not_ used in MI?
 a. interpretation of transference
 b. eliciting and reinforcing change-talk
 c. affirming and supporting the client
 d. using open-ended questions
 e. employing reflective listening

PART 3

INTEGRATION AND APPLICATION

CHAPTER SEVENTEEN

Comparisons, Contrasts, and Integration

Questions for Discussion and Evaluation

Perspectives on Goals for Group Counseling

1. How does the theoretical orientation of a group practitioner influence the group's goals and the direction it takes? How can a leader's values and beliefs influence the direction of the group?

2. In view of the many differences among the various theoretical approaches to group therapy, how is a common ground possible among groups with a cognitive behavioral orientation and experientially oriented groups? How can long-range goals and concrete short-term goals be integrated into group practice?

3. How would you strive to develop goals collaboratively with the members of your group? What problems can you foresee if a member's personal goals are not consistent with the purpose of the group?

4. Consult the overview chart of goals for group counseling (Table 17.1) in the textbook. Decide which approaches come closest to your thinking with respect to goals. Which model(s) do you find least helpful in clarifying your own vision of the purpose of a group? As you review the models, determine which goals you'd choose to incorporate in your own counseling.

Role and Functions of the Group Leader

1. In the text, review Table 17.2, which summarizes the role and functions of the group leader in the various theoretical approaches. What do you see as your specific role and functions in leading a group? To what degree does your role depend on the stage of development of your group?

2. If your group is culturally diverse, what do you see as your role in encouraging members to explore their feelings about their similarities and differences? What is your role in helping members take their cultural values into account as they explore their concerns and make decisions about their lives?

3. If you were asked in a job interview to briefly describe what you considered to be your central role as a group leader, what would you say?

The Issue of Structuring and the Division of Responsibility

1. It is clear that a group leader will provide structure for the group. What is not predetermined is the *degree* and *kind* of structure he or she will provide. The group could range from being extremely unstructured (the person-centered group) to being highly structured

and directive (a rational emotive behavior therapy group). Review Table 17.3 in the text-book on the degree of structuring and division of responsibility. Which theories come closest to your view? Why? What theories do you find the least agreement with? Why? How does structuring relate to the group's stage of development?

2. The division of responsibility, like structuring, can differ widely according to the theoretical approach used in a group. What is your position on the matter of division of responsibility?

3. The group leader needs to maintain a balance between taking on too much responsibility for the group and denying any responsibility for its direction. What problems do you fore-see for a group if the leader assumes either too much or not enough responsibility?

4. After reviewing Table 17.3, decide which approaches provide you with the most insight on this issue.

Group Leader's Use of Techniques

1. Review Table 17.4 in the textbook on techniques that flow from each of the theories. Which methods are you most inclined to employ? How would your selection of techniques depend on the kind of group you were leading? How would you adapt your methods to fit the needs of culturally diverse populations? What techniques seem to be most congruent with your personality and leadership style?

2. What kinds of interventions are you most likely to use at each of the stages of a group's de-velopment? What techniques are you inclined to use in opening a group session? in closing a group session?

3. What is the purpose of techniques in groups? When do techniques most enhance group process? When might the use of interventions interfere with the progress of a group? What are your ideas for evaluating the effectiveness of the techniques you introduce?

Theories Applied to Multicultural Group Counseling

1. If your groups are culturally diverse, which theoretical approaches would you find most useful in understanding the members? Identify several approaches that provide you with a conceptual framework and methods that would be helpful in addressing the diversity that is likely to characterize your group.

2. What group practices do you think might pose problems for some members because of their cultural background? What help could you provide to those members who have difficulty participating in your group because of a conflict between the group norms and their cultural values?

3. What do you consider to be a few of the major limitations of the theories in working with various multicultural populations? Which particular approach do you see as being the most limited in addressing ethnic diversity considerations within a group? Could these limita-tions be overcome by modifying the approach, or will these limitations preclude you from using the approach altogether?

Toward a Synthesis of Theories Applied to Practice

Review the sections of the chapter in the textbook that deal with developing an *integrative model* of group counseling. Strive to begin developing your own synthesis of theories ap-plied to groups at the various stages of development. I suggest that you use the questions below as the basis for discussion in small groups. With your fellow students, think of ways to develop a conceptual framework that can account for the factors of cognition, emotion, and behavior. Also, focus on various theoretical approaches that you'd probably draw on at each of the stages in the life history of a group. Strive for a blending and an integration of theories that will provide you with a cognitive map to explain what goes on in a group as it evolves.

1. What general *group process goals* would guide your interventions at the initial, transition, working, and final stages of a group? How might the goals for a group differ with respect to the period of development?

2. How would you describe your major *role and functions* at each of the stages of a group? What changes, if any, do you see in your leadership functions at the various phases?

3. What kind of *structuring* do you most want to provide at each of the phases of a group's development? How would you describe the division of responsibility (between you as leader and the members) at each of the stages?

4. In terms of *techniques* in the facilitation of group process at the various phases of development, what possible integration can you come up with? How can you combine theories and techniques to work on the three levels of thinking, feeling, and doing? (For example, can you think of ways to combine experiential techniques with cognitive and behavioral methods?)

5. During the *pregroup stage,* how could you draw on those approaches that stress therapeutic contracts? How might you help members formulate a contract during the screening and orientation interview?

6. During the *initial stage,* what aspects of the relationship-oriented approaches (especially the existential and person-centered approaches) could you use as a basis for building trust among the members and between yourself and the members? How might you look to the cognitive behavioral approaches in assisting members to develop specific personal goals? How can you apply solution-focused brief therapy to the tasks of the initial stage?

7. During the *transition stage,* how might you understand resistance from a psychoanalytic and an Adlerian perspective? In what ways does motivational interviewing have a unique perspective on ambivalence toward change and resistance? How do practitioners with a solution-focused model and a motivational interviewing approach typically view resistance? How could you work with resistance by using the group as a way to re-create the members' original family? Can you think of theories you could draw on to help you work with members from a thinking, feeling, and behaving perspective when a group is in transition?

8. During the *working stage,* what integration of theoretical perspectives will allow you to consider the thinking, feeling, and behaving dimensions? How much emphasis would you be inclined to place on the expression of emotion? How much focus would you place on what members are thinking and how their cognitions influence their behavior? What are some examples of techniques you'd employ to work on a behavioral level? What ways can you think of to promote interaction among the members? How could you link the work of several members? What are some ways to develop themes in a group that many members are able to work with at the same time?

9. During the *final stage*, how could you borrow strategies from the cognitive behavioral therapies to help members consolidate their learning and apply it to life outside of the group? What are some ways in which you might help members practice new learning? What are some ways of teaching members how to create support systems once they leave a group?

10. At the *postgroup stage*, how could you apply cognitive behavioral strategies for accountability and evaluation purposes? What specific follow-up procedures would you want to use for the groups you lead?

Note: Now that you have addressed these questions, attempt to develop your own questions on the applications of theory to group practice and look toward your own personal synthesis. Explain how you see groups from a developmental perspective, giving emphasis to those theories that most help you understand how groups function.

CHAPTER EIGHTEEN

The Evolution of a Group:
An Integrative Perspective

Synopsis of a Group in Action: Evolution of a Group

A DVD and Workbook for *Groups in Action: Evolution and Challenges* is available from the publishers of this textbook and student manual. The DVD program is accompanied by a workbook that illustrates the therapeutic interventions used in the group. The first program (*Evolution of a Group*) is based on a 3-day weekend residential group that Marianne Schneider Corey and I cofacilitated. Only brief segments of the weekend group could be included in the 2-hour program, yet the program does illustrate significant events in the life of that group as it progressed from the initial stage to its ending.

In the initial stage, the focus is on building trust and focusing on the here-and-now. As coleaders, we set the stage by exploring ground rules for the group and assisting members in developing goals for the 3 days. In the transition stage, identifying and challenging member fears, hesitations, and resistance is the main topic. During this stage, the level of trust deepens and members begin, reluctantly, to talk about personal material.

The working stage is characterized by a high level of trust, clearer goals, and members exploring feelings, ideas, and beliefs. As coleaders, we help members explore their issues by focusing on the here-and-now so that members are not just "talking about" their issues but actually are experiencing them. Group cohesiveness is high, and members interact with each other with less reliance on the leaders. In the ending stage, the group reviews what they have learned, discussing how they will put those learnings into action and preparing for ending the group.

Guidelines for Critiquing Various Approaches to Group Therapy

The *Evolution of a Group* program shows the stages of one group experience. Chapter 18 gives you a general picture of how different counseling approaches could be applied to the same group, providing practical examples of the advantages and disadvantages of each approach. Use the following questions as a guide in your class and discuss what aspects you like best (and least) about each approach. Then explore ways to integrate several approaches in your own leadership style—selectively borrowing concepts and procedures from all of the therapies—and begin to develop your own theory of group counseling.

Using the Psychoanalytic Approach

1. What is the psychoanalytic view of resistance? How might resistance be explored from a psychoanalytic perspective?
2. What are some ways that focusing on the here-and-now can illuminate conflicts from the past? How can working with past themes be integrated with an exploration of what is occurring in the context of the group?
3. What examples of transference can you find in the group depicted in Chapter 18?
4. With what specific kinds of groups do you think psychoanalytic concepts and techniques are most suitable? What would you most want to incorporate in your style from this approach?

Using the Adlerian Approach

1. If you were using the Adlerian approach, how would you go about getting early recollections from members, and how would you use them?
2. What possibilities can you see in using the group as a way to re-create the original family of the members? What are some ways in which work with the family constellation could be included in a group context? What family-of-origin issues did you see being played out in the *Evolution of a Group* program?
3. Adlerians are interested in the personal goals of members, including a focus on what they are working toward and what kind of life they want. Applied to the group members described in the chapter, how might you work with the various goals of members?
4. At what stage of a group's development do you think Adlerian concepts and techniques are most appropriate? What concepts and techniques would you want to draw from in this approach?

Using Psychodrama

1. How could the group leaders "warm up" the group? Would you use any of these techniques in your group work?
2. What value did you see the coleaders placing on reenacting past events or enacting anticipated situations?
3. What examples of role-playing situations stood out for you? What value do you see in encouraging members to role-play?
4. With what kinds of groups would you most be inclined to draw upon psychodrama? At what stage of a group's development would psychodramatic procedures be most effective? What do you want to take from this approach?

Using the Existential Approach

1. How might the theme "I have a hole in my soul" be explained and dealt with?
2. What are some existential themes that most struck you in the group described in this chapter?
3. From an existential perspective, how might you work with a member who expressed problems with feeling isolated?
4. At what stage of a group's development would an existentialist approach be most appropriate? With what types of group do you think an existential orientation is most useful?

Using the Person-Centered Approach

1. What are some specific things the coleaders did in this group to create and maintain trust? What lessons did you learn about how to establish trust?
2. Do you think this group or any particular members in it *need* more direction and structure than is illustrated?
3. From reading this chapter, what is your sense about the direction provided by the coleaders? Could they be seen as person-centered, and if so, how?
4. At what stage of a group's development might this approach be of the most value? What do you want to draw on from the approach?

Using the Gestalt Approach

1. What are some ways to creatively work with the metaphors group members use? How might you explore a member's wall that keeps people at a distance? How could you work with the statement, "I feel that I've been stabbed in my core, in my heart."
2. If a member in this group wanted to work on a dream that related to emptiness, how might a Gestalt leader carry this out?
3. What are some specific examples of Gestalt methods that were used in this group?
4. At what stage of a group's development do you see Gestalt therapy as being most useful and appropriate?

Using Transactional Analysis

1. How would the TA group leaders (as opposed to psychoanalytic leaders) work with a member's problem of feeling not good enough or of striving for perfection?
2. TA uses contracts between the leaders and the members. How do you think contracts will work in this group?
3. What role would examining old decisions and making new ones play in this group's work? What are some examples of early decisions made by some of the members in this group?
4. At what stage of a group's development do you think TA is most useful? What concepts and techniques do you want to use from TA?

Using a Cognitive Behavioral Approach

1. If you were a cognitive behavioral leader, how would you begin the group? What are the typical steps and sequences in a cognitive behavioral group?
2. How would cognitive behavioral leaders work with this group, as contrasted with psychoanalytic leaders? existential leaders? Gestalt leaders?
3. What are some examples of cognitive behavioral work that was done with members of this group?
4. At what stage of a group would cognitive behavioral methods be most appropriate? Which of these methods are you most likely to use in leading a group?

Using Rational Emotive Behavior Therapy

1. What are some examples of member statements where you might apply REBT techniques?
2. What are the possibilities for dealing with a member who fears rejection?

3. How might REBT leaders deal with a member with a problem pertaining to what he or she did not get as a child? How would this intervention differ from what person-centered therapists would do? from what leaders using psychodrama would do?
4. At what stage in a group would REBT be most appropriate? What might you take from REBT and use in your style of leading?

Using Choice Theory/Reality Therapy

1. From the choice theory/reality therapy perspective, how would you respond to members who blame their past for their current problems?
2. How might you get members to evaluate their current behavior?
3. In what ways would you assist members in formulating a plan for action? How is what members are doing in the present related to making plans for change and committing themselves to this program?
4. At what stage in the group's development would reality therapy be most useful?

Using Solution-Focused Brief Therapy

1. From the solution-focused therapy perspective, how would you respond to members who are intent on talking about their problems?
2. How might you encourage members to shift from a problem track to a solution track?
3. In what ways would you assist members in sharing exceptions to a problem? How might this increase group cohesion?
4. At what stage in the group's development would solution-focused methods be most useful? With what kinds of groups would this orientation be most useful?

Using Motivational Interviewing

1. From the motivational interviewing perspective, how would you respond to members who are expressing any ambivalence toward change?
2. How can you best assist members to increase their motivation?
3. If you experience any reluctance in members, how would you apply principles of motivational interviewing in working with their ambivalence?
4. At what stage in the group's development would the ideas of motivational interviewing be most useful?

Developing an Integrative Approach to Group Practice

Now that you have thought about applying specific group counseling approaches in working with the same group, consider how you can integrate several approaches in your own leadership style.

An *integrative model* refers to a perspective based on concepts and techniques drawn from various theoretical approaches. One reason for the current trend toward an integrative approach to the helping process is the recognition that no single theory is comprehensive enough to account for the complexities of human behavior when the full range of client types and their specific problems are taken into consideration. Each theory has its unique contributions and its own domain of expertise. By accepting that each theory has strengths and weaknesses and is, by definition, different from the others, practitioners have some basis to begin developing a counseling model that fits them.

Remain open to the value inherent in each of the theories of counseling. All the theories have some unique contributions as well as some limitations. Study all the contemporary theories to determine which concepts and techniques you can incorporate into your approach to practice. You will need to have a basic knowledge of various theoretical systems and counseling techniques to work effectively with diverse client populations in various settings. Functioning exclusively within the parameters of one theory may not provide you with the therapeutic flexibility that you need to deal creatively with the complexities associated with diverse client populations.

Each theory represents a different vantage point from which to look at human behavior, but no one theory has the total truth. Because there is no "correct" theoretical approach, it is wise for you to search for an approach that fits who you are and to think in terms of working toward an integrated approach that addresses thinking, feeling, and behaving. To develop this kind of integration, you need to be thoroughly grounded in a number of theories, be open to the idea that these theories can be unified in some ways, and be willing to continually test your hypotheses to determine how well they are working.

An integrative perspective is the product of a great deal of reading, study, supervision, clinical practice, research, and theorizing. With time and reflective study, the goal is to develop a consistent conceptual framework that you can use as a basis for selecting from the multiple techniques that you will eventually be exposed to. Developing your personalized approach that guides your practice is a lifelong endeavor that is refined with experience.

Explore these questions as a way of clarifying your personal perspective on working with the group described in *Evolution of a Group*:

1. What specific techniques would you be inclined to use in working with this group during the first few sessions? As the group reached a working stage, what are some cognitive, emotive, and behavioral methods you would be most likely to employ with each of the themes illustrated? What techniques might you use during the final stage as a way of helping these members consolidate their learning?

2. Select one of the themes explored in the group and think of ways you could work creatively with this theme by combining two or more models of group therapy. What theoretical approaches are you most likely to blend? What are some ways of working with the same theme with different techniques?

3. Which themes of this group do you think you might have the most difficulty working with as a group leader? Who are the members that you would find the most challenging to work with, and why?

4. If you had to select one primary theoretical orientation as a guide to your practice, which would you select? Why?

5. Using a primary theoretical orientation, what would be some of the key concepts from other approaches that you would want to incorporate into your primary orientation?

6. What do you consider to be some of the advantages of drawing concepts and techniques from various theoretical approaches as a framework for guiding your practice in group work? What are some of the disadvantages of an integrative approach to group counseling?

7. What do you consider to be some of the advantages of working within the framework of a single theoretical orientation as a basis for guiding your practice in group work? What are some of the disadvantages of working with one primary theoretical orientation to group counseling?

8. The members of the group in *Evolution of a Group* were diverse in many ways; however, they were all high-functioning individuals. How would you approach leading a group composed of members who were functioning at a much lower level? What theories may be more useful to you in working with this population?

Comprehension Check
and General Test

This test is designed to help you assess your understanding of the basic concepts of the textbook. Take it toward the end of the term to determine which areas you need to study further. Consider outlining the essay questions given after the objective test. Another set of questions, similar in format and content, is available to instructors.

A scoring sheet is provided in Appendix II. After taking this comprehension check, consult the answer key in the Appendix for this General Test and obtain your score.

This test will help you prepare for an objective test if such a test is given as part of your course. Select the *one best* answer.

Multiple-Choice Items

_____ 1. A major difference between group therapy and group counseling lies in
   a. their techniques.
   b. the group process.
   c. the goals for the group.

_____ 2. Which of the following is *not* true of psychoeducational groups?
   a. They impart information.
   b. They teach people how to solve problems.
   c. They help clients learn to create their own support systems outside of the group.
   d. They tend to be long term.

_____ 3. Which of the following is *not* a similarity between self-help groups and therapy groups?
   a. Both are led by qualified professionals.
   b. Both encourage support and stress the value of affiliation.
   c. Both aim for behavioral change.
   d. Both make use of group process.

_____ 4. In self-help groups the focus tends to be on
   a. discussing the external causes of members' problems.
   b. developing strategies to deal with environmental pressures and barriers.
   c. stressing a common identity based on a common life situation.
   d. all of the above.

_____ 5. If you are involved in group work with culturally diverse populations, it will be important for you to
   a. be an expert on each of the populations.
   b. accept the challenge of modifying your strategies to meet the unique needs of the members.
   c. be of the same ethnic background as the members in your group.
   d. do all of the above.

_____ 6. Which of the following is an advantage of group work with multicultural populations?
   a. Members gain from the power and strength of collective group feedback.
   b. Modeling operates in groups.
   c. People learn that they are not alone in their struggles.
   d. Cross-cultural universality often exists in such groups.
   e. All of the above are advantages.

_____ 7. A limitation of group work in a multicultural context is that
   a. groups have been proved ineffective in working with ethnic clients.
   b. many ethnic clients consider it shameful to talk about their personal problems in front of others.
   c. ethnic clients will not be able to develop trust in a group setting.
   d. there is no basis for sharing common struggles or common pain.

_____ 8. Which of the following is *not* an example of Western values?
   a. interdependence
   b. freedom
   c. responsibility
   d. achievement

_____ 9. Assume that you are leading a group and a particular ethnic client tends to be very quiet. Which of the following might best explain this silence?
   a. This is surely a sign of a resistant client.
   b. This is evidence that this client does not want to be in the group.
   c. The silence may indicate politeness and a sense of respect.
   d. This hesitation is best interpreted as a stubborn refusal to be open.

_____ 10. If you are intending to form a group composed of culturally diverse members, it would be important to
   a. prepare the clients for the group experience.
   b. have a general understanding of the cultural values of your clients.
   c. develop patience in accepting differences in behavior.
   d. help members clearly identify why they are in a group.
   e. do all of the above.

_____ 11. The "Best Practice Guidelines" developed by ASGW (2008) provide general suggestions for enhancing your level of competence as a group worker. Which of these suggestions is *not* included in the guidelines?
   a. Remain current and increase your knowledge and skill competencies through activities such as continuing education, professional supervision, and participation in personal and professional development activities.
   b. Utilize consultation and/or supervision to ensure effective practice regarding ethical concerns that interfere with effective functioning as a group leader.

    c. Be open to getting professional assistance for personal problems or conflicts of your own that may impair your professional judgment or work performance.

    d. None of the above; they are all suggested in the guidelines.

_____12. The principle of informed consent applies to

    a. voluntary groups only.

    b. involuntary groups only.

    c. both voluntary and involuntary groups.

_____13. On the matter of coercion and pressure in a group, members should know that

    a. some pressure is to be expected as part of the group process.

    b. they have a right to be protected against undue pressure.

    c. coercion to make acceptable decisions may be a part of group procedure.

    d. they may well be pressured to participate in threatening nonverbal exercises.

    e. both (a) and (b) are true.

_____14. On the issue of psychological risks in groups, what can be safely said?

    a. In a well-designed group, there are really no psychological risks.

    b. Because groups can be catalysts for change, they also contain risks.

    c. Members can be given guarantees that a group will not involve risks.

    d. There are risks only when members are not properly screened.

_____15. Advanced competencies have been specified by the ASGW for which groups?

    a. task work groups

    b. psychoeducational groups

    c. counseling and psychotherapy groups

    d. all of the above

    e. none of the above

_____16. A _____ group represents a microcosm of the social structure that exists in the everyday world and offers participants the opportunity to experiment with new behaviors, develop social skills, and get feedback from many diverse sources.

    a. heterogeneous

    b. homogeneous

    c. nonworking

    d. all of the above

_____17. Which of the following would *not* be considered one of a group member's rights?

    a. The right to expect protection from verbal or physical assaults

    b. The right to expect complete confidentiality

    c. The right to know the leader's qualifications

    d. The right to get help from the group leader in developing personal goals

    e. The right to expect freedom from undue group pressure

_____18. What is the recommended course of action regarding the freedom to exit a group?

    a. Members should be able to leave at any time they wish without any explanation.

    b. Members should never be allowed to leave a group once they join.

    c. Members who are thinking of leaving should bring the issue up for discussion in the group session.

    d. Members should bring up the issue of leaving privately with the leader.

    e. All of the above are true.

_____19. Regarding the right to confidentiality, which statement is *false*?

    a. Confidentiality is one of the key norms of behavior in a group.

    b. Confidentiality is often on the minds of people when they initially join a group.

    c. Members who are in an involuntary group have no rights to confidentiality.

    d. It is a good practice to remind participants from time to time of the danger of inadvertently revealing confidences.

_____20. Leaders who develop sexual relationships with current group members are

    a. acting unethically.

    b. jeopardizing their license and their professional career.

    c. degrading the profession at large.

    d. doing all of the above.

_____21. Which is the correct sequence of the stages of a group?

    a. transition, initial, working, final

    b. initial, transition, final, working

    c. initial, transition, working, final

    d. transition, initial, final, working

_____22. Which stage is characterized by dealing with conflict, defensiveness, and resistance?

    a. working stage

    b. transition stage

    c. final stage

    d. initial stage

_____23. Inclusion and identity are the primary tasks of which stage of a group?

    a. initial stage

    b. transition stage

    c. working stage

    d. final stage

_____24. Teaching participants some general guidelines of group functioning, developing group norms, and assisting members to express their fears and expectations are all group leadership functions during the

    a. working stage.

    b. transition stage.

    c. initial and exploration stage.

    d. final stage.

_____25. Which stage is generally characterized by increased anxiety and defensiveness?

    a. initial stage

    b. transition stage

    c. working stage

    d. final stage

_____26. Cohesion and productivity are most closely associated with the

    a. working stage.

    b. transition stage.

    c. initial and exploration stage.

    d. final stage.

_____27. Conflict and struggle for control are most likely to appear in the

    a. working stage.

    b. transition stage.

    c. initial and exploration stage.

    d. final stage.

_____28. Resistance in a group can be seen as

    a. a common form of defense.

    b. material for productive exploration.

    c. a bad attitude on the part of the member.

    d. something that should be avoided at all costs.

    e. both (a) and (b).

_____29. When attempting to organize and begin a group in an agency, it is important to

    a. be aware of the politics involved in the setting in which you work.

    b. give up the idea if no one else on the staff seems excited about it.

    c. expect the support and encouragement of your coworkers.

    d. do all of the above.

_____30. When working with involuntary group members, it is important to

    a. expect that they will figure out on their own the best way to participate.

    b. discuss with them ways to use the time beneficially.

    c. insist that they participate.

    d. assume that they will understand the basic group procedures after being there for a few sessions.

True/False Items

_____31. Those who seek the services in college counseling centers are increasingly older and diverse in terms of sociodemographic features and life experiences, making group work more challenging.

_____32. Structured groups are often based on a learning theory model and use behavioral procedures.

_____33. The terms *self-help group* and *support group* are often used interchangeably.

_____34. Essentially, self-help groups and therapy groups have the same goals.

_____35. Self-help groups often focus on exploring external causes of members' problems as well as developing strategies to deal with environmental pressures and barriers.

_____36. The literature dealing with multicultural counseling indicates that ethnic and minority clients are making full use of mental health services.

_____37. Group leaders may encounter resistance from some ethnic or minority clients because they are using traditional White, middle-class values to interpret these clients' experiences.

_____38. An advantage of group work with ethnic clients is that members can gain from the power and strength of collective group feedback.

_____39. A disadvantage of group work with ethnic clients is their reluctance to disclose personal material or to share family secrets.

_____40. If an ethnic client displays silence in a group, this behavior is most probably a sign of resistance.

_____41. It is best not to inform clients of their rights as members before they join a group, for this generally reduces their commitment to work.

_____42. It is clearly unethical to form groups composed of involuntary members.

_____43. It is a good practice to remind participants from time to time of the danger of inadvertently breaking confidentiality.

_____44. One way to establish trust is to reassure members that whatever they disclose in a session will never go outside of the group.

_____45. It is realistic to assume that adequately led groups, by their very nature, eliminate psychological risks to the participants.

_____46. It is unwise to forewarn participants of the psychological risks of being in a group, for this is likely to create a tense climate and lead to extreme caution.

_____47. It is important that group leaders be clear about their own values and express them openly when it is relevant and appropriate to the work of the group.

_____48. As a group counselor, you may face the need in a malpractice action to justify the techniques you have used.

_____49. Group leaders who possess personal power generally meet their needs at the expense of the members and are therefore unethical.

_____50. Research findings on leader self-disclosure clearly indicate that the more leaders disclose of their personal lives, the more their groups become self-directed and cohesive.

Definition Items

Select the group leadership skill that is described by each phrase.

_____51. Identifying with clients by assuming their internal frames of reference.
   a. sympathizing
   b. empathizing
   c. facilitating
   d. reflecting
   e. none of the above

_____52. Expressing concrete and honest reactions based on observation of members' behavior.
   a. evaluating
   b. initiating
   c. clarifying
   d. interpreting
   e. giving feedback

_____53. Attending to verbal and nonverbal aspects of communication without judging or evaluating.
   a. interpreting
   b. reflecting feelings
   c. active listening
   d. facilitating
   e. empathizing

_____54. Demonstrating desired behavior through actions.
   a. modeling
   b. clarifying
   c. facilitating
   d. evaluating
   e. none of the above

_____55. Challenging participants to look at discrepancies between their words and actions, or verbal and nonverbal communication.
  a. confronting
  b. suggesting
  c. clarifying
  d. interpreting
  e. initiating

_____56. Revealing one's reactions to here-and-now events in the group.
  a. restating
  b. empathizing
  c. confronting
  d. disclosing oneself
  e. linking

_____57. Promoting member-to-member interactions rather than focusing on member-to-leader interactions.
  a. summarizing
  b. linking
  c. suggesting
  d. reflecting feelings
  e. questioning

_____58. Safeguarding members from unnecessary psychological risks in the group.
  a. modeling
  b. linking
  c. goal setting
  d. interpreting
  e. protecting

_____59. Preparing a group to close a session or end its existence.
  a. restating
  b. terminating
  c. summarizing
  d. evaluating
  e. questioning

_____60. Planning specific goals for the group process and helping participants define concrete personal issues as the focus of work.
  a. supporting
  b. clarifying
  c. facilitating
  d. goal setting
  e. suggesting

Conceptual Items

Items 61–85 present a series of related concepts or techniques pertaining to one therapeutic approach. _One item in the series of five does not fit with the other four items._ Identify the word or phrase that does _not_ fit.

_____61. (a) life stages, (b) developmental crises, (c) psychosocial stages, (d) stress inoculation, (e) critical tasks

_____62. (a) fictional finalism, (b) basic mistakes, (c) A-B-C theory, (d) social interest, (e) style of life

_____63. (a) playing the projection, (b) the rehearsal experiment, (c) family modeling, (d) working with dreams, (e) making the rounds

_____64. (a) style of life, (b) openness to experience, (c) self-trust, (d) internal source of evaluation, (e) willingness to continue growing

_____65. (a) total behavior, (b) mistaken goals, (c) private logic, (d) early recollections, (e) family constellation

_____66. (a) congruence, (b) redecision, (c) internal source of evaluation, (d) unconditional positive regard, (e) accurate empathic understanding

_____67. (a) WDEP, (b) plan for action, (c) commitment, (d) unconditional positive regard, (e) quality world

_____68. (a) A-B-C theory, (b) irrational beliefs, (c) choice theory, (d) cognitive restructuring, (e) self-defeating thought patterns

_____69. (a) present-centered awareness, (b) the concept of the now, (c) unfinished business, (d) lifescript analysis, (e) bringing the past into the here-and-now

_____70. (a) relaxation training, (b) the dialogue experiment, (c) exaggeration technique, (d) reversal technique, (e) present-centered dream work

_____71. (a) injunctions, (b) existential anxiety, (c) early decisions, (d) games, (e) redecisions

_____72. (a) early recollections, (b) strokes, (c) lifescripts, (d) games, (e) early decisions

_____73. (a) social skills training, (b) cognitive restructuring, (c) modeling methods, (d) assertiveness training, (e) analysis of transference

_____74. (a) the dialogue experiment, (b) cognitive restructuring, (c) exaggeration experiment, (d) rehearsal experiment, (e) making the rounds

_____75. (a) games, (b) rackets, (c) scripting, (d) catharsis, (e) Parent, Adult, Child

_____76. (a) figure-ground, (b) unfinished business, (c) ego states, (d) contact and resistance to contact, (e) energy and blocks to energy

_____77. (a) a "not knowing" position, (b) exception questions, (c) scaling questions, (d) formula first session task, (e) choice theory

_____78. (a) motivational interviewing, (b) the MI spirit, (c) transference, (d) the relational context of therapy, (e) reduction of ambivalence

_____79. (a) teleology, (b) games, (c) phenomenological orientation, (d) lifestyle assessment, (e) social interest

_____80. (a) total behavior, (b) choice theory, (c) inner picture album , (d) rackets, (e) WDEP system

_____81. (a) transtheoretical model, (b) maintenance, (c) Parent, Adult, Child, (d) preparation, (e) precontemplation

_____82. (a) solution-focused therapy, (b) the miracle question, (c) exception questions, (d) focus on the future, (e) focus on the past

_____83. (a) disputation of irrational beliefs, (b) cognitive homework, (c) rational emotive imagery, (d) shame-attacking exercises, (e) dialogue experiment

_____84. (a) I/Thou relationship, (b) lifescripts, (c) redecisions, (d) injunctions and early decisions, (e) strokes

_____85. (a) reexperiencing one's past, (b) developing an action plan, (c) getting a commitment, (d) refusing to accept excuses, (e) refusing to use punishment

Multiple-Choice Items

_____86. Many analytically oriented group therapists have a leadership style that is characterized by
a. objectivity, warm detachment, and relative anonymity.
b. objectivity, aloofness, and strict anonymity.
c. subjectivity, mutuality, and self-disclosure.
d. rationality, impersonality, and coolness.

_____87. Adler stresses
a. the value of transference for group therapy.
b. the purposeful nature of behavior.
c. the role of biological determinants of behavior.
d. total behavior as a concept of control theory.
e. none of the above.

_____88. Psychodrama was developed by
a. Fritz Perls.
b. Carl Rogers.
c. J. L. Moreno.
d. William Glasser.
e. Albert Ellis.

_____89. An essential aim of existential-humanistic therapy is to
a. help clients become more present to both themselves and others.
b. assist clients in identifying ways they block themselves from fuller presence.
c. challenge clients to assume responsibility for designing their present lives.
d. encourage clients to choose more expanded ways of being in their daily lives.
e. do all of the above.

_____90. The congruence of a group leader implies
a. empathy.
b. immediacy.
c. genuineness.
d. unconditional positive regard.
e. none of the above.

_____91. Which of the following is _not_ a key concept of the Gestalt group?
a. awareness
b. unfinished business
c. understanding one's irrational beliefs
d. here-and-now focus
e. dealing with the impasse

_____92. The founder of transactional analysis is
a. Robert Goulding.
b. Eric Berne.
c. J. L. Moreno.
d. William Glasser.
e. Albert Bandura.

_____93. Which of the following techniques is *not* considered a behavioral technique?
   a. self-instruction
   b. dialogue technique
   c. cognitive restructuring
   d. self-reinforcement
   e. coaching

_____94. REBT methodology includes all of the following procedures except
   a. confrontation.
   b. logical analysis.
   c. analysis of one's lifescript.
   d. counterpropaganda.
   e. behavioral methods.

_____95. Which of the following is *not* a key concept of reality therapy?
   a. Members must make commitments.
   b. Members focus on early childhood issues.
   c. Members make an evaluation of their behavior.
   d. Members focus on the present, not the past.
   e. Members look at ways in which they are choosing their total behavior.

_____96. In an analytic group free association might be used for all of the following except
   a. working on dreams.
   b. encouraging spontaneity among members.
   c. promoting interaction between members.
   d. getting at unconscious material.
   e. getting clients to evaluate their quality world.

_____97. All of the following are key concepts underlying the Adlerian group except
   a. teleology.
   b. social interest.
   c. creativity and choice.
   d. developing a lifestyle.
   e. the A-B-C theory of personality.

_____98. Which of the following techniques is least likely to be used in psychodrama?
   a. lifestyle assessment
   b. doubling
   c. future projection
   d. role reversal
   e. soliloquy

_____99. In an existential group, which technique would be considered essential?
   a. role playing
   b. rational emotive imagery
   c. homework
   d. dream analysis
   e. none of the above

_____100. Which best captures the role and functions of a person-centered group counselor?
   a. teacher
   b. facilitator

      c. expert

      d. companion

      e. analyst

____101. Which of the following is generally *not* a technique used in Gestalt groups?

      a. experiments with dialogues

      b. making the rounds

      c. teaching rational thinking

      d. working with dreams

      e. focusing on nonverbal communication

____102. Which of the following is *not* a key concept of TA groups?

      a. lifestyle assessment

      b. analysis of ego states

      c. strokes

      d. script analysis

      e. games

____103. During the initial stage of a behavioral group, the concern of the group leader is to

      a. identify problematic behavior.

      b. develop baseline data.

      c. teach members about the group process.

      d. conduct an assessment of each member's current behavior.

      e. do all of the above.

____104. In an REBT group, role playing involves

      a. a catharsis.

      b. a cognitive restructuring of beliefs.

      c. a return to some event during early childhood.

      d. promoting an expression of feelings between members.

      e. none of the above.

____105. Which of the following is a typical procedure used in reality therapy groups?

      a. conducting an assessment of one's family constellation

      b. exploring early childhood experiences

      c. fostering transference reactions toward the leader

      d. analyzing ego states

      e. evaluating current behavior

____106. Dreams are explored in

      a. Gestalt groups.

      b. psychoanalytic groups.

      c. psychodrama groups.

      d. all of the above.

      e. none of the above.

____107. The object-relations theory is associated with

      a. behavior therapy.

      b. Gestalt therapy.

      c. Adlerian therapy.

      d. reality therapy.

      e. none of the above.

_____108. Choice is stressed in
    a. Adlerian therapy.
    b. existential therapy.
    c. reality therapy.
    d. all of the above.
    e. none of the above.

_____109. Insight is stressed in all of these approaches except
    a. psychoanalytic therapy.
    b. psychodrama.
    c. solution-focused brief therapy.
    d. Gestalt therapy.
    e. TA.

_____110. The process of skillful questioning would be used mostly by a group leader with which theoretical orientation?
    a. person-centered therapy
    b. reality therapy
    c. gestalt therapy
    d. existential therapy
    e. none of the above

_____111. Unfinished business and avoidance are key concepts of
    a. Gestalt therapy.
    b. reality therapy.
    c. motivational interviewing.
    d. rational emotive behavior therapy.
    e. none of the above.

_____112. Which type of group serves the function of re-creating the original family so that members can work through their unresolved problems?
    a. REBT
    b. behavioral
    c. psychoanalytic
    d. motivational interviewing
    e. person-centered

_____113. Individual Psychology is another name for
    a. psychoanalytic therapy.
    b. Adlerian therapy.
    c. existential therapy.
    d. reality therapy.
    e. person-centered therapy.

_____114. Contracts and homework assignments are most likely to be used in
    a. TA groups.
    b. cognitive behavioral therapy groups.
    c. reality therapy groups.
    d. REBT groups.
    e. all of the above.

____115. Which approach would be least interested in the exploration of early childhood experiences?
   a. solution-focused brief therapy
   b. psychoanalytic therapy
   c. Gestalt therapy
   d. Adlerian therapy
   e. TA

____116. Which of the following is *not* true regarding behavioral assessment?
   a. It is aimed at gathering unique and detailed information about a client's problem.
   b. It focuses on the client's past functioning and life conditions.
   c. It is concerned with taking samples of a client's behaviors to provide information about how the client typically functions in various situations.
   d. It is narrowly focused rather than dealing with a client's total personality.
   e. It is integrated with therapy.

____117. Concepts of introjection, projection, retroflection, confluence, and deflection are part of
   a. Adlerian therapy.
   b. psychodrama.
   c. Gestalt therapy.
   d. existential therapy.
   e. TA.

____118. The concept of basic psychological life positions is part of
   a. psychoanalytic therapy.
   b. TA.
   c. psychodrama.
   d. REBT.
   e. none of the above.

____119. Which theory would be most concerned with understanding and exploring an individual's developmental stages?
   a. TA
   b. psychoanalytic therapy
   c. behavior therapy
   d. REBT
   e. none of the above

____120. The socioteleological approach that holds that people are primarily motivated by social forces and are striving to achieve certain goals is associated with
   a. person-centered therapy.
   b. existential therapy.
   c. reality therapy.
   d. Adlerian therapy.
   e. behavior therapy.

____121. Which type of group counselor would tend to give the least degree of direction?
   a. REBT therapist
   b. person-centered therapist
   c. Gestalt therapist

        d. reality therapist
        e. cognitive behavioral therapist

_____ 122. The here-and-now is emphasized in
        a. psychodrama.
        b. existential therapy.
        c. person-centered therapy.
        d. Gestalt therapy.
        e. all of the above.

_____ 123. Solution-focused counseling has parallels to_____, which pays
        attention to what is right and what is working for people rather than dwelling on
        deficits, weaknesses, and problems.
        a. positive psychology
        a. object-relations therapy
        b. Adlerian therapy
        c. psychoanalysis
        d. Gestalt therapy

_____ 124. The A-B-C theory is associated with
        a. reality therapy.
        b. TA.
        c. behavior therapy.
        d. REBT.
        e. Gestalt therapy.

_____ 125. A focus on ego states would occur in
        a. Gestalt groups.
        b. Adlerian groups.
        c. TA groups.
        d. psychodrama groups.
        e. all of the above.

_____ 126. In which type of group do clients choose the goals they wish to accomplish, and little
        attention is given to diagnosis, history taking, analysis of dysfunctional interactions,
        and exploration of the problem?
        a. REBT groups
        b. Adlerian groups
        c. solution-focused brief therapy groups
        d. psychoanalytic groups
        e. none of the above

_____ 127. Cognitive homework is most likely to be assigned in
        a. psychodrama groups.
        b. psychoanalytic groups.
        c. REBT groups.
        d. reality therapy groups.
        e. Gestalt groups.

_____ 128. Modeling would be important in which type of group?
        a. reality therapy
        b. behavior therapy

c. REBT

d. existential therapy

e. all of the above

_____ 129. Choice theory is a basic part of the practice of

a. solution-focused brief therapy.

b. REBT.

c. reality therapy.

d. Adlerian therapy.

e. existential therapy.

_____ 130. The role of the family would be stressed most in which type of group?

a. motivational interviewing group

b. behavioral group

c. existential group

d. Gestalt group

e. Adlerian group

_____ 131. The miracle question is one example of

a. a future-oriented exception question.

b. a present-oriented scaling question.

c. a technique used in groups by pastoral counselors.

d. an unethical technique.

e. a technique borrowed from family systems therapy.

_____ 132. Which approach would be most likely to focus on an expression and exploration of feelings?

a. behavior therapy

b. REBT

c. reality therapy

d. Gestalt therapy

e. none of the above

_____ 133. Significant developments in dealing with borderline and narcissistic personality disorders have occurred within which theory?

a. Gestalt therapy

b. TA

c. solution-focused brief therapy

d. person-centered therapy

e. none of the above

_____ 134. Dealing with the present is stressed in

a. psychodrama.

b. Gestalt therapy.

c. existential therapy.

d. reality therapy.

e. all of the above.

_____ 135. Which approach does *not* emphasize techniques?

a. Adlerian therapy

b. psychodrama

c. existential therapy

d. behavior therapy

e. REBT

_____136. The formula first session task (FFST) is a form of homework a group leader might give members

a. to complete between their first and second sessions.

b. that puts the emphasis on future solutions rather than past problems.

c. that is used in solution-focused brief therapy.

d. to increase their optimism and hope about their present and future situation.

e. all of the above.

_____137. The miracle question is a technique used in

a. TA.

b. REBT.

c. Gestalt therapy.

d. solution-focused therapy.

e. reality therapy.

_____138. A lifestyle assessment, which would focus on family background and would reveal a pattern of basic mistakes, would be used in

a. psychoanalytic therapy.

b. Adlerian therapy.

c. behavior therapy.

d. REBT.

e. all of the above.

_____139. Which type of group leader is most likely to focus on energy and blocks to energy?

a. Adlerian leader

b. Gestalt leader

c. psychoanalytic leader

d. TA leader

e. person-centered leader

_____140. The therapeutic conditions of congruence, unconditional positive regard, and empathy are emphasized in

a. psychoanalytic therapy.

b. reality therapy.

c. TA.

d. person-centered therapy.

e. none of the above.

_____141. Role playing is likely to be used in

a. psychodrama.

b. Gestalt therapy.

c. REBT.

d. behavior therapy.

e. all of the above.

_____142. Which approach stresses the total behavior of doing, thinking, feeling, and physiology?

a. REBT

b. reality therapy

c. person-centered therapy

d. psychoanalytic therapy

e. TA

_____143. Which approach emphasizes the personal qualities of the group leader rather than the techniques of leading?

a. existential

b. person-centered

c. REBT

d. behavioral

e. two of the above

_____144. The approach that teaches members how to identify irrational beliefs and substitute for them with rational beliefs is

a. reality therapy.

b. REBT.

c. TA.

d. Gestalt therapy.

e. behavior therapy.

_____145. Social skills training groups most rely on which type of techniques?

a. behavioral

b. TA

c. psychodramatic

d. reality therapy

e. Adlerian

146. In which type of group would members focus on their lifescripts through the process of script analysis?

a. psychoanalytic group

b. reality therapy group

c. behavioral group

d. Adlerian group

e. TA group

_____147. Shame-attacking exercises are likely to be used in which type of group?

a. reality therapy group

b. person-centered group

c. Gestalt group

d. REBT group

e. psychodrama group

_____148. Motivational interviewing is best described as

a. a deterministic and directive counseling approach.

b. a school of psychotherapy.

c. a style of helping and a method of communication.

d. a set of prescribed techniques.

e. all of the above.

_____149. The contemplation stage is associated with which of the following?

a. Adlerian therapy

b. transtheoretical model of the stages of change

      c. psychoanalytic therapy

      d. psychodrama

      e. Gestalt therapy

____150. Which approach has the goal of uncovering unconscious conflicts and working them through?

      a. person-centered therapy

      b. reality therapy

      c. psychoanalytic therapy

      d. TA

      e. behavior therapy

Essay Questions for Review and Study

Directions: These questions are designed as a study guide to help you pull together some central ideas in the textbook. Strive to write your answers briefly, using your own words.

1. What are the advantages of a group format for special populations (children, adolescents, or adults)?
2. Differentiate between
   a. group psychotherapy and group counseling.
   b. group psychotherapy and self-help groups.
3. If you were working in a setting with clients representing diverse cultural backgrounds, what would you see as your major challenges as a group leader? How might you meet some of these challenges?
4. What are a few of the advantages and disadvantages of group counseling with culturally diverse clients?
5. What are some guidelines that could help you design and conduct groups with culturally diverse populations? What guidelines would you use to evaluate the success of these groups?
6. Assume that you are a counselor in a community agency. No groups are being offered, and you see a need for several types of groups. What course of action, if any, might you be inclined to take?
7. Review the section in Chapter 2 that deals with the group leader as a person. What are your personal characteristics that would help you or hinder you in your work as a group leader?
8. In the same chapter, review the section dealing with special problems and issues for beginning group leaders. Discuss your single most important concern.
9. Assume that you are working in an agency and would like to form a group. The director would like you to colead your group. What specific things would you look for in selecting a coleader?
10. Discuss what you see as your major tasks at each of the stages in the development of a group.
11. Assume that you were in a job interview and were asked this question: "Tell us about the theoretical orientation that guides your practice as a group counselor." How would you respond?
12. There are different styles of group leadership. Again, in a job interview, how might you describe your own personal style of leadership?

13. Think of a particular group that you might conduct, and describe briefly what factors you would consider in forming it.

14. The stages of a group do not generally flow neatly and predictably in the order described in the textbook. Why is it important that you have a clear understanding of the characteristics associated with the development of a group?

15. If you had to select one theory that comes closest to your thinking and that helps you in your practice as a group counselor, which would it be? Explain the reasons for your selection.

16. Dreams can be fruitfully explored by using several different therapy approaches. Show how you might work with a dream in a group format from these three perspectives: psychoanalytic, psychodrama, and Gestalt.

17. Compare the goals of psychodrama and Gestalt groups; contrast the differences in techniques between these two approaches.

18. Discuss some common denominators of these various approaches to group counseling: Adlerian therapy, TA, REBT, and reality therapy.

19. Select one of the following possible combinations and discuss what you see as the merits of merging the concepts and techniques of the two approaches as applied to group counseling: Gestalt with TA, Gestalt with REBT, or Gestalt with reality therapy.

20. Assume that you are leading a group with culturally diverse members. Are there any concepts and techniques from the various approaches that you would find particularly useful?

21. Discuss some of the ways of addressing existential themes within a cognitive behavioral framework. What are the possibilities of a merger between the existential and cognitive behavioral approaches as applied to group counseling?

22. What are some commonalities between a person-centered group and an existential group? What are some basic differences?

23. How would you describe your role as a group counselor to a new group? What do you see as your major leadership functions?

24. How would you assess the outcomes of a group that you were leading?

25. Discuss the role that theory plays in the practice of group counseling. How does the theory that a leader holds influence the interventions he or she makes?

26. What are the advantages and disadvantages of adopting a highly structured approach to group work? Under what circumstances would it be optimal to use minimal structure in the groups you lead?

27. Describe the pros and cons of forming an open group versus a closed group. How would your leadership approach and expectations differ based on whether your group is open or closed?

28. What are the major ethical concerns associated with group work?

29. What measures might you take as a group leader to prepare members for the group? Would your manner of preparing members differ according to their age, the purpose and goals of the group, the setting, and whether they were voluntary or involuntary members? If so, explain.

30. Which group counseling approaches have a strong research base and which are lacking in this respect? What topics in the group counseling literature need greater attention and seem worthy of more research?

Scoring Key for Chapter Quizzes

ANSWER KEY: CHAPTERS 1–5

1. c	2. d	3. b	4. c	5. a	6. a	7. b
8. d	9. d	10. c	11. a	12. c	13. b	14. a
15. c	16. d	17. a	18. b	19. c	20. a	21. a
22. d	23. d	24. b	25. d	26. c	27. a	28. d
29. c	30. b	31. c	32. d	33. a	34. d	35. a
36. b	37. c	38. a	39. b	40. a	41. a	42. d
43. c	44. a	45. d	46. b	47. b	48. c	49. d
50. c						

Answer key: Chapters 6–16

ITEM NO.	PSYCHOANALYTIC CH. 6	ADLERIAN CH. 7	PSYCHODRAMA CH. 8	EXISTENTIAL CH. 9	PERSON-CENTERED CH. 10	GESTALT CH. 11	TA CH. 12	BEHAVIOR THERAPY CH. 13	REBT CH. 14	REALITY THERAPY CH. 15	SOLUTION-FOCUSED BRIEF THERAPY CH. 16A	MOTIVATIONAL INTERVIEWING CH. 16B
1.	F	T	T	F	T	F	F	T	T	T	T	T
2.	T	T	F	T	T	T	F	F	F	T	T	F
3.	F	T	F	T	T	F	T	F	T	T	T	F
4.	F	F	T	F	F	F	F	T	F	F	F	T
5.	F	T	T	T	F	T	T	F	T	F	T	T
6.	T	F	F	F	T	T	T	T	T	F	F	T
7.	F	F	F	F	F	F	T	T	F	F	T	F
8.	T	F	T	F	T	F	T	T	T	T	F	T
9.	T	T	F	T	T	T	F	T	T	F	F	F
10.	T	T	F	F	T	T	T	T	T	T	F	T
11.	a	b	a	b	d	e	d	d	c	b	e	a
12.	b	e	d	c	b	c	e	b	a	a	d	b
13.	e	a	b	c	e	a	b	a	c	d	d	c
14.	c	b	c	b	e	d	d	e	a	a	b	c
15.	e	d	b	a	b	e	d	b	e	b	a	e
16.	c	b	c	b	b	c	c	a	d	b	c	a
17.	e	d	e	b	a	e	b	e	e	d	d	d
18.	a	c	e	c	b	e	d	e	d	d	d	a
19.	c	d	c	a	e	b	e	e	a	a	a	b
20.	b	b	e	a	c	b	a	a	c	b	a	a

APPENDIX II

Answer Key for Comprehension Check and General Test

1. c	2. d	3. a	4. d	5. b	6. e	7. b
8. a	9. c	10. e	11. d	12. c	13. e	14. b
15. d	16. a	17. b	18. e	19. c	20. d	21. c
22. b	23. a	24. c	25. b	26. a	27. b	28. e
29. a	30. b	31. T	32. T	33. T	34. F	35. T
36. F	37. T	38. T	39. T	40. F	41. F	42. F
43. T	44. F	45. F	46. F	47. T	48. T	49. F
50. F	51. b	52. e	53. c	54. a	55. a	56. d
57. b	58. e	59. b	60. d	61. d	62. c	63. c
64. a	65. a	66. b	67. d	68. c	69. d	70. a
71. b	72. a	73. e	74. b	75. d	76. c	77. e
78. c	79. b	80. d	81. c	82. e	83. e	84. a
85. a	86. a	87. b	88. c	89. e	90. c	91. c
92. b	93. b	94. c	95. b	96. e	97. e	98. a
99. e	100. b	101. c	102. a	103. e	104. b	105. e
106. d	107. e	108. d	109. c	110. b	111. a	112. c
113. b	114. e	115. a	116. b	117. c	118. b	119. b
120. d	121. b	122. e	123. a	124. d	125. c	126. c
127. c	128. e	129. c	130. e	131. a	132. d	133. e
134. e	135. c	136. e	137. d	138. b	139. b	140. d
141. e	142. b	143. e	144. b	145. a	146. e	147. d
148. c	149. b	150. c				